# Gender and Social Security Reform

# International Social Security Series
In cooperation with the
International Social Security Association (ISSA)
*Neil Gilbert, Series Editor*

# Gender and Social Security Reform

## What's Fair for Women?

**International Social Security Series**
**Volume 11**

# Neil Gilbert, editor

**Transaction Publishers**
**New Brunswick (U.S.A.) and London (U.K.)**

The International Social Security Association (ISSA) was founded in 1927. It is a nonprofit international organization bringing together institutions and administrative bodies from countries all over the world dealing with all forms of compulsory social protection. The objective of the ISSA is to cooperate at the international level, in the promotion and development of social security throughout the world, primarily by improving techniques and administration in order to advance people's social and economic conditions on the basis of social justice.

The responsibility for opinions expressed in signed articles, studies, and other contributions rests solely with their authors, and publication does not constitute an endorsement by the International Social Security Association of the opinions expressed by them.

Library of Congress Catalog Number: 2006040405
ISBN: 1-4128-0522-8
Printed in the United States of America

Library of Congress Cataloging-in-Publication Data

Gender and social security reform : what's fair for women? / edited by Neil Gilbert.
     p. cm.—(International social security series ; v. 11)
   ISBN 1-4128-0522-8 (alk. paper)
   1. Social security. 2. Women—Pensions. 3. Sex discrimination against women. I. Gilbert, Neil, 1940- II. Series.
HD6080.G46 2006
368.40082—dc22                                         2006040405

# Contents

# Acknowledgments

This book is an outgrowth of the Gender, Retirement and Active Aging project sponsored by the International Social Security Association (ISSA). Special thanks are due to the Mark and Carol Hyman Fund for providing supplemental support for this project. The ISSA research unit kindly facilitated efforts to organize the research team, which conducted the studies reported in this volume. Roland Sigg's good counsel and encouragement in this regard were greatly appreciated. Members of the research group presented and reviewed their initial findings during a meeting held at ISSA's Geneva headquarters in June 2004. Following their presentations, the authors enjoyed a robust exchange of ideas with the other participants in this meeting —Hye Kung Lee, Douglas Besharov, Ken Judge, Linda Bauld, Alejandro Bonilla, Mariangels Fortuny, Theo Butare, and Dalmer Hoskins–whose thoughtful insights and critical observations were much appreciated.

In the end this volume was a collaborative effort that relied on the hard work and cooperation of many people. The task was lightened by a lively and gifted research team. Special thanks are due to Dalmer Hoskins, Secretary General of ISSA, for his steadfast support and guidance. Finally the meticulous care invested by Melissa Martin in assisting with the preparation of the manuscript is gratefully acknowledged.

# Introduction

*Neil Gilbert*

When the first state-sponsored social security pension scheme was introduced in Germany by Otto von Bismark in 1889, the average life expectancy
was about twenty years less than the age at which German workers' were
slated to receive their retirement benefits. This assured the system would be
solvent. Since then life expectancy has climbed to seventy-six years in the
OECD countries. Not only are people living longer but these societies are
getting older. Between 1960 and 2040 the proportion of people over age
sixty-five is expected to more than double from an average of 9.7 percent to
22.2 percent of the populations of most OECD countries. One half of those
elderly people will be over seventy-five years of age. Aging populations are
creating tremendous pressures on social security schemes throughout the
advanced industrialized countries as looming deficits threaten to dilute the
benefits of future retirees. Responding to this challenge, policy-makers tend
to concentrate on designing reforms that will cover the projected shortfalls
and insure the fiscal integrity of the pension systems.

The fiscal challenge is serious but not critical. There are basically five
ways to restore the fiscal balance of conventional pay-as-you-go social security systems. Governments can raise payroll taxes, reduce benefits, create
incentives to increase productivity, alter the age distribution through pro-
natalist and immigration policies and borrow in the lean years against the
prospects of better times to come. Among these alternatives, increasing taxes
and reducing benefits are the most reliable and easiest to craft. Also they can
be introduced in shadowy increments through measures such as: changing
the index for raising future benefits, using income tests to tax retirement
benefits and slowly raising the age of retirement which may ease the political
costs of pension reforms. There are other reforms which essentially alter the
defined benefit model of pay-as-you-go systems. These include initiatives
that privatize all or part of the pension schemes and changing public programs from defined benefit to defined contribution schemes under which
each person's retirement benefit is directly contingent upon how much the

individual paid into the system. To insure adequate pensions for low-income workers, defined contribution schemes are often designed with minimum benefit levels which are higher than what these workers would have received based only on their contributions.

As social security programs must accommodate the fiscal demands of aging societies, they must also adapt to the changing character of modern family life. The original blueprints for social security were drawn up at a time when the norms of family life prescribed wives stayed at home; their unpaid labor invested in household management and child and elder care while husbands worked for pay in the market economy. The initial design of social security took account of the traditional division of labor, for example, by augmenting retirement benefits with a dependent's allowance. Over the last fifty years the norms governing the male-breadwinner model of family life have undergone considerable change. Increasing gender equality has fueled modern expectations women will shift their labor from the household to the market and be paid for their efforts. Women's incomes have not achieved parity with those of men but there has been palpable progress in that direction. Although the dependent's allowance remains a feature of many social security schemes, the increasing labor force participation of women has eroded the need for this benefit. Indeed, the dependent's benefit is now seen as reinforcing an outmoded traditional view of the stay-at-home housewife dependent on her husband for financial support. And it is often criticized for maintaining formidable inequities, particularly between low-income wage-earning wives who are employed and contributing to the system throughout their lives, and non-working wives of high income husbands who receive more money from the dependent's allowance than the pension benefits earned by working wives.

As they seek to reconcile social security benefits with both the fiscal demands of aging societies and the changing needs of family life, policy makers are challenged to design pension reforms that achieve fair outcomes for women. But what constitutes fairness is not always self-evident. Does it mean pension systems should be gender-neutral or compensate for inequalities in paid and unpaid labor? Is it fair to employ unisex life tables in calculating pension annuities? Should pension policies be designed to facilitate work-family balance for women and men? Is it fair to guarantee a minimum pension level that provides the most return on pension contributions to people with thin records of lifetime employment?

This book examines the different ways various countries are responding to these and other questions about the gender dimensions of pension reform. The first three chapters provide comparative analyses of the gender implications of social security as they are manifest in a range of countries at various stages of industrial development. The next three chapters focus on national case studies that furnish an in-depth picture of the interaction between gender and pension reforms. The final chapter provides an integrative perspective of the main lines of policy reform, conceptualizing the broad range of alternatives and revealing how women fare under these measures and the issues policy makers need to resolve as they seek to achieve equality of outcomes in retirement for men and women. In analyzing the gender implications of recent social security policies and practices, this book reframes, the conventional discourse of reform—from how to pay for retirement in aging societies to what is fair for women.

# 1

# Pension Design and Gender: Analyses of Developed and Developing Countries

*Ann-Charlotte Ståhlberg, Agneta Kruse, and Annika Sundén*

## Introduction

All societies have to face the problem no one can financially support her- or himself during all periods of life. Low earnings capacity may be caused by, for example, sickness, disability, unemployment, child rearing, widowhood and old age. Thus, all societies have to organize support for those without earnings capacity. Three broad ways can be distinguished: the family, the market and the state. In most societies, all three ways co-exist with one of them being dominant. The family model is dominant in developing countries while in industrialized countries a state model, in the form of a pay-as-you-go public pension, is most common.

In this chapter we focus on loss of working capacity due to old age with a special focus on gender. The main objective is to relieve poverty in old age but also to offer an insurance when life expectancy exceeds the norm.

Differences in traditions and cultures significantly affect women's level of activity in the labor market, but so, too, do economic conditions. Social and fiscal policy can be designed to economically reward and encourage women to remain in the home and "penalize" paid work by women (the breadwinner or single-earner model). Alternatively, they can be designed to encourage paid work and penalize women who remain at home (the individual or dual-earner model).

In the breadwinner or single-earner model, marriage enjoys a premium and a division of labor between husband and wife is encouraged. Economic policy supports reproductive work in the home

1

through various measures such as: supplementary allowances for spouses and children in the social insurance system, and tax relief for men with wives at home and/or children. If widowed, a woman receives a widow's pension since her pursuit of wifely duties in the home is assumed to have made it more difficult for her to re-enter the labor market. Such rules provide little incentive for women to engage in paid work thus making themelves economically independent of their husbands (Sainsbury 1996, Ståhlberg 2002a, 2002b).

In the individual or dual-earner model, the aim is to shape economic policy so that it encourages continuous participation by women in the labor market, making it possible for both men and women to reconcile parenthood with professional life. Here, both the social insurance and the tax systems are based on the individual and offer neither tax relief nor special allowances for a spouse working in the home. Earnings-related benefits in the social insurance system make paid work an attractive option. In the individual model, which promotes the goal of economic independence for all adults, the social insurance system contains no widows' or widowers' pensions.

It is rare for a country to adopt either the breadwinner model or the individual model in their pure forms. The normal case is that one of the models dominates and that legislation, taxes and transfers are designed accordingly.

In a system that is neutral to the chosen family pattern, social and fiscal policy neither favor nor disfavor market work vs. home work. Each adult gets a pension benefit in accordance with contributions. A widow's/widower's pension has to be paid for by the spouse. To safe-guard the system against the problem women may end up in poverty in old age because their spouses do not choose a survivor's benefit (free-riding), mandatory joint-survivor annuities could be a solution.

Public pension systems, be they single- or dual-earner based, are mostly pay-as-you-go systems. In the industrialized world, aging, because of decreases in fertility and increases in life expectancy, puts a fiscal strain on public pension systems organized on a pay-as-you-go basis. Both cause increases in dependency ratios. Also, decreased fertility means a declining rate of return in such a system (making alternatives more attractive). In order for these systems to be sustainable, increased longevity can be handled by:

- increases in the contribution rate
- decreases in the benefit level or the replacement rate
- deferred retirement age

As for deferred retirement, the trend is, as is well known, actually the opposite, causing further pressure. Increased labor force participation and hours of work would lead to a lesser burden for those of active age. Measures for increasing female labor force participation and working hours might be an option.

The support in old age is put under pressure in developing countries as well. They are aging rapidly as shown in table 1.1. Aging is caused both by increases in life expectancy and decreases in fertility. These are shown in table 1.2. Urbanization and changing family patterns break the former extended family- or village-based support systems and make these informal security systems less reliable. Also, the spread of HIV/AIDS might impact the sustainability of family ties. As a result, reliance on public arrangements to provide adequate retirement income is going to increase.[1] Most developing countries have public social security systems although these schemes are far less important than existing family-based systems.

To introduce or reform existing formal, mandatory systems in developing countries poses additional challenges. The introduction of an earnings-related pension scheme requires a well-organized infrastructure that can support tasks such as: the collection of contributions, recording of earnings and paying of benefits. Furthermore, the exchange of informal systems for an extended, formal, mandatory system may not solve the problem of poverty in old age. A mandatory system means restrictions are put on possible lifetime consumption patterns. In low-income groups such restrictions are likely to be binding, forcing people to a low level of consumption when young which creates a reverse incentive to continue working under the prior informal system and might actually be a contributory cause as to why the informal economy is so important in these countries. A weak connection between contributions and benefits further worsens the dilemma. For these countries it may, therefore, as a first step, be better to introduce a flat-rate minimum pension benefit to alleviate poverty in old age. However, although the challenges differ, the need to review and consider pension reforms is important to both the developed and the developing world.

We may, thus, conclude reforming the systems of support in old age has to be given top priority. In this essay we analyze different ways of organizing pension systems. We give the pros and cons of the combinations of different features with special reference to gender aspects. An aspect of special interest here is men and women have different patterns of work history with women having a lower participation rate in the formal labor market, including interrupted careers in response to child rearing, as well as lower wages in general. Also, women have longer life expectancy than men and more often become widows than men become widowers. These differences may influence the consumption possibilities in old age depending on how the pension system is designed. Pension benefits will reflect labor market behavior. However, it is important not to compensate for gender differences in the labor market in pension systems as that would merely reinforce traditional gender roles and preserve discrimination in the labor market.

We are specifically interested in: if one design favors women more than another and in what respect? The analysis will provide a basis for making decisions about pension reform.

First, we give an analytical overview on different designs and their effects on distribution. We then describe the pension systems in a number of countries trying to evaluate them by the taxonomy given.

The chapter is organized as follows: section 2 focuses on design features that are important to women's pension benefits and rate of return on their contributions and how different pension rules create incentives for different behaviors for women compared to men. The following section 3 describes pension rules in China, France, Ghana, Jordan, Mexico, Poland and Sweden. For the developing countries we focus on urban workers as pension plans in rural areas are very limited. The features of these pension systems are analyzed with respect to their expected effects on pensions and rates of return for men and women in the selected countries. Section 4 highlights gender differences in the labor market. Section 5 concludes the chapter.

**Table 1.1**

**Percent Elderly of Total Population, 1975, 2000, 2015 and 2030**

| Country | 1975 | | | 2000 | | | 2015 | | | 2030 | | |
|---|---|---|---|---|---|---|---|---|---|---|---|---|
| | 65+ | 80+ | 80+/65+ | 65+ | 80+ | 80+/65+ | 65+ | 80+ | 80+/65+ | 65+ | 80+ | 80+/65+ |
| France | 13.5 | 2.5 | 18.3 | 16.0 | 3.7 | 23.3 | 18.8 | 5.8 | 30.9 | 24.0 | 7.5 | 31.2 |
| Sweden | 15.1 | 2.7 | 17.8 | 17.3 | 5.0 | 29.2 | 21.4 | 5.7 | 26.8 | 25.1 | 8.6 | 34.3 |
| Poland | 9.5 | 1.2 | 12.4 | 12.3 | 2.1 | 16.8 | 15.0 | 3.8 | 25.1 | 22.2 | 5.5 | 24.8 |
| China | 4.4 | 0.6 | 12.5 | 7.0 | 0.9 | 13.1 | 9.5 | 1.7 | 18.0 | 16.0 | 2.9 | 18.3 |
| Mexico | 4.0 | 0.7 | 17.9 | 4.3 | 0.6 | 14.9 | 6.3 | 1.0 | 16.6 | 10.2 | 1.9 | 18.7 |

*Source:* United Nations 1999 and U.S. Census Bureau 2000 (from An Aging World 2001).

**Table 1.2**

**Life Expectancy, Fertility, and Share of Population Age 60 and Older**

| | Life expectancy at birth[1] | | Remaining life expectancy at age 60[1] | | Fertility rate[1] | Share of population age 60 and older[2] | |
|---|---|---|---|---|---|---|---|
| | Men | Women | Men | Women | | Men | Women |
| France | 75 | 83 | 20 | 26 | 1.8 | 18 | 23 |
| Sweden | 78 | 83 | 21 | 25 | 1.3 | 21 | 26 |
| Poland | 70 | 78 | 17 | 21 | 1.3 | 14 | 19 |
| Mexico | 70 | 76 | 20 | 22 | 2.5 | 7 | 8 |
| China | 69 | 74 | 16 | 20 | 1.8 | 10 | 11 |
| Jordan | 70 | 73 | 17 | 19 | 4.3 | 5 | 5 |
| Ghana | 56 | 58 | 16 | 18 | 4.2 | 5 | 6 |

1) *Source:* The World's Women 2000: Trends and Statistics
2) *Source:* United Nations.

## Gender and Pension Design Features

Before turning to the description and analysis of the pension systems in the countries selected, we describe pension systems by their combinations of features and analyze the expected effects on incentives, pension benefits and income distribution for men and women. In table 1.3 below a number of features are listed.[2]

**Table 1.3**
**Combinations of Characteristics in Pension Systems**

| Public | Private |
|---|---|
| Mandatory | Voluntary |
| Pay-as-you-go | Funded |
| Defined benefit | Defined contribution |
| Means-tested, | |
| Fixed benefit, | |
| Minimum guarantee | Earnings-related |
| Redistributional | Actuarial |
| Non-actuarial pension age | Actuarial pension age |
| Indexing by | |
|     Prices, growth rate and/or interest rate | |
|     During earnings/contribution period, | |
|     During retirement/receiving period | |
| Survivors' pension | |
| Pension credits for child rearing | |
| Annuities | |

## Public-Private

In the debate public-private is often confused with the mandatory-voluntary dichotomy, implicitly assuming that a public system is mandatory and a private one voluntary. But nothing prevents a public system from being voluntary or a mandatory system from being handled by the private sector. In fact, a number of examples show this.

The choice between public and private administration is a question of efficiency. For example, competition between companies in the private sector improves efficiency however, advertizing costs may be high thus reducing the gains from competition. Comparatively, public systems are usually uniform, i.e. not differentiated according to costs/risks. This being the case, a system that does not differentiate between different risk groups has to be mandatory as the premium of the insurance is set to reflect the risk of average individual; in this case of a pension system to the risk of an individual's living a long life. Contrarily, if such a system was voluntary, only individuals who expect to live longer than average would buy the insurance. As a result, by its nature a mandatory pension system redistributes income to individuals with longer than average life expectancies. Besides being efficient, uniform systems cost less than differentiated systems as risk dispersion information is not needed.

Private systems can, of course, also be uniform as long as they are mandatory. However, the raison d'être for a private company is to make profit. Differentiating premiums and benefits in accordance with risk differences, i.e. making the insurance actuarial, seems to be one way of doing this. However, public systems may also be actuarial.

In the face of the problems the pay-as-you-go systems are up against due to aging, privatization is often called for as a remedy. Privatization is here often confused with increased funding which, again, can take place in a public as well as in a private system.

Political risk is often assumed to be smaller in a private system than in a public one. This risk is rather a question of transparency than which sector is handling the insurance. An unsustainable system, be it private or public, has to be reformed and a restricted number of parameters can be used for this purpose. In a private system the claims are protected by a formal contract that might have to be renegotiated. In a public system, especially a pay-as-you-go system, the claims are protected by an (implicit) social contract between generations. Either of them can, and sometimes has to be, changed.

The choice of public-private in itself does not have any gender effect.

## Mandatory-Voluntary

A mandatory system forces people to save for old age, particularly those who might otherwise be too short-sighted to save on their own. Another reason for mandatory pensions is to avoid free-riders. This group may be destitute in retirement because of the lack of savings with tax payers having to support them.

In a voluntary system, premiums or annuities have to be differentiated in accordance with risk; otherwise low risk individuals will find it profitable not to join the insurance. That is, individuals who think they have shorter than average life expectancies will not join the insurance. If there is asymmetric information (the seller and the buyer not having the same information on risk) the insurance market may not be able to differentiate in accordance to risk and may not reach an efficient solution (Arrow 1974, Barr 1998). A solution to this problem is to make the system mandatory. When risks (risks vary according to sex, health, region etc) in different groups are known; i.e. when it is possible to differentiate the premiums or annuities, no efficiency reasons exist to make the system mandatory. However, if the intention is to have a common risk pool of men and women, then the system has to be mandatory. If the premiums are the same for men and women, they will be set to reflect women's longer life expectancy. This means men, on average, will pay more into the system than they receive in benefits and, therefore, will not join. In this respect a mandatory system favors women since life expectancy of women is higher than that of men.

If the system is to be used for redistribution, it has to be mandatory.[3]

A mandatory system poses a restriction on the choice of consumption profile over a lifecycle by delaying some consumption until old age. This restriction is more likely to be binding in low-income groups than for high-income earners. The higher the level of the pension system, the more binding the restrictions for low income groups especially as they usually also are liquidity-constrained. In this respect a mandatory system disfavors women as they, on average, have lower incomes.

### Pay-As-You-Go-Funded

Pension systems can either be organized as pay-as-you-go or as funded schemes. In a pay-as-you-go system, annual contributions from the working population are used to pay for the benefits of the currently retired generation. The system builds on a social contract so when those who are currently working reach retirement, younger generations will pay for their benefits. In a funded scheme, on the other hand, each generation contributes to their own benefits; that is, annual contributions are invested in the capital market, either through a common fund or in individual accounts, and used to pay for a given cohort's benefits.

Traditionally, most public pension schemes have been organized as pay-as-you-go schemes. Much of the recent debate surrounding pension reform has been about whether the current financial problems faced by public schemes could be financed by increased funding. The argument is funded schemes yield higher rates of return and thereby contribute to reducing financial shortfalls caused by an aging population.

The rate of return in a pay-as-you-go system is determined by the growth rate, i.e. changes in labor force and in productivity, while in a funded system it is determined by the interest in the capital market. Thus, pay-as-you-go systems are exposed to the risk of decreased (slow increase in) labor supply (be it caused by low fertility, decreased working hours, late entrance to the labor market, early retirement, etc.) and slow productivity growth. Even a funded system is, however, exposed to demographic risk, albeit to a lesser degree than a pay-as-you-go one as the rate of return in the capital market, to a lesser degree, is dependent of demographic structure. Financial shortfalls in a pension system must be covered by: increasing the retirement age, making other cuts in annual benefits or increasing contributions. The argument is adding more funding to a system can reduce this trend because the rate of return in capital markets is higher. Another argument is risk diversification and that a larger share of individuals should get access to capital markets.

If women, to a greater extent than men, are dependent on the public pension system, (the public pension is a greater share of their assets) women are more exposed to the risk of low growth and, vice versa, less exposed to the risk of a low rate of returns/ higher volatility in returns in the capital market. As men usually have greater assets than women, men have a larger degree of risk diversification.

## Individual Risk in a Pay-as-you-Go System

Apart from the political and financial sources of social security risks, there is another source of social security risk that is related to the way that contributions are indexed in a pay-as-you-go system (Baxter 2002). A wage index means the social security system uses a measure of aggregate labor income (or average labor income) to index individuals' contributions in the social security system. The higher the correlation between the growth rate of the social security wage index and the growth rate of the individual's own labor income, the greater the risk arising from social security will be. If the correlation is high, a period of low growth of labor income corresponds to a period in which the social security return is low. That is, a period in which low income means a reduced ability to save for the future corresponds to a period in which the value of the social security asset al.so grows by a small amount. Studies built on U.S. data indicate women's labor income tends to be closely related to movements in the social security wage index while men's labor income is much less closely related to the wage index.

### Individual Risk in a Funded System with Individual Accounts

The investments in funded schemes can be invested jointly or in fund pooling; the investment risk being spread across participants or through individual accounts. A recent trend in pension reform is the introduction of individual accounts. In contrast to a common fund, individual accounts put the risk of investment decisions on the individual.

Assets with high returns, like equities, are connected to high risk while assets with low return have low risks. In the presence of an equity premium, a lower propensity to invest in stock could translate into large differences in the accumulation of financial wealth for retirement. If women, on average, invest their money so it gives a lower return than men's, women would, as a result, also receive lower pensions than men. It could be said that women pay for this security with a lower benefit. But a too risky investment strategy can also have a negative effect on retirement income.[4]

In general, studies of risk aversion show that women are more risk averse than men which may imply that they will also invest their pension funds more conservatively.

Several studies have examined gender differences in investment decisions. Most of the studies have used data from employer-sponsored pension plans in the United States, but some recent papers have investigated behavior in the second tier of the Swedish pension system (Säve-Söderbergh 2003).

In general, the results indicate women tend to invest their funds in less risky vehicles than men. However, several of the studies demonstrate it is not gender alone that determines investment choice. Rather, investment decisions seem to be influenced by marital status and the possibility to share risks within the household.

However, in order to know what kind of risk diversification people do, it is necessary to know both their investment decisions in their pension plans and how they invest their outside assets. Individuals with all bonds in their pension account may still have a diversified portfolio if they hold stocks outside of the pension plan. Or people who hold mostly stock in their plan could also hold mostly stock in the outside portfolio. Several studies looked at these outside investments and found that the investment allocations inside and outside retirement accounts are similar.[5]

### Defined Benefit-Defined Contribution

An additional characteristic of pension schemes is if they are organized as defined benefit plans or as defined contribution plans.

In a defined benefit (DB) plan, a formula for retirement income is based on the worker's wage and service is specified. In a defined contribution (DC) plan, benefits at retirement depend on the total contribution the worker has accumulated into the plan by retirement age and the investment return on those contributions. This implies a direct link between contributions and benefits in a defined contribution plan. In a defined benefit plan, this connection can be more or less tight.

Both defined benefit and defined contribution plans can either be pay-as-you-go or funded schemes. Most commonly, defined benefit schemes have been pay-as-you-go while defined contribution plans have been funded. However, the recent pension reform in Sweden was introduced a pay-as-you-go defined contribution plan, specifically, the notional defined contribution plan (NDC).

A defined benefit pay-as-you-go system is always exposed to the risk of expansion of the system beyond its optimal level (see Browning 1975, Breyer and Craig 1997, Tabellini 2000). This means increased risk for unsustainability, i.e. a risk the system will have to be reformed in a way that reduces the former expected benefits. If public pensions constitute a greater part of income and assets for women than for men, women are more exposed to this risk than men are.

In a DB system, the benefit is specified but not the contribution rate. In the face of a deteriorating financial balance of the system, for example due to an aging population, the contribution rate has to be increased in order for the benefit level to remain unchanged (in theory, although history shows this not to be true in practice).

As women, on average, live longer as pensioners than men do, they are favored by a DB system.

In a DC system, the annuity is determined by the sum of contributions (including compound interest) divided by remaining life expectancy (also possible with other kinds of annuities, e.g., variable annuities). If the system is a pay-as-you-go system, it faces the same demographic pressures as a defined benefit plan. This means economic and demographic strain have to be met by adaptation of benefits. Increasing the contribution rate is not an option because it automatically increases benefits. Hence, the risk of financial imbalance in a pay-as-you-go defined contribution is shifted to current generations.

In a DB system that uses close to a full career earnings record, we have a similarity between DC and DB systems. With a DC system, contributions in different years are compounded by a rate of return. With a DB system, earnings in different years are compounded by some index, for example, an index of average wages. If wage growth and interest rates are similar, the outcomes are similar. In this case, the difference between defined benefit and defined contribution is likely to be smaller than the difference between defined benefit systems with long and short averaging periods (see for example Diamond 2002).

## Means-Tested, Fixed Benefit, Minimum Guarantee-Earnings Related

Basic pensions independent of former income provide a social safety net for the old, particularly the old whose lifetime income was low. To accomplish this, the benefit formula could be flat and means-tested or could provide a minimum pension guarantee.

The flat benefit is a uniform amount paid to all eligible people once they reach a specified retirement age. It is administratively simple and can be set at a level that keeps all eligible old people out of poverty. A basic pension with a flat benefit favors low earners; that is, mostly women in the sense they will get a higher rate of return and sometimes a replacement ratio higher than 100 percent. This type of benefit gives no marginal effects, though there will be incentives, mainly in the lower part of the income scale, not to supply labor to the market.

Means-tested benefits can be more clearly targeted toward those in need. All income and assets in the household are usually included in the means test. Women are disproportionately low earners with more women than men are getting benefits from a means-tested system. Thus, it favors women as a group. But it also means women are more exposed to high marginal effects (that is, the sum of the tax rate and the rate of withdrawal of the benefit) and only getting a low, if any, rate of return on any extra effort in the labor market. This affects labor supply, particularly that of women (Blundell and McCurdy 1999). Women's labor supply may be more sensitive since net wages may influence their allocation of time between market work, which is taxed, and home work, which is not.

A means test in which only the individual's own pension counts as "means," in contrast to a traditional means-tests that take account of the entire household income from all sources, is the minimum pension guarantee. If a person's own mandatory pension is below a specified amount, the government provides additional resources to top it off. Women benefit from the focus on individual, rather than family, income. A minimum pension guarantee does not discourage voluntary personal savings when young, and transfers from members of the extended family when old; in comparison with traditional means-test. Similar to a means-tested or flat benefit, a minimum pension guarantee also introduces marginal effects as well as disincentives to work.

Earnings-related benefits in the social insurance system make paid work an attractive option. By creating an obvious link between reported incomes and future benefits, employment-based social insurance schemes encourage people to participate in the formal economy. A tight link reduces the tax wedge and efficiency losses.

### Redistributional-Actuarial

The distributional effects of pension systems depend on how the system is constructed. To analyze distributional effects, it is necessary to consider both the benefits and the way they are financed. This is due to the very basic economic principle 'there is no such thing as a free lunch.' Somebody has to pay. The basis for evaluating the interpersonal redistribution is an actuarially fair insurance. An individual's lifetime contributions are compared with her or his expected lifetime benefits. Contributions are deferred wages. Irrespective of who pays the contributions, the employer or the employee; it is part of the remuneration for work. The employee's cash wages are lower in the long run than they would have been in the absence of a pension system.

If the ratio between expected lifetime benefits and contributions is greater than one for a certain socio-economic group, then there is a redistribution in favor of this group, and vice versa.

Important aspects influencing the amount of redistribution are gender, income and marital status.

The life expectancy of women is higher than that of men. An actuarially fair insurance must, therefore, have higher contributions rates or lower pensions for women than for men. Systems which treat men and women equally (rely on"unisex" life tables) as public systems often do, redistribute income in favor of women. In some countries, women retire earlier than men which also contributes to a redistribution in their favor.

Life expectancy varies between different income groups—people with high incomes have higher life expectancy at retirement; thus a public pension system redistributes income in favor of high income groups.

If pensions are closely tied to contributions, there is not much redistribution. An actuarially fair pension system does not redistribute income between high and low incomes. But there are usually clauses in the system making the relation between income and pension less strict. If the basis for calculating the pension does not comprise the income of all years, but only a part of these years, (best or final years), there is redistribution in favor of high earners because most of them have not earned high incomes through all their working life.

Studies of public plans in different countries have found little, if any, redistribution from lifetime rich to lifetime poor. In fact, in the early years of the plan, high-income groups have benefited the most. High-income people enter the labor force later and so contribute for fewer years; they also live longer and so receive benefits for more years and have steeper age-earnings profiles so they end up with a high pension relative to their lifetime contributions (Aaron 1977, Creedy, et al., 1992, Ståhlberg 1989, 1990, World Bank 1994, James 1997).

Certain rules favor certain women while putting others at a disadvantage. If an individual's pension is determined by a number of best or final years, while pension contributions are proportional to income over all years, women who alternate between non-market work, part-time and full-time market work are at an advantage. If the number of years required to qualify for a full pension is less than the number of potential years of contribution, for example, women who take a break from gainful employment while they have young children are at an advantage as is everybody who takes a break for whatever reason. Women who continuously work part-time, or have low wages throughout their working lives, on the other hand, are at a disadvantage under these rules. If there is a ceiling on benefits, but not on contributions, high earners (mostly men) are at a disadvantage.

Although few empirical studies have examined how pension systems with earnings-related benefits and contributions systematically redistribute income between men and women, one study of the Swedish public pension, as it was prior to the 1998 pension reform, found the average ratio between expected lifetime benefits and contributions was higher for men than for women, that is, men had a higher rate of return on lifetime contributions than women. Female unskilled blue-collar workers had the lowest benefit-cost ratio of all because this group includes women who both work for many years and have a weak wage progression over time. Female low-wage earners, therefore, get the least benefit out of their contributions to the earnings-related scheme (Ståhlberg 1990, 1995). Recent studies by James et al.. (2003a, 2003b) get similar results.

Why link benefits to contributions? To discourage evasion and labor market distortions and to avoid perverse income redistribution like the one in the former Swedish pension system. A tight connection between contributions and benefits encourages market work.

## Pension Age

In defined benefit plans, women are often permitted to retire earlier than men. When benefits are not adjusted in an actuarially fair manner, women could increase their lifetime benefits by retiring early. A higher retirement age would add to the supply of older workers and yield a fiscal saving.

In defined contribution plans which are actuarially fair, lifetime benefits do not increase if women retire early. Actuarially fair benefits will induce women (men) to postpone retirement voluntarily compared to a defined benefit system with early retirement subsidies.

## Indexation

Indexation before and after retirement is crucial for both men and women. With price-indexation the monetary value of the pension increases each year, just enough to compensate for price increases. With wage-indexation it increases enough to keep up with wage growth. Women, as a group, gain more with indexation of annuities since it especially benefits long-lived individuals and groups. If the growth rate is positive, it is especially important for women to have a system with wage indexation. As they have a longer retirement period, price indexation makes them fall behind the standard of living of the working generation to a greater extent than men do.

### Survivors' Pension

Most social security systems pay a survivor's pension. The majority of the recipients are women, because women's life expectancy is higher than men's, and husbands are often a bit older than their spouses. However, this is not a redistribution in favor of women. If there were no survivor's pensions, a couple would have to safeguard the income of the surviving spouse. Because most women survive their husbands and because their pensions are much lower than that of their husbands (due to lower income and lower labor market participation) any private protection of the surviving person reduces the current consumption possibilities of the husband as well. The survivor's pension is, therefore, a redistribution in favor of couples. Single men and women subsidise families. Two-career families subsidize one-career families who get the same benefit for only one contributing member. This gives incentives to wives to stay at home or to work in the informal sector. In certain social security systems women who have worked in the labor market have to give up their own pension when they receive a widow's pension. This greatly impacts women's incentive to work in the labor market.

A key question is: if the state or the husband should finance the widow's benefits? (Another one is: should it be obligatory?) Should social security be responsible for survivors' pensions or should public policy be designed in such a way it reinforces family responsibility (thereby reducing the necessary tax on others)? The defined contribution pension allows a choice of joint-life pensions (with spouses) and also allows pre-retirement transfers of pension rights between spouses. This means married men could buy joint annuities. The payout to the husband would be reduced in order to leave a reserve to fund a survivor's pension. Single men would receive a higher annuity relative to their married counterparts.

If households are myopic, or if the husband places greater weight on consumption when he is alive, the widow may not have an equivalent amount in a voluntary system. (This is likely to be the case—default in U.S. employer-sponsored pension plans changed to joint survivor benefits specifically to deal with this problem. In order to get the benefit as a single annuity, both spouses need to give their permission).

### Pension Credits for Child-Rearing

Many existing pay-as-you-go systems suffer from serious financing problems. This is partly due to the aging of populations. In some countries such as Italy, Japan and Germany, fertility has fallen below the replacement level, implying returns on contributions to the public pension system will be very low, or even negative, in the coming decades. The construction of the pay-as-you-go system in which the active generation pays the pensions of the old generation, may be blamed for this development. Because the return on social security contributions depend on average fertility in the economy, and not on individual fertility, a positive externality of having children exists. Children are necessary for a sustainable pension system but raise the return to their parents' contributions only by a negligible fraction. Further, parents generally have to decrease their labor supply to raise children. Therefore, in a system in which pensions are related to one's own contributions, the pension of parents often falls short of the pension of couples without children. The number of children also might be driven down by the social security system. Empirical evidence for the negative impact of social security on fertility is presented in Cigno and Rosati (1996) and Cigno, Casolare and Rosati (2000).

Families with an above average number of children create benefits for the rest, particularly for those without any children everybody benefits from the labor of the next generation. Families with children could, therefore, be entitled to some support for raising children regardless of their income (Sinn 1998).[6]

### Annuities

Workers who are myopic might spend their retirement savings long before they are dead. Annuities which provide lifetime insurance are important, especially to women who are expected to live longer than men. Because the voluntary nature means more of a problem for women, mandatory annuities favor women more than men.

## Overview

In table 1.4 we summarize the conclusions from this section. In particular, we show how pension design affects work and savings incentives, redistribution and benefit levels for women.

It follows that to avoid poverty among women in old age, a pension system should:

- be public and mandatory in order to make unisex life tables possible
- provide economic incentives for women to work in the formal sector
- not punish women by giving them a lower rate of return on lifetime contributions than men
- not punish child rearing
- provide a minimum guarantee
- index pensions
- provide joint-and-survivor annuities which provide continued benefit payments to a surviving spouse
- allow accrued pension rights to be divided in the event of a divorce

### Pension Rules and Gender: Selected National Experiences

In order to examine to what extent the selected countries China, France, Ghana, Jordan, Mexico, Poland and Sweden have pension schemes according to the description above, we give an overview of relevant pension rules in these countries. We focus on urban workers because pension plans in rural areas are very limited.

Coverage in developing countries is, in many cases, restricted to urban workers and certain categories of workers such as civil servants and military personnel. Rural workers have little or no pension coverage in much of the developing world. Informal (usually family) systems provide the bulk of social support for older persons in many countries, particularly in Africa and South Asia. Most developing countries have public social security systems although they are far less important than existing family-based systems (see table 1.5).

## Table 1.4
## Overview

| Feature | Consequences for women as a group | | | Pension benefits |
|---|---|---|---|---|
| | Work incentives | Saving incentives | Effects on distribution | |
| Public/Private | No effect | No effect | No effect | No effect |
| Mandatory | | Depends on the level | Pooling of risks possible; favours women (especially high income earners) as they have longer life expectancy. Poses a more binding restriction in low-income groups. Disfavours women. Life expectancy effect dominates? | Favours women |
| Means-tested; household income and assets | Reduces incentives in low income groups, especially among women as their labour supply is more sensitive | Negative in low income groups | Favours low income groups, i.e. a greater share of women than of men | High replacement rate and a high rate of return in low income groups |
| Basic pension; flat, uniform benefit | No marginal effects, though there will be incentives in the lower part of the income scale not to supply labour to the market | | Favours low income groups, i.e. a greater share of women than of men | High replacement rate and a high rate of return in low income groups |
| Minimum pension guarantee; own pension tested | Reduces incentives in low income groups, especially among women (but less than when means tested) as their labour supply is more sensitive | Does not discourage savings when young | Favours low income groups, i.e. a greater share of women than of men | High replacement rate and a high rate of return in low income groups. |
| Earnings-related, DB | Makes paid work an attractive option; how much depends on the rules: If a weak connection between contributions and benefits, a subsidy to non-market activities reduces | | The prospect of financial imbalance: contributions are raised, benefits constant; favours women with their longer life exp. If a weak connection between contributions and benefits, the rules often favour certain women while putting others at a | Low pension if low income. If the system subsidises non-market work, women get a higher rate of return than men do. If benefits are based on certain income years (best or final) men are favoured as they have steeper age earnings |

**Table 1.4**
**Overview (continued)**

| | work incentives | disadvantage | profiles. Risks in benefit level pooled |
|---|---|---|---|
| Earnings-related, DC | A strong connection between contributions and benefits, strong incentives for work in the labour market | A strong connection between contributions and benefits, no redistribution. | Low pension if low income

Individual bears the risk – could affect women more because lower income |
| Payg | By itself, no effect. In combination with means-tested, earnings related, etc., see above
If NDC strong incentives for work in the labour market | By itself no effect. Depends on how pensions are tied to contributions

Redistribution across generations. When such a system is introduced (or expanded) the initial generation makes a wind fall gain | Women are more exposed to the risk of low growth and vice versa more favoured in the event of high growth |
| Funded | By itself, no effect. If a tight connection between benefits and contributions or individual accounts: strong incentives | By itself no effect. Depends on how pensions are tied to contributions | If individual accounts: women tend to choose low risk investments. May lead to lower pensions. Can also have a funded system that is DB in which risks are pooled |
| Actuarial | Strong incentives | If an actuarial system leads to lower pension, there is an incentive to increase private savings | By definition, no redistribution | Low pension if low income |
| Redistributional | To the extent that women are favoured, work incentives are weakened | Often the rules favour certain women while putting others at a disadvantage
Benefits long lived groups. Women are favoured | Depends on the rules |
| Price index, positive real growth rate | Constant or increased incentives | Possibly an increase | Disfavours long lived groups; women are at a disadvantage |
| Wage index, positive real growth rate | ? | ? | Benefits long lived groups. Women are favoured. If women have a lower average wage |

**Table 1.4**

**Overview (cont.)**

| | | | | | |
|---|---|---|---|---|---|
| Interest (if interest rate > growth rate) | ? | ? | increase than men, wage indexation favours women more, i.e. is especially advantageous to women | | If individually handled, see funded |
| **Pension age** | | | | | |
| Actuarial | Strong incentives among the elderly | Positive effect | If women have a lower pension age than men, with no impact on contributions and benefits, women are favoured | By definition, no redistribution | Affects men and women equally. |
| Non-actuarial | Subsidises early retirement; strong incentives not to supply labour among the elderly | Negative effect | Subsidises early retired men and women. However, as women have more years with pension they are favoured | | Affects men and women equally. |
| **Survivors' pensions** | | | | | |
| Actuarial (voluntary) | No effect | Incentive to reduce savings | By definition, no effect | | Depends on the level |
| Actuarial (mandatory) | No effect if no binding restriction | As voluntary | By definition, no effect | | Depends on the level |
| Non-actuarial | No additional incentives for women to engage in paid work | | Single men and women subsidise families. Two career families subsidise one-career families. | | Favours married women as they have higher risk of becoming widows and live longer as widows than men |
| Pension credits for child-rearing | Depends on the rules | | Favours women | | Favours women |
| Annuities | | | Favour long lived groups. Women are favoured. | | |

**Table 1.5**
**Pension Coverage**

**Share of Contributors in Labor Force**

|         | Year | Share |
|---------|------|-------|
| France  | 1993 | 88.4  |
| Sweden  | 1994 | 91.1  |
| Poland  | 1996 | 68.0  |
| Mexico  | 1997 | 30.0  |
| China   | 1994 | 17.6[a] |
| Jordan  | 1995 | 40.0  |
| Ghana   | 1993 | 7.2   |

*Source:* Palacios et al.., 2000. a) May be underestimated.

# China[7]

In 1979, China announced its one-child family policy. This was relaxed in 1984 when rural couples whose first-born child was a girl were allowed to have a second birth in most parts of China. One reason for having more children in many traditional societies, such as China, is to have more boys for security and support of the parents in old age. The government in China has provided urban state employees with pensions, weakening urban demands for large families. The government prohibition of private land ownership strengthens the relative demands of rural parents for more children and for sons in particular. In the rural sector, pensions are rare. Poor, rural, elderly are most adversely affected by the birth quota, having fewer children to support them.

In 2000, covered workers comprised less than 10 percent of the total population but 50 percent of urban employees, mostly state owned enterprises (SOE) and government employees (James 2002, Whiteford 2002). Pension spending mainly benefits a relatively well-off minority of the urban population. The majority of the agricultural workers are outside the scope of the system, as is the case in virtually all developing countries. Traditional family support remains a primary source of social security in rural areas. Data from 1987 show children supported around 61 percent of people aged sixty to seventy-four in rural counties, compared with 21 percent and 16 percent in towns and cities (Marshall and Butzbach 2002). Schultz (2003) reports the level of income of persons age sixty or over from "1992 Survey on China Support System of Elderly" conducted by the China Research Center on Aging. In 1992, 61 percent of elderly women's income and 33 percent of elderly men's income in rural areas were private transfers from children compared with 34 percent of elderly women's income and 8 percent of elderly men's income in urban areas. On average, an elderly man's pension was 7 percent of his annual total income (including home production) in rural areas and a women's pension was 0.5 percent of her annual total income. In urban areas, a man's pension was 50 percent of his 1992 total income on average, for women it was 28 percent (see table 1.6).

**Table 1.6**
**Income of the Elderly in 1992 and its Percentage Composition by Income Sources**

|  | Urban | | Rural | |
|  | men | women | men | Women |
| Total income in Yuans, including home production | 2549. | 1416. | 1035. | 538. |
| Pensions (percent of total) | 49.9 | 27.9 | 7.1 | 0.5 |
| Private transfers from children (percent of total) | 7.8 | 33.6 | 32.5 | 61.0 |

*Source:* Schultz (2003).

The Chinese pension system has been subject to significant reforms over the past twenty-five years but it can still be regarded as a system in transition. The adoption of market principles in the operation of the economy, and requirement state-owned enterprises must strive to be profitable, raises the question of how to build a system that could take over the social security function from enterprises. The social security system is moving away from one in which the responsibility fell entirely on employers and the state to one in which workers themselves make contributions; and from one which was completely financed by employers as part of their operating costs to one which is partially funded through pooling at the county and city levels. However, the assistance offered by informal networks—relatives, friends and neighbors—has continued to be an important source of help for those in need.

China does not yet have national social insurance. There are three main kinds of pension schemes: the pension scheme for civil servants and employees of public institutions; the voluntary rural pension scheme; and the basic pension scheme for urban workers (Zhu 2002).

The pensions for civil servants and employees of state organizations and institutions are based on earnings and adjusted according to years of service. It is a defined benefit pay-as-you-go system.

The voluntary rural pension scheme is administered by county-level rural social insurance organizations and financed by individual contributions supplemented by a collective subsidy. An individual account is established for each participant who, at age sixty, will be entitled to a benefit based on the accumulations in the account.

The basic pension for urban workers combines social pooling at the provincial level with individual accounts. The contribution rate varies between provinces. In May 2001, the nationwide average pension contribution rate reached 27 percent of payroll. An individual account equivalent to 11 percent of payroll is established for each worker and an average of 16 percent of payroll, goes into the local fund (Zhu 2002). The main features of the current system are as follows (SSPTW 2002):

- A universal flat-rate benefit equal to 20 percent of the average wage in the region for fifteen years of work and financed on a pay-as-you-go basis. No pension is payable for those with less than fifteen years' contributions. It is uniform for all regardless of earnings. However, workers may have an incentive to evade after the fifteen-year eligibility point has been reached.
- Individual pension accounts (DC) which give a monthly benefit of one-twentieth of the accumulated employer and employee contributions plus interest. The target replacement rate for a retiree with thirty-five years of contribution is 58.5 percent. The individual account pension is paid to the retiree during his or her lifetime, although theoretically the account's accumulation is only sufficient for ten years payment. Workers with less than fifteen years' contributions receive a lump sum of the balance in their accounts.
- The retirement age is sixty for men, fifty-five for women in salaried position, and fifty for women in blue-collar jobs. Those working in arduous or unhealthy jobs may retire five years earlier.

• The basic pension for survivors involves a lump sum of between six and twelve months of the insured's wage (depending on the number of surviving dependents). If the retiree dies within ten years, a lump sum equal to the remaining balance in the account is transferred to his or her legal heirs.

## France[8]

At first sight the French pension system looks very diverse and fragmented. A multitude of schemes cover different occupational groups. However, some main characteristics can be stressed. First, the pay-as-you-go pension system is based on employment and a distinction can be made in the working population between three large groups: private sector employees covered by the general social security scheme and compulsory supplementary pay-as-you-go schemes; public sector employees (functionnaires and employees in big national firms) covered by the so-called "special schemes;" and the self-employed (for which there are several types of regimes for different categories of the self-employed including retailers, craftsmen, farmers, etc.). Second, the vast majority of the workers, private sector employees and most of self-employed ones (not employees covered by special schemes), have double coverage in the form of a basic pension and a compulsory supplementary pension in a system that can be defined as a two-tier compulsory system. Third, an old age minimum income is guaranteed to all French citizens from age sixty-five, regardless of their working record.

The general scheme can be considered as the most important scheme as it includes two-thirds of the working population. It covers employees in the private sector (areas of industry and trade). The general scheme is an earnings-related scheme which provides relatively low benefits. This scheme ensures anyone who is at least sixty years old and has contributed for forty years receives a pension equal to 50 percent of average earnings (up to the social security ceiling) over a given period. This period is currently being extended from the best ten years to the best twenty-five years. This will be achieved in 2008. The pension is paid on a pro rata basis if the contribution period is shorter. A surviving spouse receives a pension equal to 54 percent of the insured's pension (up to a ceiling). There are bonuses for women that have had at least three children (two contribution years for each child in the basic general scheme; though different in the public sector).

The social security ceiling is a little higher than the average gross earnings in the private sector and it corresponds roughly to two times the national minimum wage. In other words, the maximum pension in the general scheme is more or less equivalent to the minimum wage. In order to improve the level of wage replacement, retired private sector employees, and most of the self-employed, receive complementary pensions from compulsory complementary funds. A supplementary provision is provided to private sector employees by two federations of pension funds, ARRCO and AGIRC; AGIRC for executive/manager (white-collar) workers and for the fraction of their wages over the social security ceiling, and ARRCO for the blue-collar workers and white-collar workers' wages below the ceiling. Retired people receive complementary pensions, resulting in combined levels of wage replacement of between 75 and 80 percent of the average gross salary of the ten (twenty-five) best years.

For low-level earnings, the general scheme accounts for most of the replacement of final salary. Its pension formula, based on average earnings of the ten (twenty-five) best years at work, may even lead to an overall net replacement rate higher than 100 percent for careers in which earnings have fallen.

Nearly 25 percent of the population is insured by the special schemes. For the most part, these schemes cover employees from the public sector. The two largest cover civil servants and military personnel and local authority officials. Together, these two schemes represent 86 percent of members of special schemes (Reynaud 1997). Adding the French railway scheme and the French gas and electricity companies' scheme, the proportion rises to 94 percent.

The special schemes have provided benefits at the same level as the combination of the general scheme and the supplementary pensions for private sector employees. In the civil service and the local authorities schemes the pension is set at 75 percent of the final gross salary for a full career (thirty-seven and a half years; forty years by 2008), i.e., more or less the same as the level provided to private sector employees by the combination of general basic scheme (régime général) and supplementary pensions (AGIRC and ARRCO). Surveys at end of the 1990s confirm replacement rates are very close (slightly higher for private sector employees with low wages, slightly higher for public sector employee with high wages). However, reforms undertaken during the 1990s will lead to a decrease of private sector replacement rates and, thus, will create a growing discrepancy with public sector ones (see Benallah et al., 2003). Public employees, other than civil servants, are not covered by special schemes but by the general scheme as private sector employees and they have their own supplementary pay-as-you-go scheme (IRCANTEC instead of AGIRC/ARRCO).

Approximately another10 percent of the population, i.e., self-employed groups such as shopkeepers, artisans, independent professions and employers, but not farmers, is covered by separate schemes. Wishing to remain separate from the general scheme, these groups decide for themselves the scope of coverage and level of contribution paid. Finally, there are separate regimes for people employed in the agricultural sector and farmers. Actually, the basic scheme for self-employed is more or less aligned (same rules) to the general scheme of private sector employees. And most of self-employed regimes benefit from a compulsory supplementary pension scheme, similar to ARRCO.

The French retirement system relies extensively on pay-as-you-go to finance pension provisions. The general social security scheme does not accumulate reserves to pay future pensions. It is also the case for most supplementary schemes. The vast majority of second-tier schemes are not pre-funded. ARRCO and AGIRC schemes hold assets only as contingency reserves. They are defined contribution pay-as-you-go schemes.

## Ghana[9]

In 1965 a Social Security Act was launched in Ghana. At the outset it was a provident fund. The 1991 scheme is the one in force today. It consists of: old age pensions, disability pensions and survivors' benefits. The system is compulsory for those who work in the formal sector, i.e. for those who have an identifiable employer. It is voluntary for those working in the informal sector. It is estimated about 10 percent of the labor force work in the formal sector and is covered by social security. Self-employed are estimated to be around 70 percent of the working population. Negligibly few of these have voluntarily joined the plan.[10] A greater share of men, than of women, work in the formal sector. In 1989, 69 percent of men and 92 percent of women were engaged in non-wage employment (Sabates-Wheeler and Kabeer 2003). Women have lower wages than men. In the non-agricultural sector women's gross earnings were 92 percent of men's; in the manufacturing sector it was 87 percent (Määttä 1998).

The system is a defined-benefit, pay-as-you go system, partially funded. The benefits are financed by contributions and the returns on the fund. The contribution rate is 17.5 percent. The compliance with paying the contributions is, according to Adjei (year ?), not so good. In 1999 the ratio of overdue contributions was over 9 percent.

The benefit is determined as a percent of the average of the three best years of the contributor's covered income. It is 50 percent of that average if contributions have been paid for a minimum of 240 months. The benefit is increased with 1.5 percentage points for each twelve month period of contributions beyond the 240 months up to a maximum of 80 percent.

Retirement age is sixty, except for some specified hazardous works where it is between fifty-five and fifty-nine. It is possible to withdraw reduced benefits from the age of fifty-five. There are survivor's benefits payable to named dependants.

In 1999, there were about 31,500 persons receiving benefits, while the number of contributors were around 773,500, giving a dependency ratio of 4 per 100.

Evidently, only a small part of the population is covered by the social security system. However, there are also informal systems providing insurance. The extended family system fills such a role. Also there are village-based mutual aid systems, for example "rotatory saving and credit associations," so called RoSCAs (Maes 2003).

## Jordan[11]

There are two parallel social security systems in Jordan, PS (public system) and SSC (Social Security Corporation). PS is the pension system for civil servants and army, a system introduced in 1957. SSC is for private employees and started in 1980.

The PS is a pure pay-as-you-go system, financed by a payroll tax of 8.75 percent of 'basic' wage (equal to less than half the total wage). The payroll tax covers approximately 10 percent of the expenditures. The rest is covered by general public revenues. The SSC is a partly funded system and partly a pay-as-you-go system. The contribution to this system is 17.35 percent of total wage (SSPTW 2003).

In the PS system there is no statutory retirement age; it is possible to retire as soon as the required years of service are fulfilled which are fifteen years for female civil servants, twenty for male and sixteen for military. The SSC has a retirement age of fifty-five for women and sixty for men with thirty-eight years of work for a full pension.

In the PS, the benefit depends on status and rank. It consists of both a proportional part and a flat component. For most beneficiaries the flat part dominates (Börsch-Supan et al., p. 49). In the SSC system the benefit is determined as 2.5 percent of average monthly wage in last two years times the number of years of contribution with a maximum of 75 percent of the average monthly wage the last two years. Benefits accrue for a maximum of thirty-eight years. Contributions thereafter do not add to the pension. There is also a minimum pension in the SSC.

Both in PS and in SSC there are survivors' benefits; in the PS they are flat, in the SSC the survivors' pension is 50 percent of the average wage in the last year of contributions or, if the deceased was a pensioner, 100 percent of the insured's pension.

Civil servants and private workers working in firms with five or more workers are covered by the social insurance system. The largest part of the formal labor market is the public sector with almost 50 percent (Börsch-Supan et al., p. 19). The SSC Annual report estimates the number of participants in the social security system to be 25 percent of total labor force. The labor force participation rate is just above 50 percent, the labor force consisting of 84 percent Jordanians and 16 percent Non-Jordanians. Out of the participants in SSC, 78 percent are men and 22 percent women. The female average wage rate is 80 percent of the male one.

## Mexico[12]

In 1997, Mexico replaced its old pay-as-you-go defined benefit system with a multipillar system that includes a funded defined contribution component mandatory for all private sector workers. Under the new system rules, 6.5 percent of a worker's wage is deposited into his or her personal account. Workers have a choice among investment managers with whom they place their accounts. Investment options are severely restricted to limit risk and disparities among workers. For every day worked, the government adds a uniform amount to the worker's individual account—the "social quota" (SQ). It is indexed to the consumer price index. This daily payment is independent of both the worker's own wage rate and of how many years the worker has contributed. The SQ is 5.5 percent of the minimum wage. It is a variation of the "flat" benefit concept, but flat per day worked rather than per worker, regardless of days worked. Workers who work more, get more. This structure was designed to increase the pension levels of low-income workers while also increasing the incentive for informal sector workers to formalize their work. It redistributes primarily to people who are poor because of their low wages rather than to people who are poor because they only worked part of their lives.

For workers who reached the age of sixty-five and have contributed to the system for at least twenty-five years, the government guarantees a minimum pension (MPG) if the funds accumulated in their accounts are not sufficient to obtain at least that pension. (Under the old system, a worker qualified for the minimum pension after ten years of contributions.) This high eligibility requirement may exclude most women with many women receiving something from their own contributions and the SQ, but few qualifying for the MPG.

Both the public parts (SQ and MPG) are financed out of general revenues. The public part is targeted toward low earners but is structured to reward formal sector work and provide work incentives to this group. It encourages women to enter the formal labor market, thereby increasing their financial independence, but provides little protection for those who do not.

Workers—both men and women—can retire at age sixty-five and upon retirement have two options. One option is to use the money accumulated in their pension savings account to purchase a lifetime annuity from a private insurance company. The other option is to leave the money in their pension savings account and make programmed withdrawals based on their life expectancy and those of their dependents. If a worker choosing the latter option dies before the funds in their account are depleted, the remaining balance belongs to the beneficiaries of their estate.

Mexico requires men and women to purchase joint annuities that cover their spouses at 60 percent of their own benefit. In reality this imposes an implicit cost on married men while relieving single men of the obligation they previously had to finance widows' benefits from a common pool in the old system. Married men pay a price that takes the form of a lower monthly payout while they are alive. The joint annuity requirement can be thought of as an enforcement of the implicit family contract between husband and wives. The Mexican approach however, does not avoid poverty for the older woman who did not work "enough" to benefit much from the SQ and do not have a husband to leave her a large widow's benefit. The MPG is designed to serve this role but eligibility conditions for the MPG exclude most women.

## Poland[13]

In the pension systems of the old Soviet Union and Eastern and Central Europe, women worked almost as much as men and earned almost as much. Women were allowed to retire at age fifty-five, five years earlier than men. Full pensions (55 to 85 percent of final wage) were awarded after twenty years of work (twenty-five for men), and credit was given for child-caring years. Huge financial strains in the pension systems have required Poland and other transitional economies to reform their pensions. Crucial features are a closer linkage between benefits and contributions through the adoption of a funded defined contribution pillar and a higher retirement age for women and men.

Due to labor market changes, participation rates in the formal labor market are now 15 to 20 percent lower for women than for men. Female wages are 70 to 80 percent of male wages. Occupational segregation has increased with women concentrated in the public sector and in lower paying fields such as health and education. Men are more likely to take jobs in industry, trade and in the private sector which pay higher wages (James 2003).

Poland's new pension system gradually came into effect in 1999.[14] The old scheme was fundamentally restructured, the most important change being a shift of the entire old-age system toward a notional defined contribution (NDC) part and a defined contribution (DC) part. The new scheme is of a mixed type, combining a still dominant, mandatory public pay-as-you-go scheme, that is being downsized and made more transparent, with a mandatory individually fully funded tier. There is a minimum pension guarantee.

The NDC part of the system is based on the principle of notional defined contributions, mimicking an individually fully funded scheme while remaining pay-as-you-go financed. That is, the contributions of each worker are recorded in an account and credited with a notional interest rate that is determined by real economy (wage bill growth) but the contribution is immediately used to pay other retirees. When the worker retires his or her account value is converted into a real annuity. The pension benefit is $P = C/E$, where P=old age pension, C=virtual retirement capital of the insured, made up of the accumulated lifetime pension contributions with a rate of return that equals the wage sum growth, and E=average life-expectancy at the time of retirement (the statistical average of male and female).[15] The retirement age is sixty for women and sixty-five for men.[16]

All workers under the age of thirty have their old age contributions (19.52 percent of the contribution base) split between two individual accounts, paying 7.3 percent of their gross wage into a DC account run by a private pension company of their choice while 12.22 percent is paid into a NDC account,that is, is used in the pay-as-you-go system (Muller 2003). Pension funds are being created and managed by private pension companies. There are several safety regulations, e.g., a minimum return threshold and strict investment rules.

The guaranteed minimum pension is a pension supplement on the top of both annuities if their sum is below certain level. It is financed out of the state budget. The eligibility criteria for a minimum pension (some 25 percent of average wage) are twenty-five years of contributions for men, twenty for women. In Poland, 70 percent of recipients of the minimum pension are women, given their relatively low lifetime earnings. Women close to the minimum will have little incentive to increase their work effort beyond the years required for eligibility.

The widow is paid a public benefit after she reaches fifty, but when she retires she must choose between her own pension and the widow's pension. This depresses the wife's incentive to work.

The gender gap in annual pensions has increased compared with the previous system as a result of the interaction between new policies and changing labor market behavior (reductions in female labor force participation and wage rates). Women receive lower annual pensions than men but due to the minimum pension and the use of unisex life tables women receive a slightly higher rate of return on contributions than men (James 2003).

## Sweden

In 1998, Sweden passed pension legislation replacing the defined benefit scheme with a notional defined contribution plan. In addition, a second tier of funded benefits was established. The reformed pension system went into effect in 1999 with the first benefit payments in 2003. During a transition period, benefits will be paid both from the old and the new system.

Retirement income in Sweden comes mainly from two sources: public national pensions that cover all individuals, and occupational pensions that build on collective bargaining agreements.[17] Both national and occupational pension are organized around an individual model; that is, all individuals are expected to earn their own pension benefits.

The old national pension scheme provided a flat benefit (paid to all irrespective of previous labor market experience) to ensure income security and an earnings-related benefit to replace income in retirement. The earnings-related benefit, together with the flat benefit, replaced about 65 percent of an individual's fifteen years of highest earnings up to a ceiling. Thirty years of labor force participation was required for full benefits. The normal retirement age was sixty-five but benefits could be withdrawn from age sixty or postponed until age seventy, with actuarial adjustments. The system was financed by a payroll tax in principle on a pay-as-you-go basis although the financing of the flat benefit was supplemented by general tax revenues.

The pension reform was motivated by a severe long-term financing deficit. However, several other problems were present in the old system (see related chapter, this volume). The new pension is a defined contribution system financed primarily on a pay-as-you-go basis but with a small funded component. The contribution rate is 18.5 percent: 16 percent of earnings will be credited to the notional account and 2.5 percent will be contributed to a self-directed individual account (the premium pension). Individuals also earn complementary pension rights while having young children.

The rate of return on the notional accounts is determined by average wage growth. In the self-directed accounts the rate of return is determined by the investment allocation. Participants have more than 600 funds to choose from, most of them equity funds. For individuals who do not want to pick their own investments, the government provides a default option. The premium pension allows married individuals to transfer pension rights between spouses.

Retirement age is flexible and benefits can be withdrawn from age sixty-one. At retirement, annual benefits are calculated by dividing the balance in the notional account by an annuity divisor. The divisor is determined by average life expectancy at retirement for a given cohort and an imputed real rate of return of 1.6 percent. The divisor is the same for men and women. Benefits are price indexed plus/minus the deviation from this 1.6 percent growth norm. The account balance in the premium pension will be converted to either a fixed or a variable annuity using standard insurance practices. This annuity is nominal and not indexed for inflation.

In addition to the earnings-related benefits, the pension system also includes a guaranteed minimum pension, currently equal to approximately 40 percent of an average industrial workers wage before tax. This benefit is pension-tested and is payable from age sixty-five. The guarantee pension is only offset by the earnings-related benefit in the national scheme; at low levels of earnings-related benefits, the offset is one-for-one and then declines. Individuals without any earnings-related benefit are eligible for the full guaranteed benefit.

The pension system also includes survivor benefits which are temporary. Most of the occupational schemes provide complementary survivor benefits. In the premium pension it will most likely be possible to buy a voluntary survivor benefit (this issue is being examined currently by the government).[18]

## Overview

Table 1.7 gives an overview of the seven countries' pension rules mainly of advantage to women. Table 1.8 shows contribution rates and replacement rates.

All selected countries have a mandatory public pension. However the coverage varies from 10 percent in China and Ghana to 100 percent in countries like France and Sweden. Using unisex life expectancy tables is crucial for women. Unisex tables favor especially women in France, Sweden and Poland. At age sixty they are expected to live five to six years more than men. In Ghana, Jordan and Mexico the differences in life expectancy are small. This was shown in table 1.2.

Most countries have some kind of minimum pension. This is pension-tested in Mexico, Poland and Sweden, means-tested in France. In the basic pension for urban workers in China no pension is payable to those with less than fifteen years of work, in Poland the eligibility criteria for a minimum pension are twenty-five years for men and twenty for women, while in Mexico at least twenty-five years are required. This high eligibility requirement may exclude most women. Workers in China and Poland close to the minimum have little incentive to work in the formal sector beyond the years required for eligibility whereas in Mexico the flat benefit per day worked (the SQ-benefit) increases the incentive to work in the formal sector.

| | China | France | Ghana | Jordan | Mexico (private sector) | Poland | Sweden |
|---|---|---|---|---|---|---|---|
| **Public pension rules mainly of advantage to women** | | | | | | | |
| Mandatory | yes | yes | yes | yes | yes | yes | yes |
| Coverage | 10% of labour force[1] | all employees | 10% of labour force | 25% of labour force[1] | all employees | all employees | all residents |
| Earnings-related | Yes | yes | yes | yes | yes | yes | yes |
| Actuarial | Yes[2] | no | no | no | yes | yes | yes |
| Minimum pension[3] | yes (if 15 years of work) | yes means-tested | no | yes (private employees) | yes (if 25 years of work), pension tested | yes (if 25 years of work for men, 20 for women), pension tested | yes, pension tested |
| In percent of average wage | 20%[4] | 25% of average wage of full time employees[4] | | n.a. | 33% of average wage for men, 46% of average wage for women[5] | 25% of average wage[4] | 40% of an average industrial workers wage |
| Pay-as-you-go | yes | yes | yes | yes | yes | yes | yes |
| Funded | yes | no | no | no | yes | yes | yes |
| Mandatory actuarial survivors' pension/joint annuities | yes | no | no | no | yes | no | no |
| Credits for child-rearing | no | yes | no | no | no | no | yes |
| Normal pension age | men 60 women 55 | men 60 women 60 | men 60 women 60 | men 60 women 55 | men 65 women 65 | men 65 women 60 | men 66 women 65 |
| **Public pension rules of advantage to** | | | | | | | |

**Table 1.7 (cont.)**

| | certain women and of disadvantage to other women | | | | | |
|---|---|---|---|---|---|---|
| Non-actuarial system; benefits calculated on final years disfavour women (and men) with flat life income profiles | yes[2] | yes | yes | no | no | no |
| Mandatory non-actuarial survivors' pension | yes | yes | yes | no | yes | yes |

1. 2000
2. non-actuarial for civil servants and employees of state organizations and institutions
3. The number of years required for a minimum pension induces low income women to withdraw from the labor market as soon as the requirement is fulfilled. Thus, these women get a low life time income. It is a subsidy from women (and men) who continue working.
4. 2002
5. 1997

The earnings-related pension in Mexico, Poland and Sweden and the basic pension for urban workers in China have a tight link between contributions and benefits. These pension systems are defined contribution plans with actuarial design. In France, Ghana and Jordan the pension systems are defined benefit plans with non-actuarial design. Benefits are linked with contributions but in a very loose way. Benefits are determined by the best or final salary which means a subsidy to all kind of non-market activities. It reduces work incentives, favors certain women by giving them a high rate of return on lifetime contributions but disfavors other women giving them a low rate of return. Women (men) with uneven lifecycle income patterns win while women (men) with flat lifecycle income patterns loose under these rules.

The Swedish system provides a child credit regardless of income and it is not restricted in the sense the parent has to abstain from market work. France gives pension credits for more than three children.

Only Mexico's pension system requires men and women to purchase joint-survivor annuities covering their spouses. In reality this imposes an implicit cost on married men taking the form of a lower monthly payout while they are alive. The state-financed survivor's pension in China, France, Ghana, Jordan and Poland is a redistribution in favor of couples especially one-career couples and gives incentives for wives to stay at home or to work in the informal sector. In Poland the widow must choose between her own pension and the widow's pension which, in addition, decreases the wife's incentive to work.

Women have a lower retirement age than men in China, Jordan and Poland. In defined benefit systems women who retire earlier are subsidized.

### Pensions, Labor Force Participation Rates and Wages

Women traditionally work less in the labor market and earn less than men. Thus, a pension system that has a tight link between benefits and contributions is likely to produce lower benefits for women. The extent depends on women's labor force participation, hours of work and on women's earnings. But a high minimum guarantee may have adverse labor supply effects.

In an actuarial system, an adequate pension requires a high labor force participation rate and a high employment rate. As shown in table 1.9 Sweden has the highest female labor force participations

Table 1.8
Social Security Contribution Rates and Replacement Rates

|  | China (urban private workers) | France | Ghana | Jordan (private workers) | Mexico (private workers) | Poland | Sweden |
|---|---|---|---|---|---|---|---|
| Contribution rate | 27.0 %[1] | 14.75 % of covered earnings plus 1.6 % of total payroll[3] | 17.5 %[5] | 17.35%[7] | 6.5 %[8] | 19.52%[9] | 18.5 % |
| Replacement rate | 58.5 %[2] | 75-80 %[4] | 50 %[6] | n.a | n.a. | n.a. | 50-55 % |

1. Zhu (2002)
2. The target replacement rate for a retiree with thirty-five years of contribution (Zhu 2002)
3. The contribution rate of the general social security scheme covering private sector employees (SSPTW 2002)
4. Includes compulsory supplementary pensions
5. SSPTW 2003
6. The minimum pension. It is increased by 1.5 percentage points for each twelve-month period of contributions beyond 240 months ( SSPTW 2003)
7. SSPTW 2003
8. James et al., (2003)
9. Muller (2003)

rates followed by France and Poland with Mexico far behind. According to table 1.9 women work part-time to a greater extent than men. In an actuarial system they will, accordingly, get a lower pension. Women typically earn less per hour than men, even after controlling for age and education. In Sweden women earn 91 percent of male earnings, while in China it is as low as 54 percent. This is shown in table 1.10.

If countries want to encourage men and women to engage in paid work and enjoy economic independence they need to link pension rights to the extent an individual participates in gainful employment. However, if such a system is to yield equal economic outcomes for men and women, countries need to introduce measures to achieve equal division of time put into the home and the labor market and should abolish the gender discrimination preventing women from attaining and aspiring to higher-paid jobs. Pending such a situation, the pension system should provide economic incentives for women to gain education and paid work. The pension system is not able to fix problems in the labor market.

Table 1.9

Labor Force Participation and Part-Time Work

| | Labour force participation, percent of population age 15-64 | | | Share of part-time work in employment | | | |
|---|---|---|---|---|---|---|---|
| | Men | Women | Total | Share of total employment | Share of women's employment | Share of men's employment | Women's share of all part-time work |
| France | 75.3 | 62.0 | 68.6 | 14.2 | 24.3 | 5.3 | 80.1 |
| Sweden | 79.8 | 75.0 | 77.4 | 14.0 | 21.4 | 7.3 | 72.9 |
| Poland | 72.8 | 59.8 | 66.2 | 12.8 | 17.9 | 8.8 | 61.7 |
| Mexico | 90.2 | 42.4 | 65.0 | 13.5 | 25.6 | 7.1 | 65.1 |

*Source:* OECD Labor Force Statistics 1980-2000.

Table 1.10

Annual Hours Worked and Earnings

| | Annual earnings ($\square$)[1] | Women's earnings as a share of men's earnings[2] | Annual hours worked[3] |
|---|---|---|---|
| France | 21,884 (2002) | 78 | 1,532 |
| Sweden | 26,480 (2002) | 91 | 1,603 |
| Poland | 5,708 (2002) | n.a. | n.a. |
| Mexico | 5,099 (2002) | 70 | 1,863 |
| China | 1,149 (2001) | 54 | |
| Jordan | 3,634 (1998) | | |

1.*Source*: OECD 2002 (France, Sweden, Poland, Mexico) ILO Laborstat database (China and Jordan) Annual gross earnings, unweighted mean for all sectors (Jordan), authors' conversion to Euro (China and Jordan).

2.*Source*: The World's Women 2000: Trends and Statistics. Earnings in manufacturing

3.*Source:* OECD Employment Outlook, Statistical Annex s. 320.

## Conclusion

Old age support comes from many sources. In this paper we focus on public pensions. We have identified the following features being important to prevent poverty among women and to secure income replacements. The pension system should:

- be public and mandatory in order to make uni-sex life tables possible
- provide economic incentives for women to work in the formal sector
- not punish women by giving them a lower rate of return on lifetime contributions than men
- not punish child rearing
- provide a minimum guarantee
- index pensions
- provide joint-survivor annuities which provide continued benefit payments to a surviving spouse
- allows accrued pension rights to be divided in the event of a divorce

These features are important because women's labor market behavior differs from men. In particular women work more part-time, have more interrupted careers and are lower paid. Furthermore, women have longer life expectancy and are more likely to become widows. It is important to provide adequate pensions and income replacement but a pension system should not compensate for gender differences in the labor market as that would reinforce traditional gender roles and preserve discrimination in the labor market.

## Notes

1. Docquier et al. (2003) show a massive or a progressive migration from the informal sector to the formal sector can be obtained under reasonable assumptions.
2. Mainly from Kruse et al., 1997. The features are discussed at length in Kruse, 2002, although without special reference to gender aspects.
3. Notice that in practice redistribution does not always favor the low income earner (women). See section "actuarial – redistributional."
4. Modern portfolio theory calls for investors to diversify their asset holdings over a variety of securities and, in that way, create a portfolio that is expected to achieve some given level of expected return while minimizing the risk.
5. For example, Bodie and Crane (1997), Sundén and Surette (1998), Uccello (2000), and Weisbenner (1999).
6. Child allowances are equivalent to fertility-related pensions as instruments to achieve an efficient allocation (Fenge and Meier 2003.)
7. The description builds on Chow (2002), James (2002), James et al. (2003), Marshall and Butzbach (2002), Saunders et al. (2003), Schultz (2003), SSPTW (2002), Whiteford (2002) and Zhu (2002).
8. The description builds on Benallah et al. (2003), Palier (1997), Reynaud (1997) and SSPTW 2002. Antoine Math, Institut de Recherches Economiques et Sociales (IRES), France, has given valuable comments.

9. The description builds on Adjei (1999), Osei (2003), SSPTW (2003).
10. In 1996 the World Bank made an investigation about how to extend the insurance to the informal sector.
11. The description builds on Börsch-Supan et al.. (1999), The Social Security Corporation, Annual Report (2002) and SSPTW (2002).
12. The description builds on James et al. (2003a, 2003b).
13. The description builds on Gora (2003), James et al., (2003) and Muller (1999, 2003).
14. Strong similarity can be found to the new Swedish pension system.
15. To allow for the creation of NDC accounts, a so-called "starting capital" is assessed for every insured who has begun an employment before the start of the reform and was born after 1948. A hypothetical retirement value will be calculated for every insured, on the basis of the old pension formula adjusted for age, reflecting his/her acquired rights until the end of 1998. Post-reform contribution payments will be added subsequently to the individual starting capital. Like every partial or full shift from pay-as-you-go to fully funded financing, the Polish pension reform implies considerable transition costs.
16. The original design of the new pension system assumed equal retirement age for males and female (the age of sixty-two). According to Marek Gora, Warsaw School of Economics, it is likely that this will be achieved in the course of a couple of years to come.
17. There are four main occupational plans: for national government workers, for local government workers, for white-collar workers in the private sector and for blue-collar workers in the private sector. The occupational pensions are, in particular, important to high earners because most of the plans replace earnings above the ceiling in the national scheme. The occupational pension adds 10 to 15 percentage points to the public pension replacement rate.
18. Also most of the occupational pension systems have been fundamentally changed in recent years. Three of Sweden's four collective-agreement pension systems have followed the path taken by social insurance and have been changed from being defined-benefit to defined contribution. It is only the private sector white-collar workers who have kept the main part of their pensions defined-benefit.

## References

Aaron, Henry J. (1977), *Demographic Effects on the Equity of Social Security Benefits*, Washington, DC: Brookings Institution.

Adjei, Eric N. A. (1999), "Pension schemes in Africa. The national experience of Ghana." ISSA Regional Conference for Africa, July.

Arrow, Kenneth, J. (1974), *Essays in the Theory of Risk-Bearing*, North Holland/American Elsevier.

Barr, Nicholas (1998), *The Economics of the Welfare State,* Third Edition, Oxford: Oxford University Press.

Baxter, Marianne (2002), "Social Security as a financial asset: gender-specific risks and returns", *Journal of Pension Economics and Finance (PEF)* 1 (1): 345-52, March, 2002.

Benallah, Samia, Pierre Concialdi and Antoine Math (2003), "The French Experience of Pension Reforms," Paper presented at ENRSP (European Network for Research on Supplementary Pensions) seminar, London, September 2003.

Blundell, Richard and Thomas McCurdy (1999), "Labor Supply: A Review of Alternative Approaches," in *Handbook of Labor Economics*, Vol. 3A, ed. Orley C. Ashenfelter and David Card, Amsterdam: North Holland.

Bodie, Zvi and Dwight Crane (1997), "Personal Investing: Advice, Theory, and Evidence." *Financial Analysts Journal,* November/December 1997, pp.13-23.

Breyer, Friedrich and Ben Craig (1997), "Voting on social security: Evidence from OECD countries," *European Journal of Political Economy,* 13, 705-724.

Browning, Edgar, K. (1975), "Why the Social Insurance Budget is too Large in a Democracy," *Economic Inquiry,* XIII, 373-378.

Börsch-Supan, A., Palcios, R. and Tumbarello, P. (1999), "Pension systems in the Middle East and North Africa: A window of opportunity." Forschungsbereich 504, No. 99-44. Universität Mannheim.

Chow, Nelson (2002) "The Construction of a Socialist Social Security System in China," in M-C Kuo, H F Zacher, H-S Chan (eds), *Reform and Perspectives on Social Insurance,* 145-160, Kluwer Law International.

Cigno, A. and F.C. Rosati (1996), "Jointly determined saving and fertility behavior: theory, and estimates for Germany, Italy, UK and USA," *European Economic Review* 40, 1561-89.

Cigno, A., L. Casolare and F.C. Rosati (2000), "The role of social security in household decisions: VAR estimates of saving and fertility behavior in Germany," CESifo Working Paper No. 394, Munich.

Creedy, J., R. Disney and E. Whitehouse (1992), "The Earnings-Related State Pension, Indexation and Lifetime Redistribution in the UK," Institute for Fiscal Studies Working paper W92/1, London.

Docquier Frédéric, Ousmane Faye and Oliver Paddison, (2003), "HIV-AIDS, social security and the two-tier structure of African economies", paper presented at 4th International research Conference on Social Security, Antwerp.

Diamond, Peter (2002), *Social Security Reform The Lindahl Lectures*, Oxford, New York: Oxford University Press.

Fenge Robert and Volker Meier (2003), "Pensions and Fertility Incentives," CESifo Working Paper No. 879, February 2003.

Góra, Marek (2003), Reintroducing Intergenerational Equilibrium: Key Concepts behind the New Polish Pension System," William Davidson Institute Working Paper No. 574, University of Michigan Business School.

James, Estelle (1997), "Public pension plans in international perspective: Problems, reforms, and research issues" in Salvador Valdés-Prieto, ed. *The Economics of Pensions. Principles, Policies, and International Experience*, Cambridge University Press.

James, Estelle, (2002), "How can China solve its old-age security problem? The interaction between pension, state enterprise and financial market reform," *Pension Economics and Finance,* **1** (1): 53-75.

James, Estelle, Alejandra Cox Edwards and Rebeca Wong (2003a), "The Gender Impact of Pension Reform: A Cross-Country Analysis, *Journal of Pension Economics and Finance* **2** (2)

James, Estelle, Alejandra Cox Edwards and Rebeca Wong (2003b), *The Gender Impact of Pension Reform: And Which Policies Shape This Impact*, The World Bank.

Kruse, Agneta, Porta, Pier L. and Pia Saraceno, (1997), "A Note on Transition Problems" in Pension Systems and Reforms: Brittain, Hungary, Italy, Poland ,Sweden, European Commissions's Phare ACE Programme 1995, Research Project P95-2139-R.

Kruse, Agneta (2002), "Försörjningen på ålderdomen," in L. Andersson (ed) Socialgerontologi, Studentlitteratur, Lund.

Maes, An (2003): "Informal economic and social security in sub-Saharan Africa." *International Social Security Review*, 3-4 2003.

Marshall, Katherine and Olivier Butzbach (2002), (eds) *New Social Policy Agendas for Europe and Asia*, The World Bank.

Muller, Katarina (1999), *The Political Economy of Pension Reform in Central-Eastern Europe, Studies in comparative economic systems*, Edward Elgar. Cheltenham, U.K.

Muller, Katarina (2003), "Pension Reform in the East European Accession Countries," European Journal of Social Security, Vol 5 No 1, March 2003, 7-37.

Määttä, Paula (1998): "Equal pay policies: International review of selected developing and developed countries." ILO, Labor Law and Labor Relations Branch.

Osei, Kwasi (2003): "Extending social security coverage: The Ghanaian experience." ISSA meeting, Banjul in October 2003.

Palacios, Robert and Montserrat Pallarès-Mirrales (2000), *International Patterns of Pension Provision*, World Bank.

Palier, Bruno (1997), "A "liberal" dynamic in the transformation of the French social welfare system" in Jochen Clasen (ed) *Social Insurance in Europe*, Policy Press.

Reynaud, Emmanuel (1997), "France: A national and contractual second tier," in Rein & Wadensjö (eds), *Enterprise and the Welfare State*, Edward Elgar. Cheltenham, U.K.

Sabates-Wheeler, Rachel and Kabeer, Naila (2003): "Gender equality and the extension of social protection." ILO, ESS – paper no. 16.

Sainsbury, Diane (1996), *Gender equality and welfare states,* Cambridge: Cambridge University Press.

Saunders, Peter et al.. (2003), "The structure and impact of formal and informal social support mechanisms for older people in China," paper presented at ISSA 4th, International Research Conference on Social Security, Antwerp.

Schultz, Paul (2003) "Human Resources inChina: The Birth Quota, Returns to Schooling, and Migration," Center Discussion Paper No. 855, Economic Growth Center, Yale University.

Sinn, H.-W. (1998) "The pay-as-you-go pension system as a fertility insurance and enforcement device," NBER Working Paper No. 6610, Cambridge.

*SSC Annual Report* (2000), The Social Security Corporation, The Hashemite Kingdom of Jordan.

*SSPTW, Social Security Programs Throughout the World*, 2002, 2003.

Ståhlberg, Ann-Charlotte (1990), "Lifecycle Income Redistribution of the Public Sector: Inter- and Intragenerational Effects," in Persson, Inga (ed), *Generating Equality in the Welfare State. The Swedish Experience*, 97-121, Norwegian University Press, Oslo.

Ståhlberg, Ann-Charlotte (1995), "Women's Pensions in Sweden," *Scandinavian Journal of Social Welfare,* Vol. 4, 19-27.

Ståhlberg, Ann-Charlotte (2002a) "Gender Equality and Social Policy in Europe and East Asia," Chapter 12 in Marshall, Katherine and Butzbach Olivier (eds), *New Social Policy Agendas for Europe and Asia. Challenges, Experience, and Lessons,* pp. 203-214, The World Bank.

Ståhlberg, Ann-Charlotte (2002b), "Gender and Social Security: Some lessons from Europe," *European Journal of Social Security*, Volume 4/3, 227-239.

Säve-Söderbergh, Jenny (2003), Essays on Gender Differences in Economic Decision-Making, Swedish Institute for Social Research-Dissertation Series 59.

Tabellini, Guido (2000), "A Positive Theory of Social Security," *Scandinavian Journal of Economics*, 102 (3), 523-545.

Uccello (2000), "401(k) Investment Decisions and Social Security Reform." Center for Retirement Research at Boston College Working Paper 2000-4 March 2000.

Whiteford, Peter, (2002), "From Enterprise Protection to Social Protection: Pension Reform in China," OECD.

Whiteford, Peter, (2002), "From Enterprise Protection to Social Protection: Pension Reform in China," OECD.

World Bank (1994), *Averting the Old Age Crisis*, Oxford: Oxford University Press.

Zhu, Yukun (2002), "Recent developments in China's social security reforms," *International Social Security Review*, Vol 55, 4/2002, pp 39-54.

# 2

# Pension Policy in the European Union: Responses to the Changing Division of Labor in Family Life

*Eila Tuominen*
*Sini Laitinen-Kuikka*

## Introduction

Contemporary pension policy emphasizes high employment rates as a crucial measure for the financing of increasing pension expenditure due to an aging population in Europe. The birth rate is expected to remain low which, in combination with an aging population, would lead to an unfavorable age structure and a shortage of a young labor force. The demographic forecast is a strong argument for the growing demand for a female labor force and better work-family reconciliation in order to attract women to return to paid work. A common target for increasing the employment rate, particularly the need to increase female employment, has been clearly expressed in the pension policy of the EU. In December 2001, broad common objectives for the future pension policy of member states were agreed on. The general aim of this process is to ensure the adequacy of pensions and the sustainability and the modernization of pension systems in response to changes in the labor market and society in general. One of the eleven more detailed objectives concerning the challenge of the modernization of pension systems is especially devoted to gender equality. It says that member states should "review pension provision with a view to ensuring the principle of equal treatment between women and men, taking into account obligations under EU law" (Council of the European Union 2001). The progress made in the member states toward these objectives is monitored and evaluated by the Commission and the Council.

The EU employment strategy's target goal is for a female employment rate of 60 percent by 2010. Member states have been encouraged to set their own national target goals according to this (The Future of the European Employment Strategy, 2003). For women, these efforts mean the time spent in paid work outside the home will continue to increase as well as their lifetime earnings. In spite of the favorable prospect for women's paid work outside the home and for increasing pension accrual, there are many gendered features in labor market participation, especially caregiver work which make it more difficult for women, than for men, to get an adequate pension in old age. Women still shoulder a greater part of the household work and childcare and these family responsibilities frequently disrupt their employment. Women who move in and out of the labor force often lose pension benefits in both public and private pension schemes. The expansion of "flexible forms of working" make it likely the numbers of such workers will increase, rather than decrease, in future years and thereby increase the number of people with inadequate pension rights. The individual cost of an irregular work history can be very high. The contradicting interests related to women's traditional caregiver obligations and their increased employment should be carefully monitored.

Increasing pressures on public expenditure and aging populations have already led many EU countries to cut public pension benefits during the last decades. A central assumption in the politics of pension reform is increases in the proportions of elderly people in national populations necessarily lead to increased and unsustainable state expenditures. In pension reform, the link between lifetime earnings and benefits has been tightened. Many countries have also taken measures to encourage the expansion of private pension provision. The trend throughout the European Union, from state sponsored, pay-as-you-go pension schemes toward occupational and private pension schemes, may mean a more discriminatory future environment for women in the EU (Hutton 1998, Ginn and Arber 1999, Ginn et al. 2001). There is a risk these changes will make pension systems less advantageous for women in the future.

Many European countries have recognized the problem of linking benefits to past earnings and employment history and have succeeded in reducing gender inequality in old age to some degree by adding 'women-friendly' provisions to mandatory schemes. However, with respect to labor market participation and the family re-

sponsibilities of women there are marked differences in pension provision among European countries. The picture of these differences
is rather obscure so an exploration of these issues is needed.

## Frameworks for Comparing Pension Provision: From a Gender Perspective

*Pension Provision Through State, Market and Family*

Differences in pension provision between nations cannot be explained without paying attention to the way welfare states are
institutionalised in Europe. Comparative analyses on the origins and
development of modern welfare states have flourished over the past
two to three decades. Recent studies markedly build on the well-
known work of Esping-Andersen (1990). The three regime types:
liberal, conservative and social democratic, are based on a cluster-
ing of countries along with three dimensions of variability: state-
market relations, stratification and social rights. The key issue in the
analyses of Esping-Andersen is the principle of social rights. Social
rights permit people to make their livings independent of pure market forces. The more extensive the coverage of the bene-fits des-
ignated as social rights, and the higher the level of benefits is, the
smaller the dependency of the labor force on the market. The concept of social rights has, thus, been defined in relation to labor market depend-ence and is referred to as decommodification by Esping-
Andersen. The level of decommodification provided by the welfare
state depends on: the stringency of eligibility rules, the level of income replacement and on the range of entitlements. In sum, a highly
decommodifying welfare state is one that grants benefits irrespective of the claimant's fulfilment of given conditions such as the record
of paid contributions.

There appears to be a clear coincidence of high decommodification
and strong universalism in the Scandinavian welfare states, whereas
the continental European countries group closely together as corpo-
ratist, conservative countries and are modestly decommodifying. In
social democratic and conservative regimes, such as in Europe, all
citizens are under the umbrella of state provision, but the former
Scandinavian states are universalistic, egalitarian and provide significant public services and decommodification of labor (alternatives to participation in the labor market), while the latter European
states preserve status and class differentials, offer few public ser-

vices and condition benefits on employment. In short, direct influence of the state is restricted to the provision of income maintenance benefits related to a worker's occupational status. Another distinctive characteristic of the conservative regime is the principle of subsidiarity; the state will only interfere when the family's capacity to serve its members is exhausted.

Furthermore, in the social democratic welfare states, women—regardless of whether they have children or not—are encouraged to participate in the labor market. In contrast, in the conservative welfare states, labor market participation by married women is discouraged because this regime type is committed to the preservation of traditional family structures.

The third regime type, the liberal welfare state, is characterized by low decommodification and strong individualistic self-reliance and the primacy of the market. Within this type of welfare state, there is little redistribution of incomes and the realm of social rights is rather limited. Liberal regimes promote market provision of services, encourage dualism between the majority of market-reliant citizens and those who rely on public provision and offer few alternatives to participating in the market.

Esping-Andersen's welfare state typology inspired fruitful research. Several authors have reconceptualized institutional structures of welfare states and have formed divergent typologies. A crucial reason for reconceptualization is the criticism gender-dimension is neglected in the typology of Esping-Andersen (Arts and Gelissen 2002). It is argued a systematic discussion of the family's place in the provision of welfare and care is lacking. Not only the state and the market provide welfare, but also families themselves. According to many authors, it is the gender division of paid and unpaid work—especially care and domestic work— that needs incorporating in the typology (Orloff 1993, O'Connor et al. 1999). A large body of comparative research has developed over the 1990s showing welfare policies of all kinds are shaped by gender relations and, in turn, affect gender relations and gender differences in living conditions (den Dulk and Remery 1997, Ginn et al. 2001, Gornick et al. 1997, Trifiletti 1999, van Doorne-Huiskes et al. 1998, Anttonen and Sipilä 1996). However, the finding of many comparative analyses on gender and the welfare state is regimes seldom fully explain gender differences in labor force participation and the institutional heterogeneity of the welfare state strategies adopted by different countries.

In this chapter, we analyse pension rights in the national pension schemes of the EU from a gender perspective by using the mainstream regime-type framework based on the work of Esping-Andersen. Instead of a three-fold regime typology we, however, use a four-fold version. This is as in the Mediterranean countries the family institutions, welfare states and labor market participation of women differ from those of continental European countries in such marked ways the separation of these countries into a southern European regime is justified (Ferrera 1996, Trifiletti 1999, Anttonen and Sipilä 1996). Familialist welfare structures are most powerful in southern Europe and, for example, support for mothers' employment is clearly the lowest. Therefore, in this working paper, the Southern European countries are separated into a divergent regime from the continental conservative regime.

An important aspect of pension benefits is the extent to which they allow individual claims for benefits or 'family' recipients through derived benefits or household means testing. Individual pension rights refer to a person's own insurance record or residence-based rights whereas derived rights are based on a spouse's insurance record. From the gender perspective, we examine how policy makers have responded in pension policies to challenges due to changes in the gender division of labor and the reshaping of the family institution.

### Trends in Family Formation and Women's Employment

Demographic changes in family formation issue a challenge to pension provision based on derived pension rights and on the traditional family institution. Legal marriage has lost its weight as the only socially recognized family form in Western societies. Due to an increasing number of divorces, more people are living as singles and single parents. Also "serial monogamy" has become more widespread, i.e. people marry for the second and third time. In spite of this, there is a general trend toward decreasing marriage rates (Hatland 2001, see appendix table 1). Furthermore, new family forms have emerged as alternatives to marriage. Cohabiting, especially among young couples, has become a common alternative to marriage. A relevant question here is how pension schemes in the EU countries have responded to these new needs and risks patterns.

Due to women's increased economic activity outside the home, marriage is no longer a financial necessity for European women, even in the case of pregnancy. An obvious indicator for this is the number of extra-marital births that have increased rapidly during recent decades. This trend is seen to some extent in all EU countries: in 1980 every tenth child was born outside marriage and by 2000 it was already over one in four. The highest figures are seen in the Nordic countries and also in France and in the United Kingdom (40 to 55 percent), and the lowest in Italy (10 percent) and Greece (4 percent) (Statistics in focus, theme 3, 17/2002 European communities). Although parents often enter into marriage after childbirth, statistics do not indicate the number of these marriages.

Clearly, there are noteworthy differences in the traditional family institution between countries in the EU. Legal marriage has preserved its status quite well in southern Europe. In the Mediterranean countries, extra-marital births are rather rare and divorce rates are low in comparison to the Nordic countries and also to many other continental countries. In spite of the strong position of legal marriage, there has been a drastic decreasing trend in fertility rates in Southern Europe (appendix table 1). Paradoxically, familialist welfare in the Mediterranean countries is a major cause of low fertility rates. An important driving force behind this trend lies in the increased difficulties young adults face in starting a family. These difficulties are more and more related to high youth unemployment rates. Family formation has been postponed by a couple of years in all European countries due to longer time spent in education and then in search of stable employment. However, a recent trend has been higher fertility rates go together with high female employment (Esping-Andersen et al., 2002, 16, 63–67). Today, childcare responsibilities are not obstacles to women's paid work outside the home as much as before.

The data in figure 2.1 indicate a well-known phenomenon that one of the most profound changes during recent decades has been women's increased economic activity. Since the 1980s the activity rate of women has increased over ten percentage points in the EU while the activity rate of men, due to early retirement, has decreased nearly as much. Thus, there has been a tendency toward convergence in the labor market participation of women and men.

Still, the activity rates of women, in comparison to men, are lower in every EU country (figure 2.1). While it is tempting to speak of a converging trend toward higher levels of female employment across the EU, substantial differences in participation remain. The Nordic countries have held a leading position in women's employment rates

**Figure 2.1**

**Features of Female Labor Market Participation in in EU Countries[1]**

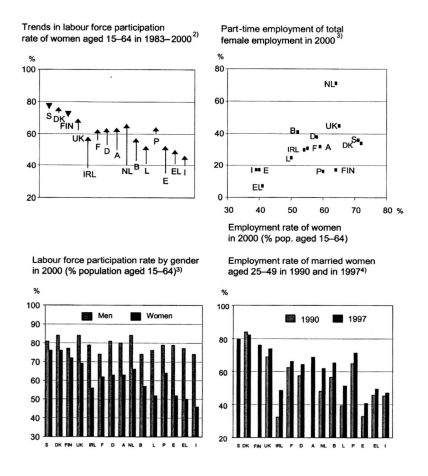

1.    A= Austria, B= Belgium, D= Germany, DK= Denmark, E= Spain, EL= Greece,
      F= France, FIN= Finland, I= Italy, IR= Ireland, L= Luxembourg,
      NL=The Netherlands, P= Portugal, S= Sweden, UK= United Kingdom.
2.    Source: OECD Employment Outlook 1997 and 2001
3.    Source: OECD Employment Outlook 2001, Employment in Europe 2001
4.    Source: Labor Force Survey 1990 and 1997 in the EU countries. The data of Sweden,
      Finland and Austria are not available from 1990.

in spite of the decreasing rates during the 1990s. The incentives to register in the labor force declined due to a recession. In Finland especially, employment rates stayed at a lower level than ten years ago (see appendix figure 1). Nevertheless, there are no signs families have returned to the house-wife and one-breadwinner model. In the Nordic countries, female employment rates still come closest to their male counterparts.

With respect to continental vs. southern European welfare states, there are clear differences in the economic activity of women. In 2000, the female labor force participation rates in the Mediterranean countries were clearly behind the EU average of 60 percent. However, Portugal constitutes an exception in the southern European regime. The employment rate of Portuguese women is closer to the countries of the continental regime where the female labor force rates are near the average of the EU (except in Luxembourg). It is worth emphasizing there has been a great deal of dynamism in female employment in the southern European countries as well (see appendix figure 1). Women have continuously increased their participation in the labor market although the institutional arrangements have not been especially conducive to female employment.

Between the Anglo-Saxon welfare states, Ireland and the United Kingdom, there are marked differences in activity rates and also in age-specific employment rates (see appendix figure 1). In the United Kingdom, a high level of female employment is associated with a large service sector. Labor market deregulation has led to a rapid growth of part-time jobs, especially for women, under relatively unfavorable conditions (Esping-Andersen et al., 2002). The activity rate of Irish women is still low and close to the southern European counterparts.

Clearly, motherhood's effect on economic activity varies considerably from one country to another, although the integration of women of childbearing age to the labor market has increased generally (see appendix figure 1). This is also seen in figure 1.

Employment rates for married women aged twenty-five to forty-nine has increased dramatically in many countries (Ireland, the Netherlands, Germany, Belgium, Luxembourg, Portugal and Spain). Female activity rates generally fall as the number of children increase, although the exact effect varies considerably among member states. In Finland, for example, the number of children makes little difference in the employment rate of women, though this does not concern women with children less than five-years-old. On the other hand, in Germany, Ireland, Luxembourg, the Netherlands and the United Kingdom, employment rates for women with at least one child are markedly lower than for those with no children. Also the age of the child makes a difference in these countries (Employment Rates Report 1998, Windebank 1996).

Due to marriage and motherhood, women face employment interruptions, which cause working career and wage penalties. For women with childcare responsibilities, full interruption in paid work has dramatic effects on lifelong earnings and, accordingly, on pension accrual. As a rule of thumb, if a full-time worker interrupts her career for a five-year interim, she will forego 1.5 to 2 percentage points per annum in potential lifetime earnings. This massive loss would, however, decline to only 0.5 percent per year if the same woman were to remain employed on a part-time basis for the same five years (Esping-Andersen et al., 2002, 78–80). For women with childcare responsibilities, the continuity of a working career is crucial in avoiding wage penalties.

In the European countries, the share of part-time employment in total female employment varies significantly. The variation is huge between countries, from 7 to 71 percent in Greece and the Netherlands respectively. There seems to be a clear correlation in the higher the female employment rate, the higher the proportion of women in part-time jobs is (figure 1). Here, the Nordic countries, especially Finland, seem to be the exceptions to the rule. Also in Portugal, in spite of a high female employment rate, the share of part-time work is low. So in this respect it remains a southern European country.

A well-known phenomenon is part-time work—which usually means working weeks of less than thirty-one hours—is often associated with poorer working conditions, job insecurity and lack of fringe benefits as well as lower hourly pay. Recent comparative research has indicated where hours are longer, part-time employment is less strongly linked to low pay, low occupational status and poor long-term prospects. Furthermore, part-time work of women tends to be in the prime earnings years when opportunities for wage gains are highest (Ginn et al. 2001). Although a motherhood effect on women's lifetime earnings and, accordingly, pension accrual, varies considerably from one country to another, this has an adverse effect on women's pension accrual, to some extent, in every country.

Over recent decades, remarkable changes can be seen in the average time spent in the labor force both among women and men[1] (table 2.1). Since the beginning of the 1980s, the average time in work has shortened generally by a couple of years for men. The only exception is the Netherlands where the average years have increased. At the same time, the average working career of women has become considerably longer. The lengthening is especially remarkable in the Netherlands, Ireland, Spain and also in Germany, Belgium and Greece.

With respect to pension policy objectives concerning the modernization of pension schemes in the EU, the challenges to national policy vary considerably. There are countries where the average years in the labor force during a lifetime are almost as long for both genders (the Nordic countries). On the other hand, there are countries where the length of female working careers is about two-thirds of that of men and a familialist welfare model is strong (Ireland, Luxembourg and the Southern European countries except Portugal). These marked differences produce differences in needs and risks patterns, which are important in the context of evaluation of pension schemes at a national level.

In European societies, the average age of exit from the labor market is lower for women than for men (table 2.1). Hence, the average years of drawing a pension after leaving the labor force are longer for women than for men[2] In addition, differences in life expectancy favoring women generally make the pension period considerably longer for women than for men. Women's contribution time in relation to the pension period is especially disproportional in countries where female economic activity is low. In the southern European countries (Greece, Spain and Italy), for example, the average pension period is longer than the time spent in the labor market: during a lifetime, the pension period is over 100 percent of the average years spent in work. Accordingly, the same ratio for Nordic women is about 60 to 70 percent, and for men generally 50 to 60 percent. The huge disproportion between the contribution time and the pension period indicates pressures on financing the pension expenditure, especially in defined benefit schemes.

Table 2.1

Average Years in the Labor Force[1], Average Age of Exit[2] and Average
Pension Period From Age of Exit[3] in 2000.

| | Years in labor force 1983 1) | Years in labor force 2000 1) | Change 1983/-00, years | Age of exit 2) | Pension period 3) | Pension period/ aver. wor years |
|---|---|---|---|---|---|---|
| | | | MEN | | | |
| EU 15 | - | 38,5 | - | 60,3 | 20,3 | .52 |
| | | | | | | |
| Sweden | 42,8 | 39,8 | -3,0 | 62,3 | 18,9 | .47 |
| Denmark | 41,8 | 41,4 | -0,4 | 61,5 | 18,2 | .44 |
| Finland | 39,6 | 37,1 | -2,5 | 59,8 | 20,2 | .54 |
| United Kingdom | 43,8 | 41,3 | -2,5 | 61,3 | 18,8 | .46 |
| Ireland | 42,9 | 39,7 | -3,2 | 61,5 | 17,6 | .44 |
| France | 39,2 | 35,7 | -3,5 | 59,2 | 22,1 | .62 |
| Germany | 40,7 | 40,0 | -0,7 | 60,5 | 19,7 | .49 |
| Austria | - | 38,6 | - | 59,5 | 20,9 | .54 |
| The Netherlands | 38,3 | 40,6 | +2,3 | 60,1 | 19,9 | .49 |
| Belgium | 38,0 | 35,1 | -2,9 | 58,6 | 21,6 | .62 |
| Luxembourg | 38,7 | 35,9 | -2,8 | 58,9 | 20,9 | .58 |
| Portugal | 43,4 | 39,4 | -4,0 | 61,5 | 17,9 | .45 |
| Spain | 42,3 | 39,2 | -3,1 | 61,0 | 20,0 | .51 |
| Greece | 40,7 | 38,1 | -2,6 | 60,7 | 20,8 | .55 |
| Italy | 39,7 | 35,6 | -4,1 | 59,2 | 21,6 | .61 |
| | | | | | | |
| | | | WOMEN | | | |
| EU 15 | - | 29,2 | - | 58,1 | 26,3 | .90 |
| | | | | | | |
| Sweden | 38,6 | 37,4 | -1,2 | 61,6 | 23,3 | .73 |
| Denmark | 35,6 | 37,0 | +1,4 | 59,9 | 23,1 | .62 |
| Finland | 35,8 | 35,1 | -0,7 | 59,5 | 24,4 | .70 |
| United Kingdom | 30,5 | 33,7 | +3,2 | 59,3 | 24,1 | .72 |
| Ireland | 17.1 | 27,0 | +9,9 | 57,8 | 24,7 | .91 |
| France | 27,5 | 29,4 | +1,9 | 58,3 | 27,4 | .93 |
| Germany | 25,6 | 31,2 | +5,6 | 58,4 | 25,5 | .82 |
| Austria | - | 30,1 | - | 56,9 | 27,2 | .90 |
| The Netherlands | 19,1 | 31,6 | +12,5 | 57,6 | 26,6 | .84 |
| Belgium | 21,6 | 26,8 | +5,2 | 56,6 | 27,8 | 1.04 |
| Luxembourg | 19,5 | 24,2 | +4,7 | 56,7 | 27,3 | 1.13 |
| Portugal | 27,7 | 31,6 | +3,9 | 59,3 | 23,6 | .75 |
| Spain | 16,6 | 25,3 | +8,7 | 57,3 | 27,6 | 1.09 |
| Greece | 19,3 | 24,6 | +5,3 | 57,6 | 26,4 | 1.07 |
| Italy | 19,5 | 22,4 | +2,9 | 56,6 | 28,0 | 1.25 |

Average years in the labor force are based on labor force participation rates of
the population aged fifteen to twenty-four, twenty-five to fifty-four and fifty-five to sixty-
four in 1983 and in 2000.

The average age of exit is calculated as fifty-five plus the average number of years in the
 labor force for persons aged fifty-five to sixty-four according to Labor Force Statistics
2000.

Average pension period= life expectancy at age sixty-five plus average years outside the
labor force between ages fifty-five to sixty-four, according to Labor Force Statistics 2000.

Source: OECD Employment Outlook 1997 and 2001, Demographic statistics 1999,
Eurostat.

## Pension Policy Responses to the Changing Division of Labor

### Changes in Minimum Pension Provision

In the EU women represent the majority of older people—nearly 60 percent of people over sixty-five and almost two-thirds of those aged over seventy-five (COM[2002],85). The oldest pensioners again tend to be more at risk from poverty than younger ones (COM(2002),28). This may be due to several factors. Older women have earned lower pension entitlements because of their lower labor market participation rates (see figure 2.1). There are probably also more widows without sufficient survivors' pensions in these cohorts (COM(2002),28). Inflation may also have eroded the purchasing power of an individual pension benefit.

Although in the future, most women will have their own earnings-related pensions complementing the minimum pension and diminishing the risk of poverty, minimum pensions will probably play a bigger role in women's pension provision than it does in that of men for a long time to come. This is indicated by women's still shorter working careers (see table 2.1). Changes in these pensions are, thus, interesting from a gender perspective.

The level of the minimum pension today is rather modest in most European countries, although the variation between the countries is large (see table 3 in the appendix). The figures compare poorly however, because there are various kinds of other benefits which may have a considerable effect on the minimum guarantee provided by the state in different countries. The adjustment of these pensions is usually either linked to a consumer price index or is made on an ad hoc basis (Laitinen-Kuikka et al. 2002). In many countries this means the longer the period of retirement, the more the pension will lag behind the general increase in the wealth of the society. As can be seen from table 1, the retirement periods of women are longer than those of men. The adjustment method is thus especially important to them.

The main difference between the welfare state regimes in the way of organizing minimum protection in old age has been the extent of universality vs. means testing as eligibility criteria. While these pensions used to be extensively universal in the Nordic countries, in the continental countries they were strictly means-tested, with the exception of the minimum pensions paid in the earnings-related schemes. In the United Kingdom the statutory minimum pension is dependent on the contribution record of the beneficiary, although women can receive a pension based on the contribution record of their husband, ex-husband or late husband (Laitinen-Kuikka et al. 2002, 73-74). The eligibility criteria have been changed lately in a way that seems to diminish the differences between the regimes.

In all Nordic countries the minimum pension is residence-based. The amount of the pension was, however, made dependent on the years of residence in Finland and Sweden when these countries applied for EU membership. In Denmark this had been made earlier. This change may affect pension provision for immigrants, especially women with many children.

Another reform, which can be considered more principal, was made in the minimum pensions in Finland and Sweden during the 1990s. In both countries the whole amount of the minimum pension was made dependent on the amount of the employment-based pension such that persons with a moderate employment-based pension receive no minimum pension at all. Previously, a basic amount of the minimum pension was paid to all residents. As the minimum pension in the Nordic countries has been considered an example of "exit out of work" policy, it seems these reforms have diminished the decommodification nature of Swedish and Finnish pension provision. This is strengthened by the fact the amount of the minimum pension is rather low and lags behind the earnings-related pension because the adjustments of the pension follow the consumer price index only.

Denmark still represents the Nordic regime well in respect to the minimum pension. A basic amount of the pension is paid to all retired residents irrespective of other income. The pension system in the Netherlands resembles the Danish system and differs from other continental countries. In both countries the replacement rate of the minimum pension is also higher than in other member states (see table 3 in the appendix). These pensions are financed by tax revenues and, thus, constitute an element of solidarity among the pensioners and between the generations. This solidarity benefits women with short careers due to child rearing and women with low incomes. Each year of employment accrues employment-related pension rights in addition to this basic pension because the amount of the pension is not diminished by other pension income. (Laitinen-Kuikka et al. 2002.)

In most continental and southern European member states the minimum pension is paid from social assistance and is dependent on the whole family income. In Austria and Luxembourg there is no special minimum pension but a general guaranteed minimum income could be paid to those without sufficient means in old age. This was previously the case also in Germany but since the pension reform of 2001, a special social assistance benefit is payable to low-income pensioners. This benefit need not be repaid by the beneficiary or by the relatives as general minimum income. From a gender perspective the difference compared to the Nordic countries and the Netherlands is that the whole family income is considered in the means test. The lack of an individual right to the benefit often means wives remain economically dependent on their husbands.

In these countries a minimum pension is also often combined to the earnings-related pension and is eligible to those having contributed for a minimum period, which is often quite long. This minimum amount helps working women with low incomes, part-time employment, etc. to accrue a moderate earnings-related pension. Because of the length of the contribution period needed, it may, however, be difficult for many women to become eligible or accrue the full amount of this minimum. If credited insurance periods are taken into account in this eligibility criterion, as in Germany, it will be easier for women to fulfil it.

In the United Kingdom the minimum income of the poorest old persons was markedly improved in 1999 when a minimum income guarantee was introduced. A Pension Credit replaced it in 2003. This social assistance benefit can be paid to people sixty or over. It will entitle single persons to an income of at least £102.10 per week (couples £155.80). The income test is less severe than before, meaning that this benefit is estimated to reach nearly half of all couples over age sixty (Council of the European Union 2003, 109). It reflects not only the generosity of the benefit but also the low level of pensions in the U.K.

It is interesting to note in Germany and in the U.K., where minimum income guarantee for the elderly has lately been improved, it has been made through the general income support system which has usually been considered more stigmatizing than social security benefits. In Germany, minimum social security pension provision was strongly demanded by some political groups but it could not be agreed on. As the minimum benefits are usually financed by taxes, regardless of the institutional organization of them, the channel of payment seems to be more a question of principle. The social security coordination rules in the EU may also affect the solutions because social assistance benefits are not transferable from one country to another. It may also be due to "path dependency"; being means-tested benefits may be easier to govern by offices used to paying this kind of benefit. From the point of view of the beneficiaries, mostly women, it would be important to know how much stigma is still connected to receiving these benefits.

To summarize, it seems minimum pension provision in the EU countries, representing different welfare state regimes, has converged somewhat. While in some of the Nordic countries the universality of these benefits has diminished, a broadening of the coverage has occurred in some of the continental countries. As the level of these benefits has been improved in many continental countries, as well as in the U.K., there is still more convergence in the amount of the benefits, irrespective of the institutional organization of them. This is not to say that the way of organizing would not be important. The economic independence given by these benefits to older persons, especially women, remains highest in the Nordic countries and the Netherlands. Also the stigma connected to receiving these benefits can be expected to be lower or non-existent in the residence-based schemes.

### Trends in Statutory Earnings-Related Pension Schemes

In most EU countries the statutory earning—or employment-related pensions—constitute the main source of income for pensioner families. With the exception of Denmark, this is the case also in the Nordic member states. In the Nordic countries, earnings-related pension entitlements are individual in the same way as entitlement to the universal minimum pensions. At the other end of the individual–derived rights axis are those continental and Anglo-Saxon countries in which a spouse supplement is added to the breadwinner's pension if the spouse has no own pension income. These kinds of higher benefits are paid in Belgium, for example, where there are two different accrual rates depending on whether the beneficiary has an economically dependent spouse or not. A supplement to the breadwinner's pension may also be paid in Ireland, the U.K. and France, and in the old Greek pension scheme (Laitinen-Kuikka et al. 2002). These supplements benefit families in which the wives have worked at home for the whole, or most, of their working age rearing children and housekeeping. Because these kinds of careers are becoming rare, the supplements are losing their importance. In some countries they have already been abolished. From an equality perspective this can be considered to be a positive development.

In the U.K., the wife of a retired husband may apply for a basic pension based partly, or totally, on the insurance record of her husband. Also, the divorced or widowed wife has this right if she has not remarried. These pensions are paid directly to the wives and are, therefore, more individual than the supplements mentioned above. Because the child-rearing years are also generously credited in the individual basic pension accrual of women, this derived pension possibility benefits mostly those women who have stayed out of the labor market for most of their lives. These features in U.K. pension provision seem to contradict our typology, where liberal welfare state regimes consider women primarily as workers and not as wives and mothers. However, this possibility is related only to flat-rate basic pensions. The level of the state pensions, the basic pension and the earnings-related pension together, seems not to support the breadwinner model of pension provision. It is, rather, low compared to continental and Scandinavian statutory pension provision.

In southern European countries the minimum insurance period for entitlement to the statutory earnings-related pension is long— fifteen years in countries except Italy, where five years are required in the new scheme (see table 3 in the appendix). Childrearing is compensated for in the pension scheme only minimally (see table 2 in the appendix). These features of the system seem to support the one-breadwinner family model strongly. The lack of institutional care for children further accelerates this. On the other hand, the levels of state earnings-related pensions are rather high compared to other European countries because they are meant to support both spouses in old age. These pension systems seem to reflect the labor market reality in these countries. As the labor market participation rate of women increases in these countries, it becomes important pension systems are modernized in a way that takes this into account.

In many countries the strengthening of the connection between the contributions paid and benefits accrued can be seen in the earnings-related pension schemes that previously have been more of a final salary type. Periods on which pensions are calculated have been lengthened, for example, in France and in Finland. In Finland earnings-related pensions of private-sector employees will be based on the total career earnings as of 2005 instead of the ten last years of employment as is now the case.

In Sweden and Italy more profound reforms have been made. The reformed state old-age pension schemes in these countries are called "notional defined contribution schemes" (NDC). They are called "notional" because the contribution, or most of it, is not funded as in "real" defined contribution schemes; only notional accounts have been established for all insured persons. However, the main principle is the same; the contribution is fixed and the amount of the pension varies depending, among other things, on the life expectancy of the cohorts in pensionable age. In these schemes the average increase in life expectancy of both women and men is used when determining the amount of the pension. This is because the schemes are part of the state social security system that is based on the principle of solidarity.

In these schemes the connection between career earnings and the amount of the pension is very clear. It may, however, be relaxed by credits admitted for certain unpaid periods such as unemployment, sickness, disability and care of children or a disabled family member (see table 2.4). Also years for which a student allowance is paid may be credited. All of these periods are made up in Sweden. In Italy, the compensation of unpaid periods is much more limited. This shows the same basic model can reflect differences in various welfare regimes.

As the example of Sweden shows, notional defined contribution schemes can combine the "workfare" principle and individual responsibility with the principle of solidarity in a new and interesting way. However, in this kind of scheme the responsibility of the state has been fixed in advance and the individuals have to bear the risk of unknown changes, like increases in life expectancy, higher than expected financial burdens on the system, etc. These are very difficult for individuals to evaluate. The younger you are the more difficult it is because so many years are left until retirement. Yet decisions concerning additional retirement savings, for example, must be made long before retirement. This uncertainty may increase the perceived need for private savings. Thus, emphasizing the responsibility of the individual, instead of the society, may, in the long-run, diminish the solidarity between individuals concerning pension provision.

In Sweden, a small part of the pension contribution is funded by private funds and thus forms a "real" defined contribution pension. For these funds no minimum return requirement is set. The individual may choose the funds into which his or her contributions are invested and also bear the investment risk themselves. This further accelerates the individual responsibility principle.

When the connection of contributions and benefits is strengthened, it is important from women's point of view, unpaid periods of care are credited in one form or another. In the next section we will look closer at the changes made in different countries in this respect.

### Compensating for Unpaid Periods

In countries like Denmark and the Netherlands, where residence-based basic pensions are generous, these pensions can be considered to moderately compensate for the losses of earnings-related pension benefits due to caregiver responsibilities. But in countries where the residence-based pension is diminished by the earnings- or employment-related pension and in countries where no residence-based pension exists, it is important that caregiver responsibilities are compensated for in some other way. Pension crediting, as mentioned above, is the most common way of doing this. It promotes the individualization of pension provision. in contrast to the spouse supplements or derived rights described earlier. It can also be applied in a gender-neutral way that gives parents more flexibility to choose how they want to organize childcare and potential care of their sick or aged relatives. This neutrality may enhance a more equal division of paid and unpaid work between the sexes and, thus, alter attitudes toward caregiver work in the labor market as well. To be neutral, the compensation must be high enough. Otherwise it will not be a real alternative to men who most often are the higher earners in the family. Even if it were added to the expenses of pension systems in some countries, the result might be a positive balance in labor market participation rates.

Details of crediting unpaid periods in different countries are described in table 4 in the appendix. These benefits have been improved during the last decade in many EU member states, e.g. in Germany, Austria, Belgium, Sweden and quite recently, in Finland, too. The latest lengthening of credited periods for childcare in Germany was prompted by the effort to encourage the labor force participation of women. If the pension rules are very strict, and a moderate pension difficult to reach, there are no incentives for women to return to the labor market after the first child is born. In Germany and Belgium, particular effort has lately been made also in pension systems to encourage part-time work connected to part-time caregiving. In Germany, pensionable incomes of parents, who work part-time because of rearing children younger than ten-years-old, have been increased by 50 percent. In Belgium, a parent of a child younger than six-years-old can be credited for three years of full-time leave or one year of full-time leave and four years of part-time leave.

It is important to note in continental countries credited periods are often also included in the insurance period requirement for the entitlement to a full pension and the special insurance period requirement for the entitlement to a minimum pension. For example, in Germany, a small pension can be paid solely based on credited periods of childcare. Credits, thus, loosen considerably the tie between the employment and the right to the amount of a pension both for men and women. This has often been left unnoticed when pension provision in these countries has been examined.

Southern European countries differ from other continental countries. In Portugal and Greece, only the maternity allowance period of a few months is credited. Even in the new Italian scheme, in addition to the maternity period, only ten months of care of a child is compensated to those women who retire before the age of sixty-five. This means childcare periods may diminish the pension of many mothers.

### Policy Responses in Survivors' Pensions

Survivors' pension benefits have been restructured during the last decade in many European countries. A trend toward gender neutrality and means-testing has been obvious. The right to a surviving spouse's pension has been extended to men and, simultaneously, the eligibility rules for the pension have been tightened to avoid the increase in pension expenditure.

In some countries the reform of the survivors' pension has been profound. For example, in Sweden the main principle after the amendment of the law in 1990 is a surviving spouse's pension is paid to the spouse only for ten months or until the youngest child is twelve-years-old. It is called an adjustment pension. A special pension may be paid to those unable to earn their living by work. The principle that earnings-related pension schemes compensate for lost earnings has, thus, been remarkably weakened.

In Finland, this change toward gender neutrality, and a compensatory role of the surviving spouse's pension, was carried out by a pension adjustment rule. Since 1990, the surviving spouse's own accrued earnings-related pension diminishes the widow's/ widower's pension through a certain formula. The effects of the pension adjustment are generally smaller on widows' than on widowers' benefits due to the gender differences in individual earnings-related pensions. Thus, pension adjustment in the surviving spouse's pension also levels out pension differences caused by childcare responsibilities.

In the Netherlands, the residence-based survivors' pension became means-tested in 1996. Also other eligibility criteria were tightened. At the same time, the coverage was extended to non-married couples and couples of the same sex. In 1998 the income-test was extended to pensions that had started before 1996.

The survivors' pension was also amended in Germany in connection with the large pension reform in 2001. The so-called small surviving spouse's pension, which is awarded to widows or widowers that are younger than forty-five, are not disabled or have no children under age eighteen, became time-limited to two years. In this context old age pension splitting was made available as an alternative to a widow or widower's pension. This splitting happens when one or both of the spouses retire. Part of the pension rights accrued during the marriage to the spouse with a higher income is transferred to the insurance record of the other. After this splitting, no widow's/widower's pension is payable to the couple. Pension splitting benefits those who have their own income that would diminish their survivors' pension. It, thus, promotes the individualization of pension rights.

In the U.K., men became eligible for a widower's pension only in 2001. The amount of the earnings-related surviving spouse's pension will gradually be reduced by half (Laitinen-Kuikka et al. 2002).

Reforms in survivors' pensions have, thus, been made in countries representing all different welfare state regimes. One difference remains after these changes, however. In continental and Mediterranean countries, the insurance more often covers a large family so not only spouses, ex-spouses and children, but also other near relatives, such as parents, grandchildren, siblings etc., may receive the pension if they were economically dependent on the deceased. This reflects the "familialist" structure of these welfare states.

## Efforts to Enhance Occupational and Personal Pension Provision

In all EU countries some effort has been made to limit the increase in public pension expenditure in the coming decades. These efforts have often been combined with reforms in legislation regulating occupational and personal private pensions. The aim of these reforms has been to make these pensions more reliable and affordable to the employees and economically attractive to organize on the part of employers. Extended second and third pillar pension provision would thus compensate for the impairments in public pensions. This was the explicit aim of the German government, for example, in the pension reform of 2001.

Simultaneously there has been a global trend to transform occupational defined benefit schemes to defined contribution schemes. The major reason for this has been it is easier for the employer to evaluate future pension expenditure when the contributions are fixed. This, again, has become more important because life expectancy has continued to increase.

In defined contribution schemes, the amount of the contribution is fixed and the amount of the pension benefit depends on the amount of contributions paid during the whole career, increased by the returns received on them during funding and diminished by administration costs. When these savings are transformed into a monthly pension, they are divided by the expected period of payment. Women, having longer life expectancy, thus receive a smaller monthly pension than men if unisex tariffs are not used. This, again, is seldom the case in company or private pensions. It is, of course, possible to stipulate a law which makes it mandatory—this has recently happened in the Netherlands (COM[2002],90).

Defined contribution pensions are strictly connected to contribution payments and, thus, to employment. Contributions are paid from the salary and directly reflect the amount of total career earnings. This is a feature disadvantageous to women with children. A feature common to all funded defined contribution schemes is the liability of the adequacy of the pension is transferred to the individual employee. If no minimum return requirement is set, as is usually the case, periods of low returns may lead to unexpected losses in the pensions. This is currently the case in the U.S. where these kinds of labor markets and private pensions are common.

Coverage of occupational pension schemes varies from 7 to 90 percent of the working population in the EU countries (see table 2 in appendix). There are also big differences in coverage between different sectors. Some companies require many years of employment before the employee will qualify as a member of a supplementary pension scheme, and she or he may lose accrued pension rights if she/he resigns before retirement age. Also the adjustment methods of pensions are often weaker than in statutory schemes. For women with children, these kinds of schemes are especially disadvantageous compared to statutory pensions.

Coverage is higher in countries where labor market organizations have established such schemes. Labor market schemes are common in Sweden, Denmark, France, the Netherlands and Greece and are also becoming more popular in Germany since the pension reform. Efforts to enhance them can be seen in Belgium, Italy, Spain and Portugal as well. In the first four countries, the coverage is high because these schemes are often mandatory to all employers and employees in the sector concerned. The larger the scheme, the more it can benefit from economies of scale. In defined contribution schemes this is reflected in the administrative costs that are easier to keep low in large schemes. The size of these costs directly affects the amount of the benefits. It may also be easier to connect features of solidarity, such as unisex tariffs, to large schemes where pension agreements are negotiated between strong partners and contributors are many.

In both Anglo-Saxon EU countries the possibility of accruing a voluntary individual supplementary pension has been advanced in recent years. In the U.K., a stakeholder pension scheme has been established especially for low and middle-income earners. The maximum amount of administrative costs in this scheme is fixed and it is supported through the tax system. This is a liberal welfare state way to promote adequacy of pension provision.

Occupational pensions and personal savings can also be combined so the labor market partners administer a fund into which contributions are paid both by employers and employees. The new German labor market schemes are an example of this kind of mix. Although women are more often disadvantaged by these schemes than by state pension provision because employers seldom have an interest in compensating for unpaid periods of childcare, they may give families more flexibility in division of labor at home and outside. It is also possible to continue paying contributions to these schemes during child/elder care periods and such a decision might be easier for families to make than to take a private pension insurance.

In Germany, a voluntary personal pension savings scheme was also established in 2001. People are encouraged to pay contributions to a pension fund by tax advantages, which favor low- and middle-income families.

### Pensions Splitting as One Solution to the Equality Problem

The diminished meaning of marriage as a lifelong contract makes reliance on a husband for an income in later life an ever more risky strategy for women. Increases in divorce, lone parenthood, remarriage and step-parenthood are unlikely to reverse. For those women who have not had the possibility to accrue individual pension rights, other mechanisms to compensate for the losses due to childcare responsibilities are needed. Splitting the pension rights between the spouses is one strategy to settle this problem. It is also a gender-neutral, and more or less cost-neutral, way of doing it. It has been used in Germany, the Netherlands and Switzerland. It is mandatory in all these countries. In Germany, the spouse with better pension accrual during the marriage can compensate this in some other way, too.

In the U.K., splitting of pension rights accrued during the marriage was made mandatory in principle at the end of the 1990s. Also, spouses there can agree on some other way of compensation. The splitting concerns both statutory earnings-related and private pensions and is important especially for women with long unpaid periods of childcare. The importance of splitting is further accentuated in the U.K. by the fact the level of statutory pensions has been low and occupational and personal pensions are diminished by career breaks. The traditional family model has also been common, but the divorce rate is still high.

Splitting of pension rights during the marriage has been made possible in Germany, as mentioned earlier, and in Sweden for part of the statutory premium pension. In the latter case pension rights can be transferred to the spouse annually. Outside the EU a very modern way of splitting pension rights was introduced in the statutory pension scheme of Switzerland in 1997. If both spouses are eligible for retirement pension, their incomes during the marriage, in addition to credits paid for child/elder care, will be split when the amount of the pension is determined.

In spite of this positive development, it is still possible in many EU countries for women who have stayed outside the labor market the greatest part of their working age because of childcare, or care of elderly relatives, and housekeeping to lose their pension safety net almost completely upon divorce. The individualization of pension rights, therefore, seems to be, by far, the best way to protect the adequacy of the pension provision of women.

## Conclusions

This examination indicated there were marked differences in the phase of change concerning both the family institution, especially women's labor market participation and the responses of pension policy to these changes. The most distinct differences are seen on the north-south axis of welfare states. The change seems to have been modest in the southern European countries. Although the labor market participation rate of women has increased, it is still lower than in northern Europe and in many other continental European countries. In the Mediterranean countries, the traditional family institution seems to have maintained its role as a social safety net. Both the economic activity of married women and the prevalence of divorces are rather low. Those women who work mostly work full-time.

In the Southern European countries changes in pension provision have also been rather modest compared to those in northern Europe. With the exception of Italy, where a comprehensive reform of the pension system has been carried out, only minor parametric reforms have been made in these countries so far. The replacement rates of the breadwinner's retirement pensions are rather high and the surviving spouse's pensions still maintain a moderate level of income to the widowed spouse's. The final salary principle is still dominating in statutory pensions and may benefit those women who return to work after years of childcare if they have years enough to fulfil the eligibility criteria. On the other hand, childcare is only minimally credited. It thus seems pension provision in these countries support the traditional on/off labor market participation of women. Women work either full-time or remain outside the labor market for most of their working age; the last alternative is still common. The "familialist" pension model responds rather well to pension provision needs in societies with traditional families; however, it simultaneously has a negative impact on women's search for economic independence. Low fertility rates are an outcome of the welfare policy of the Mediterranean countries.

The pressure to change the statutory pension schemes in these countries however, is high. In the evaluation of the Commission in December 2002, all except Portugal, were classified as countries where further pension reforms are needed to make them financially sustainable in the future (COM[2002]). When these reforms are made they should respond to the actual possibility of women to participate in the labor market.

Other continental countries seem to be, in many aspects, in the middle of the north-south axis. Today, women's labor market participation is higher than in southern Europe but clearly lower than in the Nordic countries. The durability of marriage has weakened considerably while cohabiting and extra-marital births are more common in the continental than in southern European welfare states.

Statutory pension schemes seem to reflect the phase of transformation to a modern welfare state in progress in these countries. There are various strategies for compensating women for unpaid caregiver work. Pension splitting upon divorce and upon retiring is one such method, although not used very widely so far. Also derived rights, such as surviving spouse's pensions, are still needed by elderly women. In some countries however, surviving spouse's pension's eligibility conditions have been tightened. A more modern way of compensating for unpaid caregiver work is crediting these periods to the personal insurance record of the worker. If the compensation is moderate, it may also be used by men and is, thus, neutral from a gender perspective. In many continental countries this possibility exists and the compensation is rather good. One way of enhancing women's labor market participation, used in some of these countries, is the possibility to work part-time without losing pension accrual when the children are small. For many families in continental countries, this seems to be an ideal way to reconcile work and family in a balanced way.

In Anglo-Saxon countries, labor market participation of women has increased due to low quality jobs with low pension accrual, thus risking the adequate level of pension benefits in old age. The recent increase in the level of statutory earnings-related pensions will especially benefit low- and middle-income earners, that is, the group most women belong to. Also, the new personal pension savings scheme should make it more profitable for these women to save supplementary pension benefits. The high risk of divorce in the U.K. is considered in the mandatory pension splitting upon divorce. This is an effective way to protect the equality of the spouses in families with a traditional division of labor. Yet women in the higher salary classes, who stay at home some years, are often disadvantaged in a pension system in which occupational and private personal pensions form a major part of pension provision. Different tariffs used for men and women, when changing the savings into a pension, still accelerates the disadvantage for women. The losses in pension accrual might be even higher for men taking care of the children, thus prohibiting sharing of unpaid work.

In the Nordic EU countries, women's integration into the labor market is high. Pension systems in these countries, founded both on solidarity and on individual rights, respond well to the changed position of women. In societies where the family has lost much of its stability, pension systems based on individual rights have become necessary. There are differences however, also among these countries. In Sweden and Denmark, part-time work of women is rather common and the pension systems compensate for the lost earnings moderately, whereas in Finland full-time work for women is the rule. This, combined with the fact unpaid work at home is still unevenly divided between the spouses, often puts a heavy load on women with children. The reductions in the care of the elderly make this load still heavier for those women who also take care of their own parents. In Finland, difficulties in reconciliation of work and family seem to have increased interruptions of the working career sof women with small children.

If Finnish families reflect the future of European families with both spouses working full-time, taking care of their children and helping their elderly parents, it seems paid and unpaid work must be divided more equally. More gender equality in the labor market is also needed to help the reconciliation of work and family. Except in the Nordic countries, shortage of affordable and high-quality childcare still limits the possibility of both parents participating in the labor market. At the other end of the career, the availability of social services for the elderly may be an important precondition for continuing labor force participation of especially women in their fifties and sixties. They often take care not only of their elderly relatives but also of their grandchildren. It seems in the future Europe, where a growing number of the oldest people will be in need of care, combining paid and unpaid work remains a Gordian knot to open.

In the aging societies of Europe, it is of crucial importance to examine how social protection systems can be changed so they encourage longer working careers. The long-term financial sustainability of pension systems and their ability to provide adequate pensions will heavily depend on mobilizing the full labor force potential. This would ensure a favorable balance between the active and the retired population. Advancement toward longer working careers will require a wide range of measures in the labor market, social security systems and in organizing familial care, which has so far been done in the families mostly by women.

In this chapter we have focused on the pension policy changes in the EU member states and their effect on the pension provision of women These policy changes have, so far, been mostly of parametric nature. Especially in the northern continental Europe one of the aims of the reforms has been to advance the labor market participation of women. This has meant breaking with the principle of familialism and shifting toward a more individual pension provision in these countries.

Also, a more universal shift toward more individual responsibility in pension provision is evident. This has been clearly expressed in the German pension reform of 2001 in which cuts in public pension provision were compensated by public subsidies to voluntary private pension savings. Combining the amount of the pension more closely to the contributions paid is another trend that emphasizes individual choices; the more you work, the more you get. This kind of a change has been carried out in many member states representing different welfare state regimes. In most of the countries, the unpaid care of children and disabled family members has been given a notional value on the basis of which pension accrues. This will improve the pension provision of many women in the future. It also makes the invisible work done in the families more visible and its value open to discussion.

In contrast, in occupational and personal pension schemes the work done outside the labor market is rarely compensated. Thus the trend to replace part of public pension provision with these pensions may be disadvantageous for women. The same applies to the trend of closer connection between contributions and pension amounts.

The longer average life expectancy of women is rarely compensated in private voluntary pension schemes of defined contribution type. This is not to say women-friendly solutions cannot be found in private pension schemes. There are examples, like the German one, which demonstrate this is possible when gender equality is considered a value to promote in the society.

## Notes

1.  It is worth noticing that these calculations are based on the activity rates at a certain cross-section date (cf. Palmer 1999, 463).
2.  Here, it is worth noticing that the average exit age is not necessarily the average age of retirement. Furthermore, this method of calculating the average age does not take into account early retirement before the age of fifty-five years (cf. Palmer 1999, 463).

## References

Anttonen A. and Sipilä J. (1996), European social care services: is it possible to identify models? *Journal of European Social Policy*, Vol 6 (2), 87–100.

Arts W. and Gelissen J. (2002). Three worlds of welfare capitalism or more? *Journal of European Social Policy* Vol 12 (2): 137–158.

COM(2002): Draft joint report by the Commission and the Council on Adequate and sustainable pensions. 17.12.2002.

Council of the European Union (2001). Quality and viability of pensions—Joint report on objectives and working methods in the area of pensions. 14098/01. Brussels, 23 November 2001.

Council of the European Union (2003). Draft joint report by the Commission and the Council on adequate and sustainable pensions. 6527/1/03. Brussels, 26 January 2003.

Employment Rates Report 1998.

Esping-Andersen G. (1990) *Three Worlds of Welfare Capitalism*. Great Britain. Princeton Press.

Esping-Andersen G, Gallie D, Hemerijck A, and Myles J (2002). *Why We Need a New Welfare State*. Oxford University Press.

Van Doorne-Huiskes A., den Dulk L. and Schippers J. (1998), Epiloque: Towards new patterns of responsibility for work-family policies? Amsterdam, in Work-Family Arrangements in Europe. Thesis Publishers.

Den Dulk L. and Remery C. (1997), Work-family arrangements in organisations, in K. Tijdens, A. van Doorne-Huiskes and T. Willemsen (eds) *Time allocation and Gender. The relationship between paid labor and household work*. Tilburg University Press, Tilburg, Netherlands.

Ferrera M. (1996), The "Southern" Model of Welfare in Social Europe. *Journal of European Social Policy* 6 (1): 17–37.

The future of the European Employment Strategy (EES) "A strategy of full employment and better jobs for all" Communication from the Commission to the Council, The European Parliament, The Economic and Social Committee and the Committee of the Regions. Brussels 14.1.2003.

Ginn J. and Arber S. (1996), Patterns of Employment, Gender and Pensions: The Effect of Work History on Older Women's Non-State Pensions. *Work, Employment & Society*, Vol. 10, No. 3, pp 469–490.1

Ginn J. and Arber S. (1999), Changing patterns of pension inequality: the shift from state to private sources. *Aging and Society*, Vol 19, Part 3, 319–342.

Ginn J., Street D. and Arber S. (2001), Gross-national trends in women's work. In J. Ginn, D. Street and S. Arber (eds), *Women, Work and Pensions*. Open University Press.

Gornick J. C., Meyers M. K. and Ross K. E. (1997), Supporting the employment of mothers: policy variation across fourteen welfare states. *Journal of European Social Policy*, Vol 7 (1): 45–70.

Hatland A. (2001). Changing family patterns: A challenge to social security. In M. Kautto, J.Fritzell, B. Hvinden, J. Kvist and H. Uusitalo (eds.). *Nordic Welfare States in the European Context*. London.

Hutton S. (1998). Progress Report. Incomes in retirement in the U.K.: Changes in the debate since 1996 and prospects for the future. *Aging and Society*, Vol 18, 1998, 611–626.

Laitinen-Kuikka S. (2002). Avoimen koordinaation menetelmän soveltaminen eläkepolitiikassa. In Saari Juho (et.) *Euroopan sosiaalinen ulottuvuus. Sosiaali- ja terveysturvan keskusliitto ry*. Helsinki.

Laitinen-kuikka S., Bach J., Vidlund M. (2002). Eläketurva Länsi-Euroopassa. The Finnish Centre for Pensions.

Meulders D. (1996), Individualisation of rights and social protection. International Social Security Association, European Conference: Adapting to new economic and social realities: what challenges, opportunities and new tasks for social security? Aarhus 19–21, November 1996.

O'Connor, J. S, Orloff A. and Shaver S. (1999). *States, Market, Families. Gender, Liberalism and Social Policy in Australia, Canada, Great Britain and the United States*. Cambridge. University Press.

Orloff A. S. (1993), Gender and the Social Rights of Citizenship: a Comparative Analysis of Gender relations and Welfare States. *American Sociological Review* 58 (3): 303-328.

Palmer Edward (1999), Exit from Labor Force for Older Workers: Can the NDC Pension System Help? *The Geneva Papers on Risk and Insurance* Vol. 24, No. 4 (October 1999), Oxford.

Trifiletti R. (1999), Southern European welfare regimes and the worsening position of women. *Journal of European Social Policy*, Vol 9 (1): 49–64.

Tuominen E. and Laitinen-Kuikka S. (2002), Female employment, unpaid work and retirement pensions in the EU. Paper to be presented at the XI Nordic Social Policy Research Meeting Helsinki 22–24 August 2002, WG 10: Gender, Work and Family

Van Stigt J., van Doorne-Huiskes A. and Schippers J. (1998?), European regulation and initiatives on work-family policies, in L. den Dulk, A. van Doorne-Huiskes and J. Schippers (eds.) *Work-Family arrangements in Europe*, Amsterdam. Thesis Publishers.

Vidlund M. (2001). Eläkkeistä ulkomailla: Ison-Britannian eläkeuudistus. Eläketurvakeskuksen katsauksia 2001:5.

Windebank J. (1996), To what extent can social policy challenge the dominant ideology of mothering? A cross-national comparison of Sweden, France and Britain. Journal of European Social Policy, 6, 147–161.

## Appendix Table 1
### Demographic Trends in 1980-2000 Related to Family Formation in the EU Countries

| | Crude marriage rate | | Crude divorce rate | | Crude birth rate | |
|---|---|---|---|---|---|---|
| | (per 1000 average population) | | | | | |
| | 1980 | 2000 | 1980 | 2000 | 1980 | 2000 |
| EU 15 | 6,3 | 5,1 [e] | 1,4 | 1,9 [e] | 13,0 | 10,8 [e] |
| Nordic regime | | | | | | |
| Sweden | 4,5 | 4,5 | 2,4 | 2,4 | 11,7 | 10,2 |
| Denmark | 5,2 | 7,2 | 2,7 | 2,7 | 11,2 | 12,6 |
| Finland | 6,1 | 5,1 | 2,0 | 2,7 | 13,2 | 11,0 |
| Anglo-Saxon regime | | | | | | |
| United Kingdom | 7,4 | 5,1 | 2,8 | 2,6 | 13,4 | 11,4 * |
| Ireland | 6,4 | 5,0 [p] | - | 0,7 [p] | 21,8 | 14,3 [p] |
| Continental regime | | | | | | |
| France | 6,2 | 5,2 [p] | 1,5 | 2,0 [1] | 14,9 | 13,2 [p] |
| Germany | 6,3 | 5,1 | 1,8 | 2,4 | 11,1 | 9,3 |
| Austria | 6,2 | 4,8 | 1,8 | 2,4 | 12,0 | 9,6 |
| The Netherlands | 6,4 | 5,5 | 1,8 | 2,2 | 12,8 | 13,0 |
| Belgium | 6,7 | 4,4 | 1,5 | 2,6 | 12,6 | 11,3 [p] |
| Luxemburg | 5,9 | 4,9 | 1,6 | 2,3 | 11,4 | 13,1 |
| Southern European regime | | | | | | |
| Portugal | 7,4 | 6,2 | 0,6 | 1,9 | 16,2 | 11,7 |
| Spain | 5,9 | 5,3 [p] | - | 1,0 | 15,3 | 9,9 [p] |
| Greece | 6,5 | 4,3 * | 0,7 | 0,9 [p] | 15,4 | 9,6 |
| Italy | 5,7 | 4,9 | 0,2 | 0,7 | 11,3 | 9,4 |

p provisional data
* national estimate
e Eurostat estimate
1) 1999
Source: Statistics in focus. Population and social conditions, theme 3 - 17/2002.

## Appendix Table 2
## Coverage of State and Labor Market Pension Provision by Regime
## in the EU Countries 2002

| Countries | State pensions | | | Labour market pensions |
|---|---|---|---|---|
| | Coverage | Schemes | Earnings/pension ceiling per month (in 2002) and as % of average national salary [5] | Coverage as % of working population |
| **Nordic regime** | | | | |
| Denmark | resident population, employees | national pension, contributions based pension for employees | contribution based pension max. 228 □ in month (6%) | 80 (compulsory to most employees) |
| Finland | employees and self-employed, resident population | earnings-related pension, minimum pension | no ceiling | 20 |
| Sweden | employees and self-employed, resident population | contributions based pension, minimum pension | earnings: 2619 □ (98%) | 90 (compulsory to most employees) |
| **Continental regime** | | | | |
| Austria | employees and self-employed | earnings-related pension with minimum | earnings: □2826 (121%) | 10 |
| Belgium | employees and self-employed, persons without means | earnings-related pension, minimum pension | earnings: □3223 (126%) | 30 |
| France | employees and self-employed, persons without means | earnings-related pension, minimum pension | earnings: □2352 (115%) | 80 (compulsory to most employees) |
| Germany | employees and some self-employed | earnings-related pension with minimum | earnings: □4500 (155%) | 65 |
| Luxemburg | employees and self-employed | earnings-related pension with minimum | earnings: □6451 (210%) | 30 |
| The Netherlands | resident population | national pension | - | 90 (compulsory to most employees) |
| **Southern European regime** | | | | |
| Greece | employees and self-employed | earnings-related pension with minimum | pension ceiling | compulsory to 50% of employees |
| Italy | employees and self-employed, persons without means | earnings-related pension, minimum pension | earnings: □6370 (year2001), (387%) | 10 |
| Portugal | employees and self-employed, persons without means | earnings-related pension with minimum, minimum pension | no ceiling but to those in leading position | 7 |
| Spain | employees and self-employed, persons without means | earnings-related pension, minimum pension | earnings: □2574 (176%) | 15 |
| **Anglo-Saxon regime** | | | | |
| Ireland | employees and self-employed, persons without means | flat-rate pension | full pension □638,30 permonth (23%) | 46 |
| United Kingdom | employees and self-employed (for flat-rate pensions), those aged 80 without means | flat-rate pension, earnings-related pension with minimum | earnings: □4145 (182%) | 50 |

[5] estimated average wages in 2002 (source: Commission of European Union, not published)

5. Estimated average wages in 2002 (source; Commission of European Union, not publiished)

## Appendix Table 3
## Coverage of State and Labor Market Pension Provision by Regime in the EU Countries 2002

| Countries | Full minimum pension/month (before taxes) and as % of average national wages[6] | Earnings- or contribution-based pension Minimum insurance period | Accrual period for target level/full pension | Target level/full pension | Adjustment method of the earnings-or contribution based pensions |
|---|---|---|---|---|---|
| **Nordic regime** | | | | | |
| Denmark | ▯1182 (33%) | no minimum | years between the age of 16 and 67 (52 years) | full pension ▯228 permonth | depends on the returns of the funds |
| Finland | ▯487,60 (21%) | no minimum | about 40 years | 60% of the a. e. during the last 10 years in each employment[7] | prices and wages (80/20) |
| Sweden[5] | ▯726 (27%) | no minimum | years from the age of 16, no upper limit | depends on the amount of contributions paid and partly on the returns of funds | wages |
| **Continental regime** | | | | | |
| Austria | no scheme | 15 years[2] | 40 years | 80% of the a. e.[4] of the best 15 years | wages |
| Belgium | ▯597 (23%) | no minimum | 45 years | 60% of the a. career earnings | prices |
| France | ▯569 (28%) | no minimum | 37.5 years | 50% of the a. e. of the best 25 years | prices |
| Germany | no scheme[3] | 5 years[2] | 45 years | approximately 60% of a. career earnings | wages |
| Luxemburg | no scheme | 10 years no scheme | 40 years | 71,2% of a. career earnings | prices |
| The Netherlands | ▯869 (32%) | no scheme | no scheme | no scheme | no scheme |
| **Southern European regime** | | | | | |
| Greece | no general scheme | 15 years[2] | no upper limit | after 35 years 60% of the a. e. of the last 5 years | civil servants wages |
| Italy[5] | ▯340,68 (21%) | 5 years[2] | .. | depends on the amount of contributions paid | prices |
| Portugal | ▯138,27 (13%) | 15 years[2] | 40 years | 80-86% of a. career earnings depending of wage level | government decisions usually linked to prices |
| Spain | ▯293,83 (20%) | 15 years[2] | 35 years | 100% of the a. e. during the last 15 years | prices |
| **Anglo-Saxon regime** | | | | | |
| Ireland | ▯614 (22%) | 5 years + 10 weeks per year[2] | 48 weeks per year from age 16 till 66[2] | full pension ▯638 permonth | government decisions usually linked to prices |
| United Kingdom[5] | ▯695,40 (30%) | one year | 49 years | 40 -10% of a. career earnings depending of wage level | prices |

[1] The minimum garanteed pension at the level of the year 2002. The pension is paid from the year 2002. The pension is paid from the year 2003. In som e countries this scheme replaces the old scheme only gradually. In 2002 a national pension the amount of which is lower is still paid.
[2] Unpaid (credited) insurance periods can be included in this time
[3] For those aged over 80
[4] average earnings
[5] the information considers only the latest pension schemes. In som e countries this scheme replaces the old scheme only gradually.
[6] estimated average wages in 2002 (source: Commission of European Union, not published)
[7] From 2005 average earnings during the whole career will be considered and no target level is set.
[8] A special benefit from social assistance may be paid from 2003.

**Appendix Table 4**

**Crediting Child Care Leave and Other Unpaid Periods in the Earnings-Related or Contributions-Based Pension Schemes in EU**

| Country | Child care leave | Military/civilian service | Student years | Unemployment | Sickness, disability or rehabilitation | Care of disabled family-member |
|---|---|---|---|---|---|---|
| **Nordic regime** | | | | | | |
| Denmark | maternity allowance period if contributions paid | no | no | yes | yes | no |
| Finland | unpaid period of one year within employment is usually credited[3] | no | no | yes | yes | (yes) |
| Sweden | for care of children under age 4 even if in paid work | yes | yes | yes | yes | yes |
| **Continental regime** | | | | | | |
| Austria | for care of children under age 4 | yes | yes[1] | yes | yes | yes |
| Belgium | 3 years full time leave or 1 year full time + 4 years part-time | Yes[2] | no | yes | yes | yes |
| France | paternity allowance period, 2 years per child for mother even if in paid work | yes2 | no | yes | yes | yes |
| Germany | for care of children under age 4 even if in paid work, for care of children under age 10 if in part-time work or at home with 2 or more c. | yes | yes | yes | yes | yes |
| Luxemburg | 2 to 4 years for care of children under age 4 | yes2 | yes | yes | yes | yes |
| The Netherlands | no scheme (but high national pension) | - | - | - | - | - |
| **Southern European regime** | | | | | | |
| Greece | maternity allowance period if contributions paid | yes | no | yes | yes | no |
| Italy | maternity/paternity allowance + 10 months for care of child under age 8 | .. | no | yes | yes | yes |
| Portugal | maternity allowance period | yes | no | yes | yes | no |
| Spain | 1 year of care of a child younger than 3 years | yes | no | yes | yes | .. |
| **Anglo-Saxon regime** | | | | | | |
| Ireland | for years of care of a child under age 12 (max 20 years) | no service | no | yes | yes | yes |
| United Kingdom | for years of care of a child under age 16 | no service | yes | yes | yes | yes |

[1] If contributions paid
[2] General military service terminated
[3] From 2005 the care of children under age three for a parent who stays at home.

Source: Laitinen-Kuikka, Bach, Vidlund 2002

**Appendix Figure 1**
**Employment Rates of Women (aged 15-64) in the EU Countries[1]**
**in 1990 and 2001**

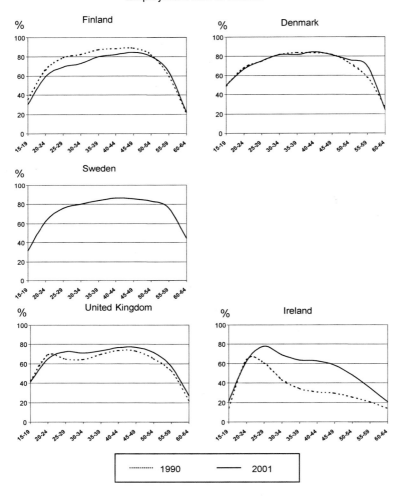

Employment rate of women

1) The data concerns the twelve EU countries in 1990 and the fifteen EU countries in 2001, therefore the data of Sweden and Austria is lacking from 1990. The Finnish data is from the national labor force survey from the year 1990.

Source: Population and Social Conditions, theme 3. Labor force survey 1990 and 2001.

**Appendix Figure 1 (cont.)**

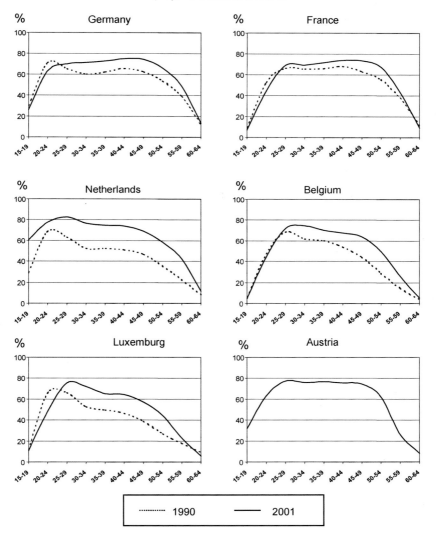

Employment rate of women

**Appendix Figure 1 (cont.)**

Employment rate of women

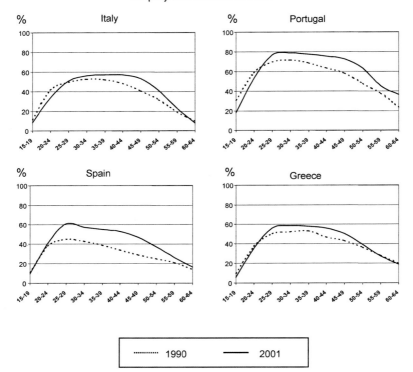

# 3

# Pensions and Gender in Latin America: Where Do We Stand in the Southern Cone?[1]

*Fabio M. Bertranou*

## Introduction

Structural reforms to pension systems were among the most profound and important social policy changes implemented in Latin America during the 1980s and 1990s. These changes have begun to be analyzed in more specific terms than the economic and financial-actuarial framework typically applied for this purpose. In the specific area of social protection, gender analysis has been limited and, in many cases, absent from the policy debate occurring in government, academic and international organizational spheres under the implicit assumption that these reforms are neutral in terms of their effects on men and women.

Recently, different international bodies and agencies have started to assume more leadership in this area, particularly the International Labor Organization.[2] A central issue during the eighty-nineth International Labor Conference, 2001, was a general debate about social security. The Conference dealt with the different aspects of social security systems in the modern world, highlighting the issue of gender equality (ILO 2002a).For the ILO, gender equality in social protection goes beyond simply guaranteeing equal treatment for men and women in the formal sense (See appendix 1: "International labor standards and gender equality"). This means gender functions in different societies should also receive adequate treatment, taking into consideration there have also been relevant changes over time in many dimensions of the work and family spheres.

The most significant change, with major implications for organizing the provision of social protection, is closely related to women's new role in the labor market. This change has accompanied modifications to the structure of employment, labor relations, and labor's contribution in modern societies. In particular, social protection systems for old age were mostly structured during the twentieth century, especially in the early years when the family and labor functions of men and women responded to cultural patterns that were significantly different from those of today. Moreover, in the past three or four decades there has been a rapid increase in the divorce rate and breakdown of the couple relationship that has had profound repercussions for income security during old age for divorced and separated women, especially if they have not personally contributed to a pension program through their own work. In this sense, if their ex-husbands remarry, women may lose all, or part, of their right to receive a survivor's pension. Also, the number of women as heads of the household has been increasing during recent years making it necessary to develop an analysis looking at the benefits women will receive in the pension system, not just as a dependent (having a survivor pension from her husband), but as a primary contributor whose own pension is her only income.

In many countries, but particularly in some Latin American countries, pension systems have achieved considerable maturity. For a variety of reasons, particularly those related to demographic and economic-financial factors, countries have reformed their systems in recent years. These reforms have covered aspects dealing with parameters (such as an increase in retirement age) and structure (i.e., the introduction of privately administered programs based on defined contributions and individual pension savings accounts). Logically enough, any reform contains elements that are not neutral for a very heterogeneous society, particularly in respect to gender.

The purpose of this chapter is to summarize gender-related aspects of the current social security reform paradigm in the area of protection against the risks of old age, disability and survival. To begin, I will summarize the main elements that justify dealing with this aspect of social protection. I will then provide a summary of the main performance aspects of these reformed social security programs in four of the region's countries in terms of providing protection for the risks of old age. Results for substitution (replacement) rates by gender are provided for Argentina, Brazil, Chile and Uruguay. I also discuss other conceptual and empirical evidence produced by other international agencies such as the World Bank and ECLAC. Finally, I will discuss some of the general implications for incorporating this dimension in the debate about public policies and reforms of social protection systems, particularly pensions and related programs. The intention of this last section is to avoid considering the debate about contribution-based pension programs in isolation, thus integrating them into a more comprehensive view of possible, financially viable, models of social protection.

## Why Worry About Gender Equality?

It is imperative social security adjusts to the current realities of the labor market and modern family organization. The changes that have occurred in these two spheres vary from one country to the next. However, several trends stand out. The current pension system structure is essentially contribution-based, so to a large degree labor history determines coverage and benefit levels. Moreover, the kind of pension scheme applied (defined contribution or defined benefit) imposes special conditions according to the worker's gender. As a result, there are two aspects relevant to the interaction between pensions and gender: the labor market and the kind of pension scheme. These two dimensions, and their interaction, produce effects that may potentially generate gaps in both coverage and benefit levels. These inequalities may be justified in terms of the structure adopted for the pension system; however, they could be considered socially unfair.

### Differences Between Men and Women with Respect to Labor

There are significant differences between the behavior of men and women in the labor market; differences affecting the pensions they will receive upon retirement. This is especially true in the context of individual capitalization accounts in which pensions are financed by the contributions that have been made during the active working life of an employee. The observed differences between men and women with respect to labor include the following: (a) labor force participation rate; (b) segmentation of the labor market; (c) part-time work; (d) short-term contracts; (e) unemployment; and (f) participation in the informal labor market.

## Labor Force Participation Rate

Historically, and all over the world, labor force participation rates of women have been smaller than those of men. Table 3.1 shows these participation rates for men and women in Argentina, Brazil, Chile and Uruguay. The lower participation rates of women consequently mean an important share of female workers cannot obtain old-age contributory pensions, limiting them to non-contributory means-tested assistance benefits, or survivor pensions, in the case of married women with a spouse that has contributed to (and is a beneficiary of) the formal contributory system. For example, Chilean labor force participation rates in 2000 show 65 percent of the women of working age (the percentage includes women outside of the labor market) do not receive pensions as a primary recipient. This result in Chile is striking because the participation rate of this country is lower than the average on the continent. However, it can be seen the gap in participation rates between men and women is closing over the years. This is most obvious in Argentina but the trend is also clearly visible in Chile and Uruguay as well.

An important factor in explaining the lower labor force participation rate of women is the interruption in their working lives due to childbearing and years spent raising these children. This limits the amount these women can accumulate in their individual retirement accounts and, thereby, the size of their pensions when they retire while also decreasing their chances of obtaining a minimum or basic pension from the contributory system because of the lower number of years contributed.

## Segmentation of the Labor Market

Traditionally, women tend to end up in specific types of jobs while men are far more evenly distributed over the labor market. This is the case in Argentina, Brazil, Chile and Uruguay. For example, in 1999 in Brazil, 67 percent of the female workers in the formal sector were concentrated in only eight different types of employment which is reflected by the low level of women in executive jobs (Rocha da Silva and Schwarzer 2003). The same story also holds for Chile where 63 percent of the women have jobs which do not require specific qualifications, such as sales personnel or office workers.

What is especially relevant regarding this labor market segmentation, with respect to the pensions men and women receive, is the salaries earned in the sectors where women are prevalent are gener-

Table 3.1
Labor Market Participation Rates: 1990-2002
Argentina, Brazil, Chile and Uruguay

| | Argentina[1] | | Brazil[2] | | Chile[3] | | Uruguay[4] | |
|---|---|---|---|---|---|---|---|---|
| | Men | Women | Men | Women | Men | Women | Men | Women |
| 1990 | 84.1 | 45.2 | ... | ... | 75.5 | 30.9 | 73.2 | 43.5 |
| 1991 | 83.6 | 44.3 | 80.0 | 44.3 | 75.7 | 30.7 | 73.3 | 43.8 |
| 1992 | 84.5 | 45.9 | 78.4 | 42.7 | 75.6 | 31.9 | 72.6 | 44.7 |
| 1993 | 84.1 | 48.5 | 77.2 | 42.5 | 77.2 | 34.1 | 71.8 | 44.1 |
| 1994 | 83.9 | 48.8 | 77.2 | 43.4 | 77.5 | 34.3 | 73.1 | 45.5 |
| 1995 | 84.1 | 51.7 | 76.7 | 43.9 | 76.7 | 34.0 | 73.8 | 46.6 |
| 1996 | 84.8 | 52.4 | 76.3 | 44.9 | 75.4 | 33.8 | 71.9 | 46.7 |
| 1997 | 83.9 | 52.7 | 74.7 | 44.3 | 74.7 | 34.6 | 71.4 | 45.8 |
| 1998 | 83.8 | 52.8 | 73.7 | 44.5 | 74.6 | 36.0 | 73.5 | 49.3 |
| 1999 | 82.8 | 54.2 | 72.2 | 43.9 | 74.3 | 35.0 | 72,0 | 48.6 |
| 2000 | 83.5 | 54.0 | 72.7 | 45.2 | 73.7 | 35.4 | 71.9 | 49.1 |
| 2001 | 82.7 [a] | 52.2 [a] | 71.0 | 43.9 | 72.2 | 33.7 | 72.2 | 50.9 |
| 2002 | | | | | 72.2 | 34.1 | 70.7 | 49.4 |

[1]Encuesta Permanente de Hogares. [2] IPEA (2002) [3]Instituto Nacional de Estadísticas [4] ILO (2004) [a] ILO (2003a)

ally below average. This has repercussions for the level of the accumulated contributions that are used to finance the pensions upon retirement, or in the level of the "pensionable" wage in defined benefit schemes.

*Part-Time Work*

The increased labor flexibility due to, among other things, increased possibilities to work part-time, is an element that has facilitated the incorporation of women in the labor market. Generally, part-time work for women is perceived as a means to combine their working lives with their family lives. However, the effects are not all positive: while it is an improvement that part-time work increases the participation rates of women, it also reinforces the idea women should be primarily responsible for non-remunerated household work and childrearing. The labor force participation of women shows a dominant pattern of part-time labor, whereas the majority of men work full-time. This results in lower levels of salaries for women and, therefore, a smaller pension at the time of retirement. In the case of Chile, for example, the percentage of females working part-time in the year 2000 was 20 percent while the same figure for men was only 9 percent.

*Short-Term Contracts*

One of the changes that the labor market has undergone in recent times is the increase in the use of short-term contracts, coupled with the decrease of long-term and permanent contracts. The increased use of short-term contracts augments the number and duration of interruptions during the working life of a person and, thus, the number of periods in which a person does not contribute to her pension account. If a person is able to obtain only a very small pension, the result is an income below the poverty line. At the same time, the interruptions in the working life decrease the likelihood a person will be able to obtain a minimum, or basic, pension from the contributory system.

This situation is especially severe for workers in the agricultural sector because they only work during the harvest, or roughly four months a year. For these workers it is very difficult to qualify for a minimum pension within the system. To illustrate this point the cases of Chile and Argentina should be considered where twenty and thirty years (respectively) of contributions are required before a person can obtain a minimum pension guaranteed by the state (Chile) or a flat-rate benefit (Argentina). This would imply a worker, who is only active during four months a year, would have to work for sixty or ninety years in Chile and Argentina, respectively, in order to fulfil the minimum contribution requirement.

In terms of the gender difference it should be noted, especially in Chile, women form the majority of the workers in the agricultural sector which reduces their possibility of acquiring a minimum pension even further. Therefore, the current pension system is not a viable option to provide old age income security for this group.

*Unemployment.* Unemployment affects a larger proportion of women than men, something that is linked to the number and duration of periods in which no contributions are made to the pension system. Table 3.2 presents the unemployment rates by sex for Argentina, Brazil, Chile and Uruguay. In these four countries, women have a higher unemployment rate then men, thereby affecting: their contributions to their pension accounts, the level of their pensions and their chances to qualify for a minimum pension. Additionally, women also have lower take-out rates with respect to other social provisions, like unemployment and disability benefits, increasing the gender inequality of the system even further.

Table 3.2
Unemployment Rates by Sex: 1990-2000
Argentina, Brazil, Chile and Uruguay

| | Argentina | | Brazil | | Chile | | Uruguay | |
|---|---|---|---|---|---|---|---|---|
| | Men | Women | Men | Women | Men | Women | Men | Women |
| 1990 | 7.4 | 7.3 | ... | ... | 6.6 | 9.2 | 7.3 | 11.8 |
| 1991 | 5.6 | 6.2 | 4.8 | 4.9 | 6.1 | 9.4 | 7.1 | 11.3 |
| 1992 | 6.5 | 7.1 | 5.6 | 6.0 | 5.0 | 8.9 | 6.7 | 11.9 |
| 1993 | 8.5 | 12.7 | 5.2 | 5.6 | 5.3 | 8.8 | 6.3 | 11.0 |
| 1994 | 10.7 | 14.5 | 4.8 | 5.5 | 6.5 | 10.3 | 6.9 | 12.0 |
| 1995 | 16.5 | 22.3 | 4.5 | 4.8 | 5.5 | 8.9 | 8.4 | 13.7 |
| 1996 | 16.8 | 20.9 | 5.0 | 6.1 | 4.8 | 6.7 | 10.5 | 14.5 |
| 1997 | 13.4 | 19.2 | 5.3 | 6.3 | 4.7 | 6.6 | 9.2 | 14.5 |
| 1998 | 12.2 | 15.2 | 7.1 | 8.3 | 5.7 | 7.6 | 8.1 | 12.7 |
| 1999 | 16.9 | 13.8 | 7.1 | 8.3 | 9.3 | 10.5 | 9.8 | 14.0 |
| 2000 | 17.2 | 14.0 | 6.5 | 8.0 | 8.7 | 10.0 | 10.9 | 17.2 |
| 2001 | 17.9 | 17.7 | 9.6 | 13.4 | 8.9 | 9.7 | 11.6 | 15.4 |
| 2002 | 21.1 | 19.4 | 9.9 | 13.9 | 8.6 | 9.6 | 14.1 | 20.3 |
| 2003[1] | 17.1 | 15.4 | 10.1 | 15.1 | 8.2 | 10.1 | 14.5 | 20.1 |

[1]Data for 2003 are based on the first semester for Argentina and on an average of the first three semesters for Brazil, Chile and Uruguay
Source: ILO (2003b)

*Participation in the Informal Labor Market.* One of the characteristics of the informal labor market is that workers are less likely to get contracts that usually provide social security coverage, including the participation in the pension system. Within this informal labor market, women have been traditionally overrepresented. Table 3.3 shows the percentage of men and women in the informal sector in Argentina, Brazil, Chile and Uruguay. The countries show very different patterns: Brazil is the only country where the participation rate of men in the informal sector exceeds that of women, but also in Argentina the gap between the two is closing rapidly. However, in Chile and Uruguay the evidence for this is not so strong.

As explained previously, this failure to contribute to the system leads to lower coverage rates, making people without additional means of income more and more dependent on non-contributory pensions when they reach their retirement age. Furthermore, this will lead to increasing fiscal pressure with respect to the financing of these types of pensions.

Table 3.3
Participation of Men and Women in the Informal Labor Market ( percent)
Argentina, Brazil, Chile and Uruguay

|  | Argentina | | Brazil | | Chile | | Uruguay | |
|  | Men | Women | Men | Women | Men | Women | Men | Women |
|---|---|---|---|---|---|---|---|---|
| 1990 | 50 | 56 | 36 | 48 | 34 | 46 | 34 | 47 |
| 1998 | 48 | 51 | 43 | 42 | 33 | 45 | 37 | 46 |

Source: ILO (2002b)

## Pension System Performance: Coverage and Replacement Rates for Men and Women

The dominant paradigm for pension reform during the 1990s consisted of promoting "multi-pillar pension systems" with principles very similar to the logic behind private insurance in which benefits are adjusted according to individual or family risk. This principle was behind the introduction of systems based on defined contribution and individual savings accounts. Benefits are calculated against the risk of individual/family survivors, identified by the sex of the beneficiary and the composition of the family (spouse and dependent children). In defined benefit systems, such as traditional public PAYG schemes, benefits depend on a formula that establishes a rate for replacing work-related income, subject to contributions prior to retirement (for example, the average salary for the last ten years).

This formula does not explicitly involve parameters affected by gender. The differences in benefits arise because of the different retirement ages or simply due to differences in the individual's work life. Thus, there was a significant implicit redistribution from men to women since, in general, the latter survived the former and received the benefits of the higher actual replacement rates of rules establishing minimum benefits. One way of evaluating this would be to compare the estimated present value of contributions made to benefits received throughout the life cycle.

The most noteworthy change in pension systems has to do with the introduction of benefits based on individual savings, which involves these amounts being paid out gradually using a formula that explicitly employs gender-related parameters. The annuities obtained based on the retirement age are directly related to the survival table by age and sex. This is a particular characteristic of the structural pension reforms introduced in Latin America. It is important to note, however, mortality rates by sex have generally been considered discriminatory in developed countries such as the United States and some European countries.

Given the financing arrangements of individual capitalization schemes, the higher life expectancy of women, compared to men, further worsens the situation of women, who, on average, already receive lower pensions due to their condition and behavior in the labor market. When women retire at a younger age compared to men, this implies in an advanced funding schemes, a smaller fund of accumulated contributions has to pay for a larger number of years in retirement. In Argentina, Brazil and Chile, the legal retirement age of women is lower than the one for men while their life expectancy is higher. In Uruguay, the retirement age is sixty for both men and women. This is notable, particularly for men, since this country has a high life expectancy.

An important characteristic of the new pension legislation in Latin America, therefore, is the establishment of "joint annuities," that is, benefits are calculated not only on the basis of the beneficiary's age and sex but also dependents'. Thus, to some degree, there is redistribution within the family as possible discrimination against women—due to expectations they will live longer—is offset by the lower benefits received by men while they have a spouse. In this sense, the most noticeable differences arise when comparing benefits for single men and women, who have similar labor histories. In the case of spouses, the effects of sex tables tend to offset each other because of the legal requirement the spouse be considered when calculating the benefit. Therefore, it is possible "joint annuities" reduce the difference in pensions between men and women.

The results of the new pension system make it possible to evaluate distinct indicators which include: the level of coverage during both the active working life and retirement, and the received pension as expressed by the replacement rate (the relation between pension and salary). The remaining part of this section will focus on these two issues.

*Pension System Coverage.*Considering the coverage of the pension system during retirement should reflect the level of coverage present during the active working life, it is interesting to look at these two indicators. One interesting case is Chile, because it not only applied the region's most radical reform, but also as its economic performance since has been outstanding and, as a result, the macroeconomic environment has not negatively affected the overall performance of the pension system.[3]

In terms of coverage, there are two relevant aspects to consider: its current composition and its trends. In terms of the former, in Chile, men are better covered by contribution-based programs used to deal with the risks of old age (Table 4). For the year 2000, coverage had reached 70.9 percent of men compared to just 36.9 percent of women. This was because men had spent more time in the labor force. However, this gap was offset by improved coverage of women in the case of survival benefits (22.5 percent versus 0.3 percent). This last gap was particularly large in Chile, compared to other countries, because men have no right to survivor's pensions unless they are invalids. In this sense, this type of legislation could be seen as discriminatory against men.

In terms of trends in coverage, it is important to start by mentioning in Chile, as in other countries, reforms have tended to reinforce the contributory nature of the system, establishing stricter entitlement conditions (for example, contributions must occur over longer periods in order to gain access to public guarantees or benefits) or a stronger link between benefits and the amount of contributions. Thus, if we examine the trends in coverage for older adults (over sixty-five years) from 1992 to 2000, the coverage of the contributory system has fallen by similar amounts for both men and women. Meanwhile, coverage of the non-contributory system has increased for men and women, although most of the beneficiaries receiving this kind of assistance continue to be women. Thus, total coverage has risen because non-contributory benefits rose more than the decline in contributory benefits, revealing a reduction in the coverage gap for older men and women (from 9.3 to 7.6 percentage points). As a result, it is worth reflecting on trends for the future of coverage and the weight of the contributory, as opposed to the non-contributory, pillar as also occurred with the number of beneficiaries (by gender) who have access to the minimum pension established for the contributory component.

When looking at the coverage figures of the Chilean pension system during the active working life, it turns out the effective and occupational coverage rates[4] are higher for women than for men. In 2000 the effective coverage rate was 51.2 percent for women, as opposed to 44.6 percent for men while the occupational coverage rates were 56.2 percent and 48.5 percent respectively. However, these figures should be interpreted with caution because the figures for effective coverage rates depend on the size of the labor force while

Table 3.4
Chile: Pension System Coverage By Sex and Type of Pension
1990-2000
(Population 65 years and over)

| | | 1992 | 1994 | 1996 | 1998 | 2000 |
|---|---|---|---|---|---|---|
| Old age | Men | 73.7 | 76.9 | 75.3 | 71.4 | 70.9 |
| | Women | 39.8 | 39.6 | 37.4 | 36.7 | 36.9 |
| | Total | 54.5 | 55.8 | 53.5 | 51.5 | 51.5 |
| Survivor | Men | 0.7 | 1.4 | 0.4 | 0.4 | 0.3 |
| | Women | 21.6 | 21.6 | 25.0 | 24.1 | 22.5 |
| | Total | 12.6 | 12.8 | 14.6 | 14.0 | 12.9 |
| PASIS | Men | 6.2 | 7.5 | 12.3 | 11.6 | 12.4 |
| (welfare) | Women | 10.0 | 11.5 | 16.3 | 15.0 | 16.5 |
| | Total | 8.3 | 9.8 | 14.6 | 13.5 | 14.7 |
| Total | Men | 80.6 | 85.8 | 88.0 | 83.4 | 83.5 |
| | Women | 71.3 | 72.7 | 78.7 | 75.8 | 75.9 |
| | Total | 75.4 | 78.4 | 82.6 | 79.0 | 79.2 |

Source: Arenas de Mesa and Gana (2003) based on CASEN surveys, 1992 – 2000.

the occupational coverage rates depend on the number of employed workers. Since the labor force participation rate of women is considerably lower than that of men, and because coverage of the pension system is mainly based on participation in the labor market, one could argue the coverage rate of women is considerably lower than of men when looking at the total number of women of working age (Arenas de Mesa and Gana 2003).

In Brazil there is a very pronounced difference between men and women in the coverage of the social system during their working lives. In 1999, the coverage rate for women was 26.6 percent while it was 46.6 percent for men[5]. With respect to the coverage of the pension system at older ages (benefit recipients), it turns out in 1999 the proportions of people sixty or older receiving benefits from a system of social security were 79 percent and 75 percent for men and women, respectively (Rocha da Silva and Schwarzer 2003).

With respect to Argentina, where the coverage of the system of people sixty-five or older has to be considered, 1999 showed coverage figures of 78 percent for men and 68 percent for women. However, when survivor's pensions are also being incorporated in the calculation of the coverage rate, women actually have a higher coverage than men. In 1999, these coverage rates would be 78.5 percent and 83.3 percent for men and women, respectively (Bertranou, Grushka and Rofman 2001).

*Replacement Rates.* Argentina, Brazil, Chile and Uruguay have implemented pension reform under different criteria. Chile, Argentina and Uruguay implemented structural reforms. Chile applied a substitute model while Argentina and Uruguay applied a mixed one (Mesa-Lago 2001). Brazil carried out a non-structural reform. Unlike the other three Latin countries, Brazil did not introduce a privately managed defined contribution scheme opting, rather, for reforms to the public PAYG scheme.[6]

One way of evaluating pension system performance, and its ability to provide suitable coverage to the risks of old age, is to use the benefit substitution or replacement rate. This is the percentage of the wage replaced by the pension benefit. Logically, this concept is applicable to contributory pension schemes. Undoubtedly, there are other important aspects that should also be considered, given the financing crisis affecting these systems has made it necessary to cover the gaps in contributory systems using general revenues, but these go beyond the scope of this paper. This situation has meant social security systems have become more contributory in the sense of requiring more years of contributions while also requiring more and more resources from outside the system. This means more general tax revenues, particularly indirect taxes on consumption. The best example of this situation is in Argentina where, because of several factors, include including the costs of the transition involved in the structural reform, its public system is financing more than 70 percent of its benefit expenditure directly from tax revenues. This means a lower percentage is financed using contributions, thus raising profound questions about the distributive impact of this policy which naturally will have a regressive effect in terms of income distribution.

*Chile: Substitution by an Individual Saving Pillar.* Before the pension reform in 1981, the replacement rates for the public system were legally established according to retirement age and years of contribution. There were no gender differences—that is, both men and women received a guaranteed salary substitution of 80 percent, if contribution density was at least 80 percent, while the retirement age was sixty-five for men and sixty for women. Moreover, the replacement rate did not vary if the man had a dependent spouse.

With the reform and the introduction of the individual capitalization system, more gender differences appeared. Several studies have calculated the replacement rates for different assumptions regarding the behavior of the relevant variables for determining pension benefits: the level and amount of contributions, the commissions, retirement age, gender, fund yields, etc. The purpose of this section is not to question the validity of these assumptions but, rather, to highlight the differences that emerge when examining the new system. Logically, larger or smaller gaps result according to each assumption because each variable has a different effect on the different types of representative male and female workers that can be considered.

Based on estimates by Arenas de Mesa and Gana (2003), table 3.5 indicates women obtain lower replacement rates than men. Moreover, these fall as pension fund yields decline and when there are dependent family members at retirement age. Because the retirement age affects both the quantity of funds accumulated, and the period over which savings disbursements will be distributed, postponing the retirement age for women from sixty to sixty-five years improves the substitution rate, pushing it up from 32 percent to 46 percent (assuming the contribution density is 60 percent and the yield on the pension fund is 4 percent). In summary, at sixty-five years of age, a man obtains better benefits (replacement rate) than a woman of the same age. However, because of the joint annuity phenomenon, the man's benefit will be worse than the woman's if he has a dependent spouse five years younger than himself.

Thus, we can conclude women will receive lower pensions than men for reasons arising from the nature of the labor market on one hand, and due to the chosen pension system on the other. However, the family structure may alter this result. In particular, it should be

**Table 3.5**
**Chile: Estimates for the Replacement Rate Under**
**the Individual Capitalization System**
*(Percentage)*

| Year | | 2001 | |
|---|---|---|---|
| Contribution density | 80 | 80 | 60 |
| Yield | 4 | 3 | 4 |
| Men 65 (18) | 74 | 50 | 53 |
| Men 65 (18)-Women 60 | 58 | 40 | 44 |
| Women 60 (18) | 43 | 30 | 32 |
| Women 65 (18) | 62 | 43 | 46 |

(·) Age at which men or women enter to the labor market.
Source: Arenas de Mesa and Gana (2003).

noted the most important reasons stem from the effects of the period for accumulating pension saving: (i) lower wage income; (ii) fewer years of contributions; (iii) lower retirement age; and (iv) less growth in the wage profile. These impacts need to be combined with the unfavorable effects implicit in the period during which saving is disbursed: (v) longer life expectancy (Arenas de Mesa and Gana 2003)

*Argentina and Uruguay: Mixed Reforms.*Argentina restructured its pension system in 1993, introducing a mixed system the following year based essentially on two pillars: one involving the public sector and providing defined benefits in the form of a basic universal benefit (*pensión básica universal, PBU*); and another involving, according to the insured choice, either a defined benefit (PAP)—pay-as-you-go system—or a privately managed defined contributions scheme based on individual accounts providing an ordinary pension (*jubilación ordinaria, JO*)—capitalization system. The system also provides compensatory benefits (*prestación compensatoria, PC*) consisting of a defined benefit for those workers who made contributions to the system before the new system came into effect in 1994.

The old system involved two types of differentiation with regard to gender: explicit and implicit. The explicit differences affected the rights of survivors of deceased workers to receive pensions. Thus, while workers' widows had the right in any case, widowers only had this right if they were unable to work and dependent on their deceased spouse. Likewise, the legislation provided pensions for children but discriminated by gender: while sons had the right, in general, until they turned eighteen years, women under eighteen years of age only received this if they were single while daughters over eighteen also had this right if they were single, widowed or separated and dependent on the deceased. Another explicit differentiation arose from retirement age, because women could retire from work five years before men, at the age of fifty-five (Rofman and Grushka 2003).

In terms of the implicit differences under the old system, these were associated with the existence of a minimum benefit. The formula for calculating the benefit was uniform (the benefit amounted to 70 percent of the average salary earned during the three best of the past ten years of work for those retiring at the minimum age, rising to 82 percent in the case of those postponing retirement for five or more years). However, calculating these benefits in an inflationary context resulted, in practice, in many workers receiving the minimum benefit. In this case and because, in general, women tended to have lower income than men, the effect was often that the actual substitution rate for women was higher than for men (Rofman and Grushka 2003).

Under the new system, the requirements for access to public benefits (PBU, PAP and PC) include: thirty years of contributions and a minimum retirement age of sixty-five for men and sixty for women. That is, the explicit requirements for access to benefits were maintained. In terms of the benefits provided by the capitalization system through its individual saving component, the characteristics are similar to those for Chile. As a result, because the two different kinds of benefits are combined, evaluating the distributive effects, and how these affect men and women differently, is more complex. In the case of public benefits, the explicit differentiation in terms of retirement age has been maintained thus benefiting women. However, the increase in the required years of contributions makes it more difficult to meet this objective by sixty years of age. Another mechanism, which was modified, affected the rights arising from the beneficiary's death. In this sense, rights were equalled permitting survivors' pensions for both genders and eliminating the special treatment of unmarried daughters.

In terms of evaluating implicit mechanisms, Rofman and Grushka (2003) empirically estimate the replacement rates this set of benefits would generate for representative female and male workers. For benefits arising from the capitalization scheme, there are two factors affecting each gender differently: first, as in Chile, the different life expectancies; second, the impact of fixed commissions on pension saving capacity, because these affect low-income workers more and women account for a higher percentage of this group.[7]

The results of empirical estimates of replacement rates indicate once the system matures (that is, for those retiring in 2040 and thereafter), women, in general, will receive somewhat higher substitution rates than men within the pay-as-you-go option for the second pillar, thanks to the indirect effect of the Basic Universal Benefit (PBU) and the neutrality of the bonus for years of contribution (*Prestación Adicional por Permanencia, PAP*). In contrast, within the capitalization system, this effect is the reverse because the advantage obtained from the PBU is more than offset by the difference in the ordinary pension (*annuity*).

As with Chile, the enormous number of variables influencing the substitution rate make evaluating these, and comparing different population groups, extremely complex. A representative case would be to evaluate the system after the transition, i.e. for those workers who will not receive the PC and who will be retiring in 2040 under the current system's conditions. Table 3.6 provides the results for the capitalization system, assuming workers enter the labor market at age twenty and then remain active until they reach retirement age, although with a contribution density of 80 percent. That is, it is assumed those who retire at sixty years of age have forty years in the labor market but just thirty-two years of contributions, and those who retire at sixty-five years have forty-five years in the market but just thirty-six years of contributions. Thus, the substitution rate for married men is 63 percent in the capitalization system and 53 percent in the public pay-as-you-go system. For single women, sixty years of age, the rates are 60 percent in the capitalization and 66 percent in the public system.

As mentioned above, the capitalization system includes two specific factors when determining benefits. For annuities, the gender of those insured is considered along with the presence of dependent family members (rights holders). Upon reducing the benefits of those expected to live longer (women), or generating pensions for death (those married and/or with children who are minors), a clear disadvantage appears affecting these population groups. Table 3.7 presents the monthly benefit a sixty-five-year-old worker can acquire with an accumulated fund of $100,000, depending on marital status[8] and gender.

One factor important to noteagain, in the case of Argentina, is the significant number of years of contributions required to obtain a public benefit: this rose from twenty to thirty years. This restriction affects men and women differently because the latter normally post a lower density rate for contributions, thus limiting their access to coverage by these benefits.

The case of Uruguay is similar to the one of Argentina. Both countries changed their pay-as-you-go pension systems into a mixed system. In Uruguay, this system consists of a public first tier, called "Intergenerational Solidarity" which is run by the BPS (Bank of Social Insurance) and a second tier, called "Mandatory Individual Saving" managed by AFAPs (Administrators of Social Insurance Saving Funds) which can be either private or public. Furthermore, there are five independent pension funds for special occupational groups like policemen and teachers. Contributions are mandatory and the BPS collects these contributions in the form of payroll taxes (15 percent) and employer contributions. It keeps the part that goes into the public system and transfers the rest of the contributions to the AFAP of choice.

The Uruguayan system shares most of its gender issues with Argentina. However, there are a few notable differences. One of the most important ones is the legal retirement ages for men and women have been equalized, thereby broadening the scope for women to contribute to their pensions due to their longer presence in the labor force. However, still no compensation is given to women who tem-

**Table 3.6**
**Argentina: Substitution Rates in 2040**
**abd Socio-Demographic Characteristics**
*(percentage)*

| Case | Substitution rate by type of benefit | | | Total substitution rate | |
|------|------|------|------|------|------|
| | PBU | PAP | JO | PAYG | Capitalization |
| | (1) | (2) | (3) | (1) + (2) | (1) + (3) |
| Women 60 years | 29 | 37 | 31 | 66 | 60 |
| Women 65 years | 29 | 31 | 46 | 60 | 75 |
| Men 65 years | 22 | 31 | 71 | 53 | 93 |
| Men 65 years Married | 22 | 31 | 41 | 53 | 63 |

Source: Rofman and Grushka (2003)
Note: It is assumed that wages rise 2 percent annually until fifty years, contribution density is 80 percent distributed uniformly from twenty years on, and funds yield 4 percent annually. PBU: *Prestación Básica Universal* (basic universal benefit). PAP: *Prestación Adicional por Permanencia* (bonus for years of contribution). JO: *Jubilación Ordinaria* (ordinary pension).

**Table 3.7**
**Argentina: Annuity Obtained from a Fund of $100,000,**
**by Socio-Demographic Characteristics**

| Gender | Marital Status | |
|--------|------|------|
| | Married | Single |
| Men | $ 552.43 | $ 724.73 |
| Women | $ 583.58 | $ 621.77 |

Source: Rofman and Grushka (2003) based on the GAM71 table.

porarily drop out of the labor market in order to care for their children. It is estimated only 23.5 percent of the domestic workers (of which 98 percent are women) are actually covered by the BPS because of the frequent changes in jobs and the difficulties in negotiating with employers. The discrimination with respect to survivor's pensions, like in Chile, is also present in Uruguay: men have to be financially dependent on their wives in order to qualify for such a pension while such a restriction is not placed on women.

The replacement rates of the first pillar are similar for both men and women (50 percent for regular pension at sixty with thirty-five years of contributions, and 55 percent for advanced age pensions at seventy with twenty years of contributions). This means replacement rates are gender neutral, however failing in compensating women for their spells of absence in the labor market. Differences arise when the AFAP-second tier is considered, likewise in Argentina, the level of all pensions (old age, incapacity and survivors) is determined by the amount deposited in the insured individual account and the contract signed with the insurance company that will pay a life annuity based on gender-specific life expectancy tables and a given interest rate.

*Brazil: Non-Structural Reform.* While the 1998 to 1999 pension reform in Brazil reinforced the contributory relationship as the basis for the system's functioning, this differed from other reforms within the region because it was of a non-structural nature. Essentially the private sector did not get involved in managing compulsory pension savings, nor did Brazil implement a defined contribution system with individual capitalization accounts.[9]

The reformed system continues to be based on a pay-as-you-go scheme, but how benefits are calculated was changed to adjust the system to demographic trends and the contribution record of each worker. Before the reform, the "benefit by age" was calculated using the contribution wage for the three years prior to retirement for men (sixty-five years) and women (sixty years). The reform established this calculation should be carried out over 80 percent of the best taxable wages since entry into the labor force. The other reform involved the *Bonus for years or length of contribution* (replacing the benefit for time in service), with men required to show at least thirty-five years of contributions and women thirty years. Thus, the so-called *Fator Previdenciário* (pension factor) is applied to calculate pensions, adjusting the benefit to the moment in time when this is received (that is, the insured person's life expectancy). To avoid introducing gender inequality, some specific mechanisms were introduced. Thus the *Fator Previdenciário* is calculated using unisex mortality tables and maintaining women's rights to receive benefits after thirty years of contribution, i.e. five years less than required for men. In this case, the system explicitly recognizes women find it harder to certify their years of contribution.

One way of evaluating the reforms' impact, as with Chile and Argentina, consists of estimating probable trends in replacement rates by gender in the two types of awarded benefits (by age and by length of contributions) according to the rules in effect before and after the reform introducing the *Fator Previdenciário* (Law 9876/99). According to Rocha da Silva and Schwarzer (2003), the results most relevant for the purposes of this evaluation have to do with the pension by length of contributions. Estimates for before and after the pension reform by retirement age and gender indicate no significant differences as they rise by similar percentages for both men and women. That is, the substitution rates improve for both men and women without widening the gaps between both.

Comparisons of substitution rates for length of contribution benefits take into account a premium for five years of contribution enjoyed by women due to the effect of using the same *Fator Previdenciário*. Table 3.8 compares the replacement rates for women and men, revealing there is a substantial improvement in every case, except where both men and women retire at sixty years with the same number of years of contributions (men thirty-five years and women thirty years but with the five-year "premium"). This means with the reform, the replacement rates for both genders should tend to converge. As a result, the large inequalities would continue to arise due to labor market conditions, rather than the way pensions are calculated.

When considering the situation of the four different countries described in this section, it can be concluded, especially in Chile and Argentina where radical reforms of the pension system have taken place, little attention has been paid to the gender aspect. The result in these countries is the differences in labor market participation between men and women not only cause discrepancies in income between those groups during their active working life, but also exacerbates the problem at retirement.

Table 3.8
Brazil: Comparison of Pension Reforms' Effects on Replacement Rates for
Length of Contribution Benefits by Gender
*(for the average population, in percentage)*

| Cases compared | | Comparison of substitution rates (Women/Men) | |
| --- | --- | --- | --- |
| | | Pre-Reform | Post-Reform |
| M 55 yr, 30 cont. | W 55 yr 25 cont. +5 | 86.9 | 96.3 |
| M 55 yr, 35 cont. | W 55 yr 30 cont. +5 | 83.2 | 94.9 |
| M 60 yr, 30 cont. | W 60 yr 25 cont. +5 | 94.2 | 97.4 |
| M 60 yr, 35 cont. | W 60 yr 30 cont. +5 | 102.9 | 99.0 |

"yr." indicates age; "cont." indicates years of contributions
Source: Rocha da Silva and Schwarzer (2003)

Only in Brazil, where the reforms were undertaken in a less drastic fashion, has attention been paid to the increase in the retirement age of women. Brazil has also made an effort to deal with the differences in life expectancy between men and women which negatively affects the income of women. However, there are persistent differences between the situation of men and women due to the different behavior of both sexes in the labor market.

Another interesting point to notice is the perceived role of women is implicit in the establishment of these reforms. They are still being considered dependent on their families and are not recognized as being the provider of families which is becoming more and more common. In this respect, little has changed since the origin of the first pension systems in the first half of the twentieth century; the role of women in society is mainly in non-market work activities, i.e., taking care of home and family responsibilities. This point is perfectly illustrated by the example of survivor's pensions. In Chile, unless men suffer from complete invalidity, they will not receive this pension when their wives die, even though she pays into a monthly survivor's insurance fund.

### Incipient Attention of Other International Organizations

International organizations have recently started to fuel the discussion on the issue of gender and pensions in developing countries. A number of studies and projects on the subject have been undertaken and experts in the field have actively participated in several seminars and workshops dealing with these issues. In 2003 the

---

**Box 1: ECLAC project on pensions and gender**

In 2000, ECLAC started a project on the gender impact of the pension reforms in Latin America, in an attempt to contribute to the recommendations on social security that were adopted at world conferences, most notably the Platform of Action in Beijing, which focuses on the majority of Latin American countries that have completed their pension reforms. This project has been developed in Argentina, Bolivia, Chile, Colombia and El Salvador and tries to attract attention to the gap between the different sexes in the pension system and to supply recommendations to the social security sector on how to correct these inequalities in the system. The intention is to look at the situation from a juridical-institutional point of view, while at the same time using a demographic and labor perspective.

One of the methods CEPAL used in their project was the organization of seminars in the different countries to raise awareness. One of these took place in Santiago, Chile on June 17-18, 2002. In order to illustrate some of the results of the projects, some of the main conclusions of the seminar in Chile are presented below:

- The system of individual account does not recognize the disadvantages women face in the labor market or the higher life expectancy they have.
- It is necessary to increase intergenerational transfers and transfers between the two genders to increase the coverage of social protection and to allow for reproduction.
- A possible solution to the low coverage rates and inequity might be to increase the attention being paid to the redistributive aspect of the system.
- The pension system still uses the traditional role model with a nuclear family and a dependent mother which no longer corresponds with the reality in these countries, thereby disadvantaging women.
- In order to close the gap between the pensions of men and women, unisex life expectancy tables in combination with equalized legal retirement ages should be considered.

Some of the recommendations for the future include:

- Collection of more reliable statistical data, especially with respect to the new types of family structures and the size of contributions, pensions and coverage disaggregated by sex
- Evaluation of the interaction between formal and informal systems of social protection and the differences between men and women
- Consideration of the legal structure and an evaluation of both the purposes of the system and the effects on the two genders as well as on different incomes.

Although it is difficult to assess the impact of the ECLAC Project on the discussion on gender and pensions, it is clear it has at least helped to get the topic on the political agenda and to encourage developments that will help to reform the system to solve the inequality between genders. There is still a long way to go in this respect, but by considering both the technical and political aspects of the pension systems, ECLAC has managed to involve both experts in the field of social protection and politicians in the process, which is definitely a further step in the right direction.

Source: http://www.eclac.cl/mujer/proyectos/pensiones/antecedentes.htm

ILO published two sub regional studies on social protection and gender, including pensions, for three Latin American countries (summarized in this article) and three Central and Eastern Europe countries: Bertranou and Arenas de Mesa (2003) and Fultz et al. (2003). The UN Economic Commission for Latin America and the Caribbean (ECLAC) carried out a regional project (see box 1) and the World Bank conducted a series of country studies.

The World Bank (2002) series of studies on pension systems incorporated the gender issue into their analysis. In a summary paper by James, Cox and Wong, the authors conclude women are the main beneficiaries of the pension reforms in the countries studied (Chile, Argentina and Mexico). The authors argue that even though the accumulated funds and annuities of women are only 30 to 40 percent of those of men, women benefit because of the guaranteed minimum benefits of which women are the main beneficiaries due to their situation in the labor market (interruptions in their working life due to pregnancy, lower wages). Furthermore, the inclusion of shared annuities in the calculation of the pension of a spouse has improved the situation of women. Additionally, the authors argue that when a woman receives a benefit from their individual account, together with a survivor's pension, her total benefits would be 60 to 80 percent of those of a man. In the case of women with full-time careers, actual benefits would equal, or even exceed, those of a man.

When evaluating this study, it is obvious that an assumption is made that the majority of women are married and, more specifically, their husbands will provide a survivor's pension. Furthermore, the study only provides a relative comparison between the new systems in the different countries, but not an absolute comparison with respect to the previous pension systems. This is justified by arguing that these systems were financially unsustainable and, therefore, under the old system, benefits had to be reduced or taxes increased. However, the following points need to be taken into consideration when analyzing this particular study.

First of all, the benefits that are assigned through a pension system need to be evaluated from a perspective of social security. However, the study of James et al. considers the situation from a perspective of actuarial fairness, in which contributions should equal benefits, instead of looking at replacement rates and the relationship to the minimum guaranteed pension. Furthermore, it is argued that women are favored by the system because they receive survivor's pensions from their husbands. These arguments are obviously flawed for two reasons. Firstly, in a system of individual accounts, the stream of benefits is by definition equal to the accumulated contributions so actuarial fairness is not an issue. Secondly, the reason why women receive survivor's pensions is, on average, they live longer than men, so this has nothing to do with being favored by the system.

Secondly, the analysis on the effects of the pension system on women is based on the image of a dependent woman. The analysis fails to pay attention to the large number of women who are not married and only receive a pension based on their own contributions. Over the past years, the role of women and the structure of families have changed dramatically. The image of a nuclear family with a dependent mother is less applicable to modern societies. Therefore, the analysis done by the World Bank, which fails to address these changes in the social structure, should be reconsidered.

Thirdly, the authors believe it is unnecessary to compare the benefits in the new system with those in the old system because the latter was not financially sustainable. However, they fail to recognize other opportunities to finance a PAYG system such as increasing taxes. Most countries that continue to use such a pension system have found ways around the problem of financing.

Fourthly, both in the old and new system women receive a survivor's pension. The difference between the two is the new system guarantees the payment of the accumulated funds in the individual account, independent of the number of years of contribution of the spouse. On the other hand, the old system only paid survivor's pensions to the spouses of men satisfying the requirements for obtaining a pension. If this was not the case, neither the contributor nor his wife would receive any benefits. Consequently, when looking at the situation from the perspective of a man qualifying for a pension under both pension regimes, the new system does not bring any additional benefits in terms of higher income from his wife.

Finally, one of the principles of social security is solidarity. Nevertheless, James et al. argues one of the benefits of the new system is it terminates the financial transfers from men to women and creates an intra-family transfer. When considering this from an inter-temporal perspective, this is not an improvement for the family, since the income of the family during the active working life decreases in order to finance a survivor's pension in the future (which, in the case of Chile, is not even going to be paid in the event of the wife dying before her husband does). Therefore, the solidarity between the sexes in the old system should be considered as something positive; compensating the women for their dedication in bearing and then raising their children, work valued by the whole of society.

## Public Policy and Agenda for Social Protection, Pensions, and Gender

Old age social protection in Latin America, as measured by old age pensions, is generally lower for women than for men. This is the result of the mainly contributory nature of social security systems in which labor trajectories vary substantially between genders. Women have had, and continue to have, lower participation rates and lower income profiles which lead to lower pension saving and reduced entitlement to benefits and public guarantees. The reasons for this poorer performance in the labor market are widely known: occupational segregation, higher and longer unemployment rates, more participation in the informal wage-earning sector, interruptions in the work record due to maternity, more responsibility for the care of disabled family members and the elderly, etc. Despite this, social protection systems have normally been capable of providing other types of income security to offset the effects of strictly contributory systems. Minimum pension guarantees, more advantageous entitlement rights (lower retirement ages and required years of contributions), non-contributory and/or welfare benefits, are the main examples of programs particularly favoring workers and families with lower incomes from labor with women accounting for a higher percentage of these than men.

The other source of gaps in social protection coverage during old age arises from the introduction of new ways of calculating pension benefits in reformed pension systems. The introduction of systems with defined contributions based on individual accounts, blended with benefits calculated using mortality tables by sex, leads to a gap between men and women that from a social perspective may be considered unfair. A male and female worker with the same labor profile who retire at the same age will receive different benefits solely on the basis of their gender: the woman will be at a disadvantage compared to the man because of her longer life expectancy and, as a result, a longer period that must be covered by disbursement of savings. However, these gaps are cushioned by benefits from private systems (annuities) corresponding to the "joint annuity" method, that is, the incorporation of a calculation for the life expectancy of spouses and/or dependent children. This way, within marriage these effects tend to balance out, while they are more evident in the case of single male and female workers with no dependent children. Nevertheless it could be argued: (i) an evaluation of the pension system should be viewed from a perspective where the received monthly pensions replace the income from work; (ii) the role of women has changed over the last few years both in terms of their participation in the labor market and with respect to their role in the family structure (higher divorce rates and increasing number of women as head of household) which creates the necessity to reconsider the system in order to account for women that do not receive a survivor's pension; (iii) the old systems also supplied eligible women with survivor's benefits and (iv) the income of women from survivor's pensions is not collected from men, in the case of Chile, during the period when they receive a pension. Therefore the solidarity between men and women present in the old system has disappeared or diminished. In particular, joint annuities do not offer any additional guarantees to women in the individual capitalization system as compared to the old pension systems.

This article discussed comparatively the gender situation arising from four major reforms in the region (Argentina, Brazil, Chile and Uruguay). The replacement rates and the gaps resulting from new calculation formulae were estimated for the reformed systems. One important aspect that should be noted, which goes beyond the objectives of this study, is within each gender there is an enormous heterogeneity and a variety of conditions that should be taken into consideration. Thus, "affirmative action" programs for women (for example, the use of unisex tables or minimum pension guarantees) or for men (for example, access to the right to a widower's pension) must be treated as supplementary to other social protection policies in a context involving actions giving priority to the welfare of sectors marginalized or excluded from the system.

The estimates carried out, and the evaluation of the social protection profile foreseen for, each of the three countries' systems are, in part, confirmed by the PSS socio-economic security surveys carried out by the ILO in 2001 (Bertranou and Arenas de Mesa 2003). Women had the most negative expectations regarding their entitlement to a pension in their own right during old age. However, expectations regarding standard of living during old age did not vary significantly by gender. It can be speculated this is the result of the fact the basic social protection unit is the family and there is important redistribution of resources within it, particularly from men to women. Moreover, the convergence of standard of living expectations is the result of the application of protection programs tending to favor women. Thus, social policy and social protection programs must constantly consider this aspect, not only to extend social security to everyone, but also to ensure it is applied equally across genders.

## Appendix: International labor standards and gender equality [10]

In the ILO's early years, standards related to women were aimed primarily at protecting female workers in terms of health and safety, conditions of work and special requirements related to their reproductive function. Over time, there has been a change in the types of standards relevant to women—from protective conventions to conventions aimed at giving women and men equal rights and equal opportunities. The adoption of the Equal Remuneration Convention, 1951 (No. 100), the Discrimination (Employment and Occupation) Convention, 1958 (No. 111), and the Workers with Family Responsibilities Convention, 1981 (No. 156), marked a shift in traditional attitudes concerning the role of women and a recognition family responsibilities affect not only women workers but the family and society as well. The mid-1970s marked the emergence of a new and more ambitious concept aimed at equality of opportunity between men and women in all fields. This concept found its expression in the debates and texts coming out of the Sixtieth Session of the International Labor Conference held in 1975. Since then, the protection of working women has been based on the principle women must be protected against the risks inherent in their job and profession on the same basis and according to the same norms as men. The special protective measures remaining permissible are those aimed at protecting women's reproductive function.

Most of the ILO social security instruments contain no provision forbidding discrimination on the basis of sex, having been adopted at a time when the prevailing opinion (often at variance with reality even then) was men were the breadwinners and women would normally stay at home to take care of the family. Two social security Conventions do, however, prohibit discrimination. One is the Maternity Protection Convention (Revised), 1952 (No. 103), which states any contribution shall be paid in respect of all men and women employed by the enterprise without distinction on the basis of sex. The other is the Employment Promotion and Protection against Unemployment Convention, 1988 (No. 168), which requires equality of treatment for all persons protected without discrimination on the basis *inter alia* of sex while allowing member states to adopt special measures to meet the specific needs of categories of persons who have particular problems in the labor market.

Other ILO Conventions not specifically relating to social security do, of course, expressly prohibit discrimination on the basis of sex, namely Conventions Nos. 100, 111 and 156 mentioned above. With a view to creating effective equality of opportunity and treatment for men and women workers, Convention No. 156 prescribes all measures compatible with national conditions and possibilities shall be taken to take account of the needs of workers with family responsibilities in social security. The Discrimination (Employment and Occupation) Recommendation, 1958 (No. 111), recommends all persons should, without discrimination, enjoy equality of opportunity and treatment in respect of social security measures.

The protection of the reproductive function of women is intimately linked with the promotion of gender equality. Maternity insurance benefits are critical for allowing women and their families to maintain their standard of living when the mother is unable to work. Throughout its history the ILO has been concerned in ensuring women workers enjoy this entitlement, from the adoption in 1919 of the Maternity Protection Convention (No. 3) to the adoption in 2000 of the Maternity Protection Convention (No. 183) and Recommendation (No. 191).

# Notes

1. This chapter is mainly based on Bertranou and Arenas de Mesa (2003), ILO (2002a) and Bertranou (2001). Pamela Gana contributed in the completion of sections 2 and 4 of this version, while Sander Huizinga provided invaluable research assistance. I thank Wouter van Ginneken and Carmen Solorio for their valuable comments to previous versions. The usual disclaimer applies.
2. Others who have dealt with this issue are the Economic Commission for Latin America and the Caribbean (ECLAC 2002) and the World Bank (World Bank 2002).
3. There is still debate about whether there is some causal relationship between pension reform and macroeconomic performance, specifically: its impact on national saving, the development of the capital market and the generation of new financial instruments. It would seem the causal relationship is more difficult to reject in the case of the latter, than in the case of national saving, because of the enormous costs involved in the transition to these new fully funded schemes.
4. "Effective coverage rate" relates contributors to economic active population while "occupational coverage rate" relates contributors to employment.
5. For this purpose only the workers covered by both the social security pension system for private sector workers (INSS) and the scheme for public servants.
6. Studies by Arenas de Mesa and Gana (2003), Rofman and Grushka (2003), and Rocha da Silva and Schwarzer (2003) summarize the main characteristics of the reforms introduced in these countries.
7. Argentina eliminated fixed commissions in 2002.
8. It is assumed that in the case of marriage men are five years older than women.
9. It should be noted at the time of the reforms, a supplementary private pension system had already been functioning in Brazil. This system is voluntary and organized separately from the public pension system. This system is called the "private pension system" (*Previdência Privada*).
10. ILO (2002a).

# References

Arenas de Mesa, Alberto and Verónica Montecinos (1999). "The Privatization of Social Security and Women's Welfare: Gender Effects of the Chilean Reform." *Latin American Research Review*, Vol. 34. Nº 3, Fall.

Arenas de Mesa, Alberto and Pamela Gana (2003). "Protección Social, Pensiones y Género en Chile," in Bertranou and Arenas de Mesa (2003), pp. 137-225.

Bertranou, Fabio M. (2001). "Pension Reform and Gender Gaps in Latin America: What are the Policy Options?" *World Development*, Vol. 29, No.5, pp. 911-923.

Bertranou, Fabio M., Carlos Grushka and Rafael Rofman (2001). "Evolución reciente de la cobertura provisional en Argentina," in Bertranou, F. (Ed.) *Cobertura Provisional en Argentina, Brasil y Chile*. Santiago de Chile: International Labor Office.

Bertranou, Fabio M. and Alberto Arenas de Mesa, Eds. (2003). *Protección Social, Pensiones y Género*. Santiago de Chile: International Labor Office.

ECLAC (2002). "Proyecto Impacto de Género de la Reforma de Pensiones en América Latina." Santiago de Chile.

Fultz, Elaine, Markus Ruck and Silke Steinhilber, Eds. (2003). *The Gender Dimensions of Social Security Reform in Central and Eastern Europe: Case Studies of the Czech Republic, Hungary and Poland*. Budapest: International Labor Office.

ILO (2002a). *Social Security. A new consensus*. Geneva: International Labor Office.

ILO (2002b). Políticas de Empleo. Salarios y Género en Chile. Textos de Capacitación. Santiago de Chile: International Labor Office.

ILO (2003a). Key Indicators of the Labor Market. Geneva: International Labor Office.

ILO (2003b). *Panorama Laboral 2003*. Lima: International Labor Office.

ILO (2004). *Protección Social en Uruguay: Financiamiento, Cobertura y Desempeño 1990 – 2002*. Santiago de Chile: International Labor Office.

IPEA (2002). Boletin de Mercado de Trabalho. Brasilia. November.

Mesa-Lago (2001). "Structural reforms off social security pensions in Latin America: Models, characteristics, results and conclusions," *International Social Security Review*, Vol.54, No.4.

Rocha da Silva, Enid and Helmut Schwarzer (2003). "Protección Social, Jubilaciones, Pensiones y Género en Brasil" in Bertranou and Arenas de Mesa (2003), pp. 65-136.

Rofman, Rafael and Carlos Grushka (2003). "Protección Social, Jubilaciones, Pensiones y Género en Argentina," in Bertranou and Arenas de Mesa (2003), pp. 31-64.

van Ginneken, Wouter (1999). "Pensions for Women in the Informal Economy: Options for Developing Countries." Workshop on social protection for women in the informal Economy, ILO, Geneva, 6-7 December 1999.

World Bank (2002). "The Gender Impact of Pension Reform: A Cross-Country Analysis." Washington, DC.

# 4

# Gender, Employment and Social Security in Norway

*Espen Dahl*
*Axel West Pedersen*

## Introduction

In this chapter we discuss how gender equality is influenced by the interaction between structural changes in the Norwegian society, particularly in the labor market, and changes in social policy and family policy programs.

Norway is often considered one of the more family- and women-friendly societies in the Western world. This perception is based on facts like a high proportion of women in the Parliament and among cabinet ministers, a high female labor force participation extending into older age brackets and a welfare state providing benefits and services enhancing the reconciliation of work and family. In the recent Human Development Reports, the UN has declared in a comparative perspective women in Norway are ranked on top in terms of welfare, social equality and opportunities, as compared with men. This has prompted Norwegian media to portray Norwegian women as "super women" because they, to a large degree, combine paid work with the roles of wives and mothers. As might be suspected however, this picture is one-sided and misses many nuances and ambiguities. In this chapter we analyze how social policy and welfare reforms affect women's life and living conditions within the context of women's socio-economic position.

The central question is how "gender blind" reforms influence women's labor market activity, living conditions and welfare, in both the short- and the long-run, in a situation where important gender differences exist at the outset. This question is closely related to a profound dilemma between the utopian ideal of promoting full equality in actual labor market behavior and labor market pay-offs of males and females, and a concern for compensating females here and now for their de facto weaker position in the labor market and their disproportionate share of unpaid care and domestic work.

We proceed as follows: In the first section we give an account of the institutional features of the Norwegian welfare state model. This is followed by a description of women's social and economic standing relative to men in the Norwegian society with a particular focus on women's position in the labor market. The reason for this exercise is welfare and income maintenance for men and women in Norway is, to a large extent, linked to their labor market activity. Today, most Social Insurance rights are closely linked to labor market activity, performance and earnings, and will be so at an increasing rate according to recent White Papers commissioned by the Government. The third section includes a presentation of the major Social Insurance programs in Norway, recent reforms in these programmes and our assessments of how these reforms may impact the lives of men and women differently. The fourth section addresses the very recent proposal to reform—"modernize"—the old age pension system. Lastly, in section five we summarize our main findings and discuss whether there is a change in the philosophy of social welfare and how Social Insurance and social policy influence the labor market participation, living conditions and welfare of men and women differently.

## The Norwegian Welfare State in Comparative Perspective

The Norwegian welfare state conforms to what has come to be known as the social democratic regime type. Titmuss (1974) made a distinction between 'three contrasting models or functions of social policy (Lødemel and Trickey 2001). These were developed to analyze differences in welfare state provision and the ideas and ideologies of the role of the state underlying them. First, 'The Residual Model of Welfare' sees the function of social services as one of dealing only with people who are unable to help themselves. Second, "The Handmaiden Model" rests on the view social services are functional to other institutions, that "social needs should be met on the basis of merit, work performance and productivity." Third, "The Institutional Redistributive Model" "sees social welfare as a major integrated institution in society, providing universalistic services outside the market on the principle of need." However, it was not until the publication of Esping Andersen's (1990) exceptionally influential *The Three Worlds of Welfare Capitalism*, the work and discussion about typologies became mainstream in comparative research. The basic claim was we cannot understand welfare state variation linearly but there are qualitative differences in the way social provision is provided and welfare states tend to cluster into three different regimes forming interconnected configurations of state and market and, later, the family. His three ideal-types of welfare state *regimes* are defined according to two dimensions; extent of decommodification, i.e. the extent to which social policy makes individuals independent of the market; and stratification and labor market participation, that is, the extent to which the welfare state differentiates in the treatment of different groups. The first distinctive regime type is labelled 'conservative-corporatist' and it is characterized by strong emphasises on the role of social partners, on the principle of family subsidiarity and, in consequence, on an underdeveloped service sector, and on the existence of labor market "insiders" and "outsiders." It is empirically illustrated by the cases of France and Germany. The second regime type is labelled 'liberal' and it is characterized by minimal and targeted assistance measures, re-enforcement of job-seeking behavior and promotion of systems of private welfare provision. The primary cases of reference are the U.K. and the U.S. The third idealised type, the "social-democratic regime," exemplified by the above mentioned Nordic or Scandinavian countries, is characterized by institutionalized redistribution in which the welfare state provides universal social rights based on full employment (Esping-Andersen 1990).

The defining criteria are the degree of universalism and generosity of Social Insurance Programs such as unemployment benefits, pension insurance and sickness pay. Because in the Nordic model such programs are expensive, the model is based on the premise of "full employment" since its sustainability depends a broad tax base. Thus, also pertaining to this model, are features like relatively high employment rates among women and the elderly and active labor market policies (Huber and Stephens 2002).

The Nordic welfare state model is characterized by a low degree of social inequality; a large body of empirical evidence shows the Nordic welfare states enjoy a high level of social equality. For example, a large number of analyses based on the Luxembourg Income Study (LIS), probably the best database on comparative income and poverty studies, indicate income inequality, as measured by the Gini index, is consistently lower in these countries than in most others. The same applies to poverty: poverty rates among people in their working ages, as well as poverty rates among vulnerable groups such as aged and single mothers, are low compared to nations in the other welfare regimes (Atkinson 2000; Fritzell 2001; Smeeding 2002; Huber and Stephens 2002).

Although not one of Esping-Andersen's defining criteria, but highly relevant in the present context, is social democratic welfare states are characterized by a large public sector predominantly occupied by women. This has contributed to the particularly gendered labor market segregation in Norway, among the highest in the OECD area (Leira 2003, Kjølsrød 2003).

In a comparative perspective, the Nordic welfare states are considered to be family- and woman-friendly (Esping-Andersen 1999). Several institutional features contribute to this: opportunities for paid maternal leave, entitlement to days off when children are sick, subsidized child care, cash allowance for families with small children and pension credits for care for family members. As we will discuss below however, the actual impact of some of the existing welfare arrangements may be ambiguous for gender equality. Birkelund and Petersen (2003:146) claim the so called "state feminism" has enhanced women's opportunities to be both workers and mothers but has not necessarily contributed to more equality between the genders. This has been variously dubbed "the Norwegian equity paradox" (Birkelund and Petersen 2003), and "gender equity light" (Skrede 2004).

Obviously, the way welfare state institutions function and impact upon gender equality will depend on other contextual factors such as culture, gender roles and labor market demand and structure. Our main analytical point is interplay between social structures and gender differences in employment and family obligations on the one hand, and the embeddedness in the welfare state institutions on the other, might have undesired consequences for gender equality in present society and, perhaps, even more so in the future; equal treatment of population groups who are unequal at the outset leads to inequality in result. The next section addresses the gendered employment structures and trends in Norway and relates them to some features of the welfare state.

## Employment Structure and Labor Market Outcomes

A high female labor force participation is one of the hallmarks of the Scandinavian model. The influx of married women into paid employment started somewhat later in Norway than in the other Scandinavian countries. It did not take off before the early 1970s and by the end of the 1980s Norway was still lagging behind Denmark and Sweden in terms of female employment rates. In the course of the 1990s however, Norway finally appears to have caught up with, and even surpassed, the Nordic neighbors in terms of female labor force participation and (in particular) employment rates. Women still have lower employment rates than men but the difference has shrunk to less than 10 percentage points (see table 4.1).

**Table 4.1**
**Employed as Percentage of Whole Population Age Sixteen to Seventy-Four**
**1980 to 2000**

|       | 1980 | 1985 | 1990 | 1995 | 2000 |
|-------|------|------|------|------|------|
| Men   | 78.3 | 76.4 | 71.8 | 71.3 | 75.1 |
| Women | 53.8 | 57.7 | 59.4 | 61.1 | 66.6 |

Source: Statistics Norway 2003

In table 4.1, people with just a few hours of paid work per week, not only those with employment as main activity, are counted as employed. According to Birkelund and Petersen (2003), who refer to the latest data from SSB 82 percent of women and 89 percent of men in the economically active ages are currently employed.

The growth in female employment taking place during the 1970s and 1980s is a good example of the Scandinavian pattern of employment growth through the expansion of publicly financed services (see Esping-Andersen 1990).

One could describe this fundamental change as a relocation of traditional female care work from the informal economy of the family sphere and into the formal economy of the public sector. Once set into motion, this process is facilitated by strong self-reinforcing mechanisms. When females (housewives) enter formal employment, the demand for public services rises (kindergartens, nursing homes, etc.), and the resulting expansion of these public services will then lead to a further increase in the demand for (female) labor.

## *Educational and Occupational Segregation*

However, the apparent convergence in participation and employment rates between males and females coexists with significant gender differences in the nature of employment. In Norway, men and women have about the same level of education but the choice of educational types are markedly gendered and have been so for decades (Birkelund and Petersen 2003): Men have chosen, and still choose ,subjects like technical trades, engineering, math and science while women still prefer subjects in humanities, social care, health care and welfare (Mastekaasa and Nordlie Hansen 2003).

These pervasive and persistent differences in the choices of educational tracks are reflected in the gendering in the occupational and industrial structure. The Norwegian Labor market turns out to be among the most gender-segregated in the OECD area (Birkelund and Petersen 2003). In 2000, women constituted only about 25 percent of the employees in manufacturing and are also clearly underrepresented in private businesses such as finance. On the other hand, 83 percent of employees in health and social services are women. High proportions of women also work in educational institutions. This pattern has been stable for thirty years (Kjølsrød 2003).

This kind of segregation is often called horizontal segregation. Another dimension is vertical segregation, a term alluding to the degree to which men and women hold leading positions in the labor market. In private businesses, less than ten percent of the CEOs are women (www.likestilling.no). Birkelund (cited in Birkelund and Petersen 2003) has shown also along this vertical dimension, Norwegian women are worse off than women in several Western countries and lag, for example, far behind their North American counterparts.

## *Part-Time Work*

Another distinctive feature of employment among Norwegian women is the high prevalence of part-time work, that is, less than thirty-five hours per week. As already mentioned, the entry of married females into the labor market in the 1970s and 1980s was closely linked to the expansion of public service employment and of part-time jobs (Ellingsæter and Rubery 1996). While part-time work is almost non-existent among male employees, the part-time share among female employees continues to be high. The part-time ratio among employed women aged sixteen to seventy-four was 43 percent in the year 2000 compared to 53 percent in 1980.

However, more than half of all female part-timers have regular working hours between twenty and thirty-six hours per week and only about 20 percent of all female employees work less than twenty hours per week (Torp and Barth 2001). There has been a tendency since the 1980s for "long part-time" employment to grow at the expense of "short part-time" employment (Ellingsæter 1989). Research on the preferences of part-time workers indicates part-time work is very often a voluntary arrangement and the prevalence of part-time work cannot, therefore, be taken as an indicator of underemployment in any meaningful sense of the word. While part-timers, on average, report preferring to have higher working hours than the amount of hours actually worked, the difference is rather modest and it is matched by a reverse tendency among full-time workers who, on average, would prefer to work less than they actually do (Torp and Barth 2001).

Actual average working hours per week have been reduced somewhat among men (from 41.5 in 1980 to 38.8 in 2000), primarily due to a reduction in the standard working hours, while average working hours per week increased slightly among women (29.2 in 1980, 30.6 in 2000), due to the observed decline in part-time work (SSB 2003, table 11).

*The Gender Gap in Wages*

Against this background it comes as little surprise the gender gap in wages is significant. On average it is about 20 to 30 percent (Birkelund and Petersen 2003), but varies quite substantially between industrial sectors as indicated in table 4.2.

Table 4.2 also shows in many sectors, there has been a slight closing of the gender gap in wages over the last years (see also www.ssb.no/emner/00/02/10/likestilling/).

Although some disagreement remains on the issue, it seems most of the gender gap in wages is due to differences in working hours and occupational segregation and not to gender discrimination within occupations. It has been shown the gender gap in wages between men and women in matching occupations and rank positions is negligible (Petersen 2003, Birkelund and Petersen 2003). Occupational segregation is extremely important and accounts for a substantial part of the gender gap in wages. It has been estimated if there was

**Table 4.2**
**Average Annual Wages for Women as Percentage of**
**Average Annual Wages for Men in Selected Industrial Sectors**
**1990 and 1998**

| Industry | 1990 | 1998 |
|---|---|---|
| Manufacturing | 89,7 | 90,9 |
| Clerks in retail | 70,6 | 75,3 |
| Insurance | 70,7 | 74,4 |
| Municipalities | 86,6 | 88,0 |
| School sector | 89,6 | 89,8 |
| Transportation | 93,4 | 94,8 |

Source: Statistics Norway 2000.

no segregation in Norway, the differences in wages would have been reduced to 1 to 4 percent instead of the observed 20 to 30 percent (Petersen 2002 in Birkelund and Petersen 2003:143). It is also speculated a compressed wage structure in Norway is one reason why Norwegian women so seldomly acquire the top jobs in private companies, and also the highest ranked jobs in the public sector, because the incentives are too weak (Petersen 2003).

The gender gap in wages is strongly tied to differences in wage levels between the (predominantly male) private and the (predominantly female) public sector. It has been shown wage levels in the public sector have been lagging systematically behind the private sector over the last decades. Typically, female para-professions, like nursing and primary school teaching, have lost out compared to skilled, typically male occupations in the private sector (Høgsnes 199?).

One could argue that the comparatively high public sector employment which, in turn, is an important factor behind the high female employment rate, rests on a complicated equilibrium between macro and micro factors. The relatively low wage levels found in the public sector help to make the very high public sector employment financially sustainable at the macro level. At the micro level, the comparative low wage levels are (at least to some extent) balanced by friendly employment relations appearing to have a special appeal to female wage earners since it helps to facilitate the combination of (almost) full-time work and family obligations. Norwegian women continue to carry out a disproportionate share of unpaid household work, despite the almost universal participation in the labor market (Aslaksen and Koren 1995).

This equilibrium is presently under pressure in different ways. Unions and professional organizations in the public sector are no longer willing to accept the wage gap said to exist in comparison to the private sector and they challenge the hegemonic position. The Confederation of the Trade Unions (LO), and in particular the unions in the export-oriented sectors, have held in the latter half of the twentieth century in the national system of wage bargaining (Barth, Moene and Wallerstein 2003). The equilibrium is also under pressure to change due to current attempts to improve the efficiency of the public sector through experiments with privatization, exposure to competition and similar measures in the spirit of "New Public Management" (NPM). A great deal of the female employment is tied to the public sector in which welfare arrangements and employment relations have traditionally been particularly friendly. The traditional friendliness includes more generous schemes for parental leave, sick leave, pension schemes as well as a higher degree of job protection, insulation against turbulent market forces and a lower pressure to improve productivity and efficiency. Administrative reforms in the spirit of NPM are likely to erode the traditional friendliness of employment relations in the public sector and put an end to the role of the public sector as a women-friendly "employment machine."

*Trends in Retirement Ages*

One should note although employment rates among elderly men have decreased steadily over the last decades, the opposite is true for elderly women. Today, the employment rates for both genders in their senior ages are among the highest in the OECD area (Esping-Andersen 2002). Despite this, there has been a long-standing concern for labor market participation among the elderly in Norway. By 1992, the Government had commissioned a working group to discuss reforms in disability pension and old age pension system. The initiative was motivated by the fact, at the time, the average age of retirement had fallen to about sixty-two years. The public and official retirement age in Norway is sixty-seven. The working group proposed remedies aimed at pushing the average pension age up to sixty-four years. However, since that time, the average retirement age has fallen further to slightly less than sixty years (RTV Rapport 06/2002).

Average pension age however, gives a misleading picture of the central tendency of when people retire. Among other things, the measure is influenced by demographic changes and is, thus, not a reliable indicator of the retirement pattern in the population. Expected retirement age is a more appropriate measure that, like life expectancy, reveals the central tendency of when people retire and takes account of changes in the population's age composition as well as changes in mortality. As for "life expectancy," it is not a prognosis but a hypothetical measure based on the retirement experiences during one year among a population within a certain age range. Table 4.3 shows expected retirement ages for women and men for selected ages and years.

**Table 4.3**
**Expected Retirement Age for the Years 1995 to 2002**
**The figures include transitions to disability pension, contractual pension and old age pension.**

Women
Retirement after turning

| | 50y | 55y | 60y |
|---|---|---|---|
| 1995 | 64.2 | 65.0 | 66.0 |
| 1996 | 64.0 | 64.9 | 65.9 |
| 1997 | 63.5 | 64.5 | 65.5 |
| 1998 | 62.5 | 63.6 | 64.7 |
| 1999 | 62.5 | 63.7 | 64.9 |
| 2000 | 62.7 | 63.7 | 64.7 |
| 2001 | 63.4 | 64.3 | 65.2 |
| 2002 | 63.3 | 64.2 | 65.1 |

Men
Retirement after turning

| | 50y | 55y | 60y |
|---|---|---|---|
| 1995 | 64.1 | 64.9 | 65.8 |
| 1996 | 64.1 | 64.8 | 65.7 |
| 1997 | 63.6 | 64.3 | 65.2 |

**Table 4.3 continued**

| 1998 | 62.7 | 63.4 | 64.3 |
|------|------|------|------|
| 1999 | 62.8 | 63.6 | 64.5 |
| 2000 | 62.9 | 63.6 | 64.4 |
| 2001 | 63.6 | 64.2 | 65.0 |
| 2002 | 63.4 | 64.1 | 64.9 |

(Source: Social Insurance Rapport 06/2002).

Two important traits stand out from table 4.3. First, among both men and women a decline in the expected retirement age can be observed over the entire period covered, although a very fast decline during the first years appears to have been replaced by a partial recovery over the later years. This applies to all three age cutoffs displayed. In 2002, the expected retirement age for a fifty-year—old is slightly above sixty-three years as compared to sixty-four years in 1995. Secondly, the table shows the gender differentials in expected retirement age are negligible.

One should be aware however, in table 4.3 transitions to disability pension are counted as "retirement." If expected retirement age is calculated for the non-disabled population, the figures are markedly different and much less dramatic; in 2002 expected retirement age is sixty-six years for men as well as for women, i.e. only one year below official retirement age in Social Insurance (RTV Rapport 06/2002). This illustrates what drives early retirement in Norway and, thus, expected retirement age is primarily transition to disability pension.

We have shown the expected retirement age is remarkably similar for men and women. In several works, Midtsundstad has analyzed patterns of early retirement among men and women employed by the state in different industries, branches and occupations. In the state sector she documented interesting differences between the genders: First, men retire earlier than women, at least outside the school sector. This is primarily because of special age limits in occupations men traditionally hold. Second, when women retire early they receive a disability pension while when men retire they receive a contractual pension. This suggests poorer health among elderly women than among men. Thirdly, the longer education and the higher the occupational rank, the higher the expected retirement age is. The main reason is those with lower social status are granted a disability pension (see Midtsundstad 2002).

To sum up this section: In Norway economic activity rates among men and women in the working ages are high, above 80 percent for both sexes. However, more often than men, women work in the public sector, have lower paid jobs and work part-time. This is also the background for understanding why women on average earn about 20 to 30 percent less than men in Norway. Because women still tend to choose traditional educational tracks, these patterns are likely to prevail in the foreseeable future. Many women are employed in the women (and family) friendly public sector. Because of general fiscal austerity and the NPM reforms implemented here, this sector is expected to grow less in the future. Over the past decades, the employment rates among elderly women have reached, or exceeded, those of elderly men. Today men and women have very similar expected retirement ages. Since many Social Insurance benefits in general, and old age pensions in particular, are linked to (former) economic activity and earnings records, women are, on average, entitled to lower benefits and pensions than men.

## Recent Social Policy Reforms

The main architecture of the Social Insurance system was developed during the first three decades after World War II. During the 1990s, attempts were made to tighten eligibility criteria for receiving disability benefits and a stronger emphasis was put on labor market reintegration, activation and workfare—summarized in the policy slogan "The Work Approach" (Dahl and Drøpping 2001, Drøpping et al. 1999, Lødemel and Trickey (eds.) 2001. However, in the Norwegian Social Insurance system, there was always a fairly strong emphasis on the primary obligation to find work and be self-sufficient and experiments with activation and workfare are still relatively marginal. Thus, as we will return to in the discussion section, it is not justified to talk of a paradigmatic shift like the one that has taken place in countries such as the Netherlands and Denmark.

In the 1990s, The Work Approach was, and still is, the major principle underpinning welfare reforms and rhetoric. Most reforms point in the same direction. They may be described as iterative adaptations to the overarching ideology of the Work Approach. This reform wave reflects a commitment to change the profile of the programs in "work friendlier" directions. It re-emphasises the obligations of the citizens to be "active;" backed by sanctions ("stick") and programs and remedies are (re)designed to provide stronger work incentives ("carrot"). However, not all social policy reforms launched over the last decade are justified by reference to the Work Approach. In particular, family policy reforms have been implemented without much consideration for the consequences for women's (or men's) labor market activity in the short- and long-run. These programs are however, likely to affect men's and women's labor market participation differently. Therefore, two such programs will be described and their consequences will be discussed. In what follows we will describe and discuss the gender implications of four Social Insurance Programs and two family policy programs having a bearing on gender inequalities in labor market participation and (future) welfare.

*Sickness benefits*

Statutory sickness benefits replace 100 percent of the previous wage and they can be claimed for a maximum period of twelve months. Since the late 1980s, a number of measures have been introduced to limit the growth in sickness absenteeism—mainly by tightening the demands for medical certification. In 1988, the Medical Certificate II was introduced making eligibility for sick pay exceeding eight weeks dependent on reassessment. The formal authority to make this reassessment was eventually transferred to the National Insurance Administration. In a similar vein, a second checkpoint was introduced in 1993, namely, in cases where sick pay exceeded twelve weeks it became dependent on confirmation from the national insurance authorities in addition to an assessment by a doctor. In 1993 the so-called "active sick leave" was introduced as an amendment to the ordinary sickness benefit scheme. "Active sickleave" means a person on sickness benefits is allowed to return provisionally to work and put in as many hours as he or she is capable of doing while continuing to uphold full sickness benefits. This arrangement can be extended to a maximum of twelve weeks as the main rule but it can be further extended if the person in question has to undergo training to retain his/her position in the firm.

Two other modifications were introduced to the sickness benefit scheme in the early 1990s. The first was the benefit level of sickness benefit for the unemployed was reduced to match the compensation level of mainstream unemployment benefit. The main purpose of the revision was to avoid a situation in which a de facto, able-bodied unemployed person could avoid the typical requirements otherwise placed on the unemployed—while at the same time enjoying a relatively more generous benefit. The second change was the advisory role of medical doctors was strengthened to enable them to make more accurate medical diagnoses and contribute to drawing up rehabilitation plans at an early stage of a person's illness. Recently (July 1, 2004), the eligibility criteria for sickness certification beyond eight weeks were tightened. Employers, employees and physicians are now obliged to prepare an "action plan" after six to eight weeks. Further: all possibilities for partial sick leave shall be assessed and exploited; the employer shall seek to adapt the working place and working conditions to the special needs of the sick employee; and the medical criteria for prolonged sick leave shall be tightened. These new requirements are enforced by sanctions. If violated, the employee may loose the right to sickness benefit, the physician may lose the privilege to issue sickness certificates and the employer may be fined.

Reforms in the sickness benefit system are bound to affect more women than men as they have higher prevalence of illness and substantially higher sickness absence rates, and, as described above, they have lower earnings and more frequently disrupted work careers. Although the intentions of the recent reforms are to prevent sick leave, shorten its duration and promote occupational activity, the actual effects may be negligible, mixed or outright the opposite. Higher thresholds imply more women than men will be excluded from sickness benefits because they are more distant from the labor market. Women also tend to have so-called "diffuse" ailments and are, thus, more prone to be ineligible for sickness benefit beyond eight weeks. "Everything else being equal," women's welfare is likely to be lower in the short-run and, in the long-run, their old age pension credits will be reduced (as sickness benefits grant pension credits) and thus their old age pension benefits will be lower.

*Disability Pension*

In an attempt to curb the growth in (permanent) disability pensioning, a so-called temporary disability benefit was introduced early in 2004. In the existing scheme, the general presumption has been the disability condition is permanent and almost all recipients stay on benefits until they die or reach the official pension age. The purpose of the new scheme is to prevent life-long receipt of disability benefits and to enhance work activity among claimants with a less severe, potentially reparable condition. Benefits are granted for a specific period of time for those who are considered to have "residual" work ability and/or who are expected to recover from disease. In order to stimulate work activity, the benefits of this new scheme are lower than that of the permanent scheme. Since women, and especially younger women, have higher risks of becoming disability pensioners, and they often have "diffuse" ailments, it is likely more women than men will be offered this new disability scheme. Figures from the first quarter of 2003 verify this. They show that women constitute about 66 percent of the recipients of this new benefit (http://trygdeetaten.no/hovedside/kjonn.pdf). How this will influence women's and men's welfare is, however, disputed. The proponents argue the stronger work incentives and better social support will lead to increased work activity and, hence, to higher earnings. The critics contend that the most likely result of the reform is people who previously would have been granted a decent and permanent benefit will have problems finding a job in the labor market and, thus, have to accept a lower and less certain disability benefit. The effects of the new scheme have not yet been evaluated. However, the experience from a similar reform in the early 1990s suggests that the latter scenario is the most likely. At that point, rules were introduced tightening the pure medical criteria for granting disability benefit. A study of refused applicants found women were over-represented in this group. Further, of those who were rejected, only about 20 percent returned to work during the subsequent three-year period. This percentage was somewhat higher among women than among men probably because many women (re-) entered part-time jobs. On the other hand, more than 20 percent of the women became economically dependent on their families (Andersen, Grimsmo, Westin 1995). A more recent analysis of administrative data covering the entire Norwegian population reinforces this finding by demonstrating that among those who were refused access to disability pension in the early 1990s, "paid work hardly occurs" and after four years almost 60 percent was eventually granted a disability benefit (Fevang et al. 2004).

*Unemployment Benefits*

Entitlement to the Unemployment Benefit (UB) is determined by earnings in the year(s) previous to unemployment. The compensation rate is normally 62.4 percent of the calculation base. Both the income requirements and the time limits were recently restricted.

The maximum duration of benefits is now 104 weeks after which re-qualification is contingent upon a new period of ordinary work or participation in a temporary employment program and given that your earnings prior to the employment spell exceed two times the Base Amount in Social Insurance (G), that is, 117 556 NOK. The minimum income requirement was raised from 1.25G to 1.5G. Un-employed earning between 1.5G and 2G are now only eligible for UB for fifty-two weeks. The present legislation differs from its pre-decessor in two important respects: first, the new rules impose stricter time limits for all, but in particular, for low income earners; second, the earnings threshold are raised, thus excluding groups of part-time workers and low-income earners from entitlement, i.e. many women.

The UB is (still) a relatively comprehensive and generous system for income maintenance. As such, and according to common ortho-doxy, it may undermine work motivation. Thus, recipients of UB are required to accept job offers or a place in a labor market pro-gram and the rules emphasise benefit recipients shall be available to the labor market. This implies the claimant is expected to *move* to areas where jobs are available. This requirement was strengthened in 1995, particularly for young people (Directorate of Labor, 1996: 5). Benefits may temporarily be suspended if the person concerned is considered to be unemployed by their own choice, refusing to take a suitable job or participate in labor market measures or failing to go to the employment office when summoned.

In a gender perspective, the increases in the earnings thresholds and the stricter time limits are likely to disfavor women as compared with men. In the short-run, and under equal conditions, this means more women than men no longer will have entitlement to this ben-efit if thrown into employment. In the long run, this implies reduced benefit rights and pension credits among women as sickness benefit give these rights.

*Transitional Benefit for Lone Parents*

Unlike other Western countries, a transitional benefit for single parents is an integral part of the Social Insurance system in Norway. Until 1998, a single parent had the right to receive a transitional benefit until the youngest child was ten years old. This was reduced to three-years-old in September 1998. When the youngest child is three-years-old, the parent must be in work-related activity to preserve benefit eligibility. Work-related activity comprises formal job-seeking or working/studying at least part-time. In cases where the single parent is studying, it is possible to extend the eligibility period to five-and-a-half-years. Maximum time of receipt is eight years. In tandem with the introduction of a stricter time limit, annual benefits have increased by about Nkr 10,000 from September 1998. Furthermore, Social Insurance provides a childcare benefit and an education benefit for single parents. Childcare benefits are  granted until the child is ten-years-old. The number of lone parents receiving transitional benefit have declined gradually over the past few years reaching about 25,000 recipients in 2002 (Basisrapport 2002:116). As nearly all lone parents are women, the reform influences primarily the life of women and their children and not men. If this reform functions as intended, more lone mothers will improve their  economic activity and earnings and, therefore, earn more pension credits. One evaluation of this reform concludes the "users" of the reform, to a large degree, support the intension. Nonetheless, they report the new arrangements impose too strict time limits and that requirements are enforced with too little flexibility. (Fjær and Syltevik 2002).

*Parental Leave*

Effective in 1994, parents with a newborn child are granted a full-year leave with a compensation rate of 80 percent. Alternatively, the parents can take forty-two weeks off with 100 percent compensation. Nine weeks are reserved for the mother around the time of birth and four weeks are reserved for the father. If he does not take out his quota, it is withdrawn. The parents can share the remaining months between them as they wish. Research shows however, the large majority of the available months are taken by the mothers. In 1999, the mothers took 90 percent of the period and there has been little change in this pattern over the past years (Skrede 2004:167). The degree to which mother's occupational careers and future labor market participation are affected by this arrangement is hard to tell. Probably, the effect of this scheme alone on gender equality in the long-run is negligible but if added to the "de-commodifying" effect of the next program the effects may be more pronounced.

*Cash Benefit to Families with Small Children Who Do Not Utilize Subsidized Daycare*

A new cash allowance for families with small children was introduced in 1998. This benefit is paid to all families (lone parents as well as couples) with small children (up to three-years-old) provided they do not use a daycare center receiving a state subsidy. A full monthly cash benefit is equivalent to one month's state subsidy of care for one child in a public pre-school (about 3700 NOK). If the child is in a state-sponsored daycare center for less than thirty hours weekly, the family will be entitled to a reduced cash benefit. Combined with maternal allowance for one year, this benefit, thus, enables (one of the) parents to stay at home to take care of a child for three years. The cash benefit has three major objectives: first, to allow the families to spend more time taking care of their children; second, to enhance the freedom to choose the childcare of preference; and third, to increase equity in the subsidies to families with small children (Ot.prp. nr. 56 1997-98: 1).

This reform has been quite extensively evaluated. In short, the evaluators conclude this big reform has had a surprisingly small effect on the behavior among parents in general. Although evaluations of this reform indicate it has not resulted in a manifest drop in employment rates among women, as some predicted and feared, one group seems to be affected, namely immigrant women. In this group there was a tendency to take the children out of pre-school (Kavli 2001). Moreover, the first wave of evaluations has not been able to assess the long-term consequences. A plausible hypothesis is especially low-paid women will be tempted to accept the cash benefit and take care of the child themselves. More recent evaluations support the suspicion mothers' economic activity is reduced due to the cash benefit (Social Insurance Basisrapport 2002:43). This type of behavior is more likely to occur where places in pre-schools are hard to find and, in many municipalities, there is a shortage of pre-school openings especially for children one- to two-years-old (Ellingsæter and Gulbrandsen 2003:83, Leira 2003). Thus, a likely effect of the cash allowance, in combination with lack of childcare, is the development toward larger differentials among women with respect to participation in the labor market with consequences for their living conditions, benefit rights and later pension credits.

While these programs formally give both parents the same opportunity to stay home to take care of their children the first three years after they are born, it is in practice almost exclusively the mother who exploits these opportunities.

There are some interesting differences between policy developments in the area of social insurance discussed above and the family policies pursued over the last decade. The former have become more conditional, there are more strings attached; they aim at modifying behavior to a larger extent and they are explicitly normative: paid work or activity are the expected and politically-preferred behaviors. The result is that there is less freedom of choice for the recipients of these benefits. The family-related benefits however, are offered without any conditions; there are no strings attached, no type of behavior is explicitly preferred over another and the decisional latitude of the recipients is wide. As mentioned, the main argument put forward for introducing the cash allowance for families who choose not to send their minors to pre-school facilities was to increase the families' freedom to choose. Skrede (2004) has emphasised that these family-related benefits are provided as offers without norms. The contrast to the Social Insurance programs we have discussed is quite striking.

Finally, we will mention a recent reform of a more general level. In 1999, a tripartite agreement was struck by the social partners, i.e. the organizations of the employees, employers and the central Government. The overarching end of this agreement is threefold: to reduce sickness absence rates, increase the pension age and to include more occupationally handicapped into the labor market. An army of counsellors has been built up in the local social insurance administrations. This initiative has no gender focus but in as much as women are over-represented among the target groups, which they are to some extent, these new measures may enable more women to gain a stronger foothold in the labor market if they prove successful. A first-phase evaluation has mostly looked at the effects on the sickness absence rates (Dahler, 2003). This evaluation documents the sickness rates have continued to rise. Nonetheless, there are examples from single companies indicating it is possible to achieve significant reductions in the sickness absence rates. It is worth noting thus far none of the other two objectives have been subjected to evaluation. Thus, the overall effects, in general, and the gender-specific effects, in particular, are largely unknown.

## The Present and Future of the Old Age Pension System

Norway is in the midst of a major pension reform process that is likely to have profound distributional effects both within and across generations and with gender issues at the very forefront of the political debate and public attention. Before turning to the current reform debate, it is necessary to provide some historical and institutional background on the present system and the dynamics of change to which it has been subject over the last three decades.

### Historical Background

The present National pension system is representative of the much-celebrated Scandinavian model, combining a rather generous minimum protection with earnings-related benefits offering additional income security for all wage earners and the self-employed. The present system was introduced in 1967. It originally consisted of two components: a universal flat rate benefit supplemented with an earnings-related second tier. It was strongly inspired by the Swedish "superannuation" reform introduced in 1959 but with more modest benefit parameters in the earnings-related second tier. The Norwegian system was originally designed to replace 45 percent of earnings above lower threshold equal to the basic pension for a single pensioner. The right to full benefits was made conditional on forty years of contribution and benefits were to be calculated on the basis of the twenty years of the individual's career with the highest earnings.

The Norwegian National Insurance system was from the beginning characterized by a rather unclear and undecided structure of financing (Pedersen 1990). A few years after the introduction of the earnings-related second tier, initial ambitions to build up a buffer fund, and to smooth out the financial burden over time, were abandoned and a full-fledged pay-as-you-go strategy was adopted. This meant contributions to the system could be kept low during the extended period of maturation (the requirement of forty years of contribution to receive full benefits meant the system would not be scheduled for maturation before the early decades of the twenty-first century).

### The Rise in Women's Employment as a Force of Change

As we have discussed in the previous sections, married woman starting to enter the workforce in the 1970s and the rise in female employment, spurring the associated move from the one-earner to the dual-earner model of family life, had a tremendous influence on both economic and political aspects of the pension system.

On the financing side of the system, the influx of female wage earners over the last three decades has helped to ease the financial burden and counteract the tendencies toward population aging that have in fact been present since the 1960s.[12] Thanks to the growth in female employment rates, there were more workers to shoulder the costs of current expenditures on benefits to the present generation of retirees. However, the cohorts of women who have become economically active during the last decades will eventually retire and be able to claim benefits from the earnings-related system and this will be a strong component in the growth of pension expenditures over the coming decades in Norway. One might say the growth in female employment has meant the well-known effect of expanding a pay-as-you-go pension system—that all current generations stand to gain—has been prolonged, or, perhaps, restarted and that the advent of a steady state, in which current expenditures will catch up with the current accrual of pension rights, has been postponed.

Simultaneously, the growth in female employment, and the rise of the dual-earner model of family life, has had important consequences for the demand for income security in old age and, in addition, to incremental changes in the benefit profile. This is an important factor explaining the growth in private and occupational pensions—particularly since the mid 1980s (see Pedersen 1997).

## Developments in Benefit Generosity and the Benefit Profile

The 1960s was the golden age of the male-breadwinner model and this was clearly reflected in the preparation and design of the Norwegian superannuation reform of 1967. Official calculations of the prospective compensation levels offered by the system took only two family types into consideration: one-earner couples and single-pensioners (St. meld. nr. 75, 1963-64 and Ot. prp. nr 17, 1965-66). In particular the traditional one-earner couple would be very well catered to in the new system—despite the relatively modest parameters chosen for the earnings-related part of the system. The reason is in addition to replacing a substantial fraction of the male breadwinner's wage, the system grants the wife a basic pension and this pension benefit had no equivalent in the couple's previous earnings history. The prospective combined replacement for a couple used to living on one average full-time earnings would amount to 73 percent while the replacement rate for a single-pensioner with average earnings would amount to 60 percent (see table 4.4).

**Table 4.4**
**Gross Replacement Rates in the Norwegian National Insurance Scheme***

|  | Single person | One-earner couple | Two-earner couple |
|---|---|---|---|
| Official calculations of prospective replacement rates in 1967** | 60 % | 73 % | *(57%)*** |
| Actual replacement rates under the current system (2003) | 52 % | 73 % | 48 % |

*All calculations assume a full contribution record (forty years). **Source: Ot. prp. nr 17, 1965 to 1966. ***No official calculation was done for this family type, and the figure is calculated on the basis of the actual 1967 parameters.

The earnings-related second tier of the Norwegian National Insurance scheme is gradually approaching maturity. Only from the year 2007 will the first cohort of pensioners be able to retire with a forty-year contribution record and, hence, with full pension rights. The very process of maturation of the earnings-related part of the system implies average benefit levels increase for every new pensioner cohort while simultaneously the degree of differentiation according to previous labor force participation and earnings will tend to increase.

Alongside this programmed maturation of the earnings-related second tier, the system has, over the last three decades, undergone an almost infinite series of incremental changes significantly changing its overall profile. One important trend has been a gradual weakening of the (prospective) replacement rate and income security for wage earners with a full contribution record while simultaneously strengthening the quality of minimum protection. This obviously implies the redistributive character of the system has been strengthened at the expense of the insurance analogy and the "ideal" of actuarial fairness.

The fact that the degree of income security offered to wage earners has deteriorated is exacerbated by the transition from the traditional one-earner couple to the modern two-earner, or more accurately, the "one-and-a-half-earner" couple. As can been seen from table 4.4, the Norwegian National Insurance system is—even as it was originally conceived—not particularly generous towards this more modern family type.

The level of minimum protection has been raised through the introduction and gradual expansion of a third element in the benefit formula: a targeted Pension Supplement functioning as a minimum pension guarantee. The Pension Supplement is granted to individuals without any, or relatively low, benefits from the earnings-related part of the system and taper is set to 100 percent. The Pension Supplement is only tested against earnings-related benefits, as opposed to a general income test, and it is a strictly individual benefit as earnings-related benefits received by the spouse are not taken into consideration. Initially, when it was first introduced, this Pension Supplement was very modest compared to the two other elements in the system—the universal Basic Pension and the earnings-related benefits—but it has gradually been increased to the present level of almost 80 percent of the Basic Pension for a single pensioner.

The Pension Supplement is very important both politically and economically as it defines a category of old age pensioners who receive the minimum benefit only (so-called Minimum Pensioners) and who do not benefit from the earnings-related part of the system. For the classic housewife and the one-earner couple, the Pension Supplement represents an unequivocal good. It raises the income of the wife without infringing on other income sources and the pension rights earned by the bread-winner husband.[3] For women who have joined the labor force—often as part-time workers—the Pension Supplement has a much more ambiguous economic impact and symbolic significance. While the Pension Supplement will typically add to their pension income, it effectively nullifies the contributions they have made to the earnings-related part of the system and it defines them as belonging to the bottom of the benefit distribution together with people who have had no earnings and contribution history whatsoever.

Table 4.5
**Share of male and female old age pensioners who are Minimum Pensioners
(receive the Pension Supplement) and the ratio between average old age benefit
received by men and women pensioners. Selected years.**

| | Share of old age pensioners receiving Minimum Benefits | | Ratio of average benefits received by men and women pensioners |
|---|---|---|---|
| | Men | Women | |
| 1980 | 53.5 | 88.5 | n.a. |
| 1985 | 39.6 | 79.8 | 1.19 |
| 1990 | 22.3 | 67.0 | 1.30 |
| 1995 | 15.6 | 58.7 | 1.34 |
| 2000 | 12.7 | 55.1 | 1.34 |

Sources: Pedersen 1999, Koren 2001

As shown in table 4.5, the share of old age pensioners who receive the minimum benefits has decreased over time—but much more rapidly for males than for females. Still, more than half of all female pensioners receive minimum benefits only. Furthermore, it is shown the difference in average benefit levels received by males and females has increased over time.[4] These figures are the result of a complex interaction between three independent forces of change:

- System maturation implies a decrease in the number of minimum pensioners, in particular among men, and a widening of the gap in average pension benefits received by male and female pensioners.
- Increasing female labor force participation will (particularly in the long-run) tend to decrease the share of Minimum Pensioners among female pensioners and to narrow the gender gap in average pension benefits
- Systemic changes in the direction of a more redistributive system tend—all other things being equal—to increase the share of Minimum Pensioners and to limit the gender gap in average benefit levels

Concerning the gender gap in average pension benefits, one can see from the last column of table 4.5 system maturation has, so far, been stronger than the other forces and responsible for a widening of the gender gap despite increasing female labor force participation and incremental moves toward a more redistributive benefit profile. However, as we shall see below, the increase in female labor force participation taking place over the last three decades will eventually lead to a narrowing of the gender gap in pension benefits under the rules of the current system.

System maturation is, of course, also responsible for the decline in the share of Minimum Pensioners among males. Among females the decline has been very slow and still in the year 2000 with more than half of all female pensioners receiving Minimum Benefits only. Even among the cohorts of women who currently enter retirement and who clearly belong to the generation entering the labor force, although often as part-time workers, well over 40 percent end up as Minimum Pensioners (Koren 2001). If the present system were continued into the future and core parameters indexed with average wages, it has been estimated the share of Minimum Pensioners will decline to about 10 percent among female pensioner and 5 percent among male pensioners in the year 2040 (Frederiksen 1998).

*The Current Reform Debate*

Like in almost all OECD-countries, population aging has put pension reform on the political agenda in Norway. This is so even though Norway currently does not belong to the group of countries with the highest spending on public pensions. Total public spending on old age pensions amounts to 4.5 percent of GDP as compared to an OECD average of 7.4 and as compared to about 12 percent in Germany and France and 14.2 percent in Italy (see table 4.6).

There are three main reasons why current expenditures on public pensions are relatively modest in Norway: The first factor is the high formal retirement age of sixty-seven for both males and females which is combined with a comparatively high effective retirement age and a corresponding high labor force participation among the population aged fifty-five to sixty-seven as we have seen in section 3 above. Secondly, the current National insurance scheme offers rather modest replacement rates for typical wage earners as was shown in table 4.4 above. Thirdly, the Norwegian pension system is comparatively young and still very far from reaching steady state maturity. This latter point also helps explain why Norway ranks among the OECD-countries with the highest projected growth in public pension expenditure over the next half-century—according to official estimates public pension expenditure is expected to increase with 10 percentage points of GDP to a total of almost 15 percent of GDP in the year 2050.

Table 4.6
**Expenditures on old age pensions as percentage of GDP in selected countries.
Actual figures for the year 2000 and projections for 2050**

|  | 2000 | 2050 |
|---|---|---|
| Norway | 4.5 | 14.8 |
| Sweden | 9.2 | 10.8 |
| Denmark | 6.1 | 8.8 |
| Germany | 11.8 | 16.8 |
| Italy | 14.2 | 13.9 |
| France | 12.1 | 16.0 |
| Spain | 9.4 | 17.4 |
| UK | 4.3 | 3.6 |
| US | 4.4 | 6.2 |
| OECD average | 7.4 | 10.8 |

Source: NOU 2004:1.

Under the current system average benefits per pensioner are expected to increase by 32 percent relative to average wages between 2001 and 2050. For male pensioners the expected increase in relative benefit levels is 18 percent while it is no less than 44 percent for female pensioners. In addition, the number of old age pensioners is expected to double. The underlying demographic projections assume a very strong increase in the longevity of both men and women. It is assumed that the remaining life expectancy for a sixty-seven-year-old will have increased from 15.1 to 20.1 for men and from 18.7 to 23.7 for women by the year 2050.

*The Reform Proposal*

In 2001 a Pension Commission with representatives of all parliamentary parties was launched with a mandate to develop proposals for reforms in the existing pension system. The achievement of long-term economic sustainability was clearly pointed out as the main concern. In a preliminary report published in the fall of 2002, the Commission sketched two alternative reform strategies: (1) To dismantle the earnings-related second tier and return to a public pension system providing universal flat-rate benefits while leaving the need for income security among the working population to be the responsibility of the private sector (occupational pension systems and individual savings arrangements). (2) The second alternative suggested by the Commission was to follow the lead of other OECD-countries, like Sweden and Italy, to change the existing public system toward actuarial neutrality: to reinforce the link between contributions and lifetime earnings, on the one hand, and retirement benefits on the other. This latter strategy was dubbed "modernization" and it turned out to command the support of a majority of the Commission.

The final report from the Pension Commission was published in January 2004 and it contains a majority proposal for a comprehensive reform of the Norwegian old age pension system (NOU 2004:1). The majority's proposal is very strongly inspired by the Swedish pension reform put in force in 1999 and inspiringmilar pension reforms in several other countries including Italy, Latvia and Poland (Williamson 2004). A core element of these reforms is a switch from the traditionally defined benefit formula for accumulating pension rights to a "defined contribution" formula, otherwise seen in fully funded occupational pension schemes. The point of these schemes is they build on pay-as-you-go financing and, hence, avoid the well-known double payment problem and the transition costs associated with a switch from a mature pay-as-you-go system to a fully-funded system (Fox and Palmer 2001, Disney 1999, Cichon 1999, Barr 2002). In these so-called Notional Defined Contribution (NDC) schemes members of the economically active population pay a fixed annual contribution rate to the pension system. While these contributions are de facto used to finance current old age pension expenditures, each contributor is credited with the value of his/her contributions to a "notional" account and the accumulation of credited contributions on this account then defines the accrual of pension rights. When the participant eventually retires, the accumulated assets are transformed to a lifelong annuity.

The NDC formula secures a very strong link between contributions and benefits and one of the main ideas is the contributions to the system will be perceived not as a tax but as a form of forced saving. Hence, the hope is that the negative effects on labor supply and general economic performance that economists assume to follow taxation will be avoided. The approach secures that pension rights are linked proportionally to lifetime earnings and the somewhat arbitrary redistribution toward wage earners with relatively short employment histories and fluctuating or rising annual earnings, built into many traditional social insurance schemes, are effectively removed.

The proposed reform of the Norwegian National Insurance system can be briefly summarized in the following points:

- Switch to the NDC formula with a suggested contribution rate of 17.5 percent
- The introduction of a rather generous system of pension credits for people who are temporarily inactive due to caring obligations for children under six or elderly or disabled persons.[5]
- The universal basic pension is to be replaced by a guaranteed minimum pension tested against benefits from the NDC-scheme. One might say this is a guaranteed minimum pension, a generalization of the already existing Pension Supplement.
- The formula for converting accumulated NDC-rights to a lifelong annuity will be adjusted to changes in the remaining life-expectancy of sixty-seven-year-olds
- Indexation of accumulated NDC-accounts with average wages and indexation of NDC benefits after retirement with an average of changes in wage and price indices. The level of the guaranteed minimum benefit will be indexed with wages less a factor taking account of increases in the life-expectancy of a sixty-seven-year-old
- Introduction of a flexible retirement age from age sixty-two with almost full actuarial deductions for those who retire before the normal retirement age of sixty-seven and corresponding premiums for those who postpone retirement from that age.

Although the Swedish inspiration is indeed very strong there are some important deviations from the Swedish reform:

1)  In Sweden, the minimum guarantee is to be indexed only with prices and, hence, it is programmed to decrease relatively in the event of a general rise in productivity and affluence of the Swedish society. The Norwegian Commission has suggested an indexing formula insuring the guaranteed minimum will keep in line with pension rights accumulated in the NDC-scheme. The high level of minimum protection is to be preserved also in relative terms.

2)  In the Norwegian Commission's proposal the suggested pension premium of 17.5 percent will not act as a hard budget-line for future pension expenditures. This follows from the suggestion to let the pension system be fully integrated in the state budget and, hence, not the let the development in total contributions have any relation to the development in total outlays. The system is not required to keep contributions and expenditures in balance, and, hence, while the risk of changes in longevity is placed with each successive pensioner cohort,

the remaining demographic and economic risks are to be carried by the general state budget and the taxpayers. In fact, the figure 17.5 percent was chosen not as a functional pension expenditure but as an approximation to a defined benefit scheme with a yearly replacement rate increment of 1.25 percent. This link, with an equivalent defined benefit scheme with an annual accrual of pension rights equal to 1.25 percent, has made it rather easy to compare the distribution of pension benefits under the new system with the present system and other alternative reform proposals.

Of course, the basic principle of moving toward a system less redistributive and more accurately reflecting differences in lifetime earnings is highly controversial from a gender perspective. However, a number of modifications are built into the proposal—as in the Swedish blueprint—intended to maintain a certain redistribution toward low income groups and women in general. The most important are:

- The minimum pension guarantee
- The system of pension credits for caring
- Rules securing a surviving spouse might, under specific circumstances, inherit a part of the husband's accrued pension rights

As far as the first of these modifications, the majority faction of the Commission finally decided to opt for a softer integration between the minimum guarantee and the NDC-scheme. From a certain level the taper is reduced from 100 percent to 60 percent and this implies fewer individuals will end up with the minimum benefit only. This modification has helped to secure the reform proposal appearing not to deviate radically in its distributive profile from the present system as indicated in figure 4.1 below.

Nevertheless, distributive concerns and, in particular, the implications for the gender gap in pensions, are at the center of continued controversies. Table 4.7 shows the results of an attempt to estimate how gender inequalities in retirement benefits will be affected by the proposed reform as compared with the current system. Here, inequalities are calculated as Gini indices for men and for women, respectively and also as the "gender gap." We see inequalities in retirement benefits in the proposed system will be somewhat higher than in the current system. This applies to both the degree of inequality found within the male and the female population and to the difference in average benefits between the genders. Although the projected changes are not dramatic, a reform contributing to widening the gender gap rather than narrowing it, is bound to be controversial.

**Figure 4.1**
**Projected Annual Retirement Benefit for a Single Pensioners with Constant Earnings Over a Forty-Year Earnings Career**

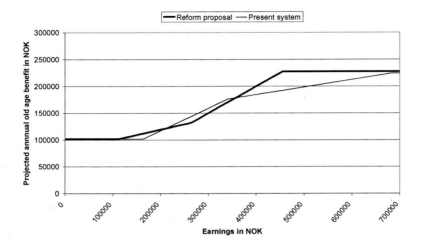

**Table 4.7**
**Projected distribution of lifetime earnings for cohorts born between 1950 and 1970 and projected distribution of retirement benefits in the year 2050. Gini coefficients for men and women and gender gap in average benefits.**

|  | Gini coefficient | | Gender gap (men/women) |
|---|---|---|---|
|  | Men | Women |  |
| Lifetime earnings | 0.26 | 0.28 | 1.44 |
| Pension    Present system | 0.10 | 0.12 | 1.11 |
| benefits    Reform proposal | 0.15 | 0.14 | 1.16 |

## *What About Work Incentives?*

An important downside of the solution of a minimum pension guarantee and, in particular, with the modified taper being suggested is more people, and particularly women, will be affected by the taper and, hence, have less than full effect of pension rights accrued in the earnings-related NDC system. While the effective NDC accrual rate is 17.5 percent for higher incomes it is zero for very low-income and reduced to 40 percent of the full accrual rate (40 percent of 17.5

percent=7 percent) for an earnings interval likely to comprise a significant proportion of the population with a strong over-representation of women. Based on a longitudinal micro-simulation model, about 37 percent of the 1970 cohort of females, and 18 percent of the males, will be affected by the gradual taper. The proposed reform will, hence, lead to a polarization of work incentives. It will clearly strengthen work incentives for well-paid, full-time workers but it will provide very weak incentives to individuals belonging to the lower parts of the income distribution due to a combination of low wage levels and part-time work. Needless to say, women are over-represented in this group. The reform can, therefore, be seen to lead to a polarization of the incentive structure; providing stronger incentives to middle- and high-income earners (i.e., men), while weakening incentives in the lower part of the income distribution, (i.e., women), where, arguably, people tend to be more sensitive to high effective marginal tax rates (Røed and Strøm 2002).

### Summary and Discussion: Social Policy Reforms in a Gender Perspective

In this chapter, we have addressed the question of whether gender differences in welfare in Norway will change as the result of recent reforms in Social Insurance, family policies and old age pensions. We have approached this question by describing the ways in which the socio-economic structures are gendered combined with a description of recent social policy reforms and an analysis of how these reforms will affect labor market activity and welfare differences between the genders.

As in many Western countries, women started entering the labor market in the 1970s. Some thirty years later, economic activity among men and women in their working ages are high and similar, above 80 percent. However, in general, women tend to work in the public sector, have lower paid jobs and work part-time. For this and other reasons, Norwegian women earn 20 to 30 percent less than men. The proportion of female CEOs and women at company boards is low as compared with other Western countries. Political equality in status between the genders (*"likestilling"*) is not matched by economic equality in Norway but economic equality between the genders remains an official objective of high priority.

Welfare is closely related to labor market activity and earnings, both in the short- and in the long-run, i.e. over the life course of men and women. Labor market activity and earnings are influenced by many factors, social policy and social security amongst others but also labor market conditions, labor market structures, business cycles, work environment, rules and regulations, culture and family patterns, to mention some crucial factors. Thus, it is hard to isolate how welfare institutions and reforms impact gender welfare in a precise way. Modern welfare states are complex configurations of the state, markets and families. This implies that a minor change in one component might be counteracted by changes in others or, on the contrary, a small change in one part of the system may set in motion dynamic repercussions throughout the entire system. Important aspects of our arguments are based on rather soft evidence. The most obvious reason for this is that reforms are to be implemented in the future, as is the case for the reform proposal for a "modernized" old age pension. Further, other reforms are so recent that no effects have appeared yet; and in other cases, gender specific effects are poorly analyzed and evaluated. Thus, our discussion and conclusions will inevitably be of a reflective, and even speculative, nature and, therefore, must be seen as hypotheses yet to be "tested."

We have quietly assumed the reforms in Social Insurance and family policies are gender neutral. Our rationale for this approach is the official and explicit aims and intentions put forward by the authorities when proposing the reforms. Some critics would not endorse this approach. Rather, they would argue, the underlying intentions of the reforms, and of the cash benefit in particular, are far from gender neutral but aimed at giving incentives so more women can stay at home and take care of their children when they are small. We do not have to choose sides in this debate as it is beyond the scope of this paper. Our focus is on the gendered consequences of reforms, and not the actual underlying or hidden agendas and reasons for their emergence. This would require a very different approach and different data.

All reforms in the Social Insurance Programs during the 1990s and up to today are, with few exceptions, anchored in "The Work Approach" which emphasizes that paid work should be the first choice of all able-bodied citizens in working ages. With the exception of families with infants, remunerated work is the expected activity for all, for women as well as for men. Since many Social Insurance benefits in general, and old age pensions in particular, are linked to (former) economic activity and earnings records, women are, on average, entitled to lower benefits and pensions than men. Proposals for reforms in Social Insurance arrangements in general, and in the old age pension in particular, will probably exacerbate these tendencies. Our simulations indicate the proposed reform in the old age pension system will increase the gender gap in retirement benefit, although not dramatically. Simultaneously however, inequalities among women are also projected to widen somewhat. The projected increase in the gender gap in future pension benefits has spurred debate, but it is less certain whether the projected rise in inequality among women will exert similar controversies.

The proposed old age pension reform is designed to pursue "actuarial fairness," that is, a close connection between contributions and benefits among individuals. Because women, on average, contribute less than men, they will inevitably receive less. In the wake of the proposal, this principle has received quite a lot of critical attention, not the least from the Government body having the responsibility to serve as a "watchdog" over gender equality in Norway, that is, "*Likestillingssenteret.*" One should note, however, the notion of actuarial fairness pursued by the Commission does not take into account the fact women tend to live longer than men and, hence, can expect to receive benefits over a longer period. Currently, the life expectancy of Norwegian women is about five years longer than that of men and it could very well be argued the Commission proposal entails a considerable redistribution from men to women simply by insisting on maintaining of sex-neutral principles for the calculation of benefits also in the reformed system. Also, other aspects of the Commission's proposal entail a considerable amount of income redistribution. Granting pension credits for caregiving responsibilities, and the provision of a Minimum Pension guarantee, are the most important examples. These modifications raise the classical dilemma between the provision of economic incentives and the pursuit of egalitarian objectives. We fear the Commission's proposal will tend to feed tendencies toward a polarization of female labor market behaviors. Women who stay home during childrearing and with low labor force participation over a lifetime will generally be well-served by the reformed system and so will those women who behave, perform and last, but not least, are rewarded completely like men. The losers are to be found among the majority of women who do not conform to either category; their benefits will be curtailed and they will face weak incentives to increase their labor market participation.

This issue, change in social inequality amongst women, extends beyond the proposed reform in the old age pension system. As indicated above, in several respects social inequalities in women are larger than in men. This is illustrated by the larger lifetime earnings Gini shown in table 4.7 above. Social policy reforms that increasingly rewarding full-time employment over a lifetime, and family policies that predominantly providing work disincentives for more marginal women, and for many immigrant women in particular, will probably increase disparities in living conditions and welfare among women in the future. Our simulation of the "modernized" old age pension system also predicts this might occur. Thus, it might be that, given the current circumstances, welfare state reforms may lead to a polarization among women as well as a wider gap between the genders. The degree to which this will take place, and what the social and political implications will be, should be addressed in future gender analyses of welfare reforms.

Can we observe a new "philosophy" of welfare emerging in Norway? One major feature of the Nordic welfare state is the high degree of de-commodification. This means that most citizens have the opportunity to opt out of the labor market and still lead a decent life because they are entitled to relatively high benefits. Special benefits and services for women and families have granted these opportunities to a higher degree to women than to men. One unintended and undesired side effect of this might be that women are less active in the labor market than they otherwise would have been. Most, if not all, reforms in Social Security and social assistance that were introduced during the 1990s and the early 2000s have moderated or weakened the de-commodification aspects in the Norwegian welfare state. There has been a move towards *re-commodification* of labor within the welfare benefits and services. This has been accompanied by a strengthening of the idea of the importance of "independence" of Social Insurance and social assistance benefits. Most political parties have endorsed this shift but, of course, some are more committed than others. Increasingly, the labor market is trusted to solve many social problems, including poverty and low-income problems and, according to the official view, public services and benefits should be designed to enhance this kind of independence.

The measures launched to achieve this end vary; both sticks and carrots are used and counselling services and organizational reforms are implemented. The actual reforms in transitional benefits, sickness benefit and disability benefits fits neatly into this account, as do the proposed reforms to the old age pension system. Here, there is a change toward a stronger emphasis on duties, conditions, behavioral requirements, activation schemes, work, earnings records, the use of economic incentives and, as in the proposed old age pension system, a tighter link between contributions and benefits. Still, despite the many steps taken toward re-commodification, all have been rather tiny; the de-commodifying elements of the welfare architecture prevail. At any point in time, it is estimated about 25 percent of people in their working ages are out of work, i.e. "de-commodified," for shorter or longer periods of time. Further, it should be kept in mind the productivist ethos has always been central to the ideas about welfare, work and economic progress in Norway as it has been in other social democratic welfare states. The slogan has been, and still is: work *and* welfare. This leads us to conclude although we witness a shift in the balance between work and welfare, the philosophy has hardly changed.

This conclusion is strengthened if we add to the picture recent reforms in family policies. While there is little doubt that the work approach has provided the ideological ammunition for reforms in Social Insurance over the last decade, the situation is different for family policy reforms. As indicated, Social Insurance programs have become more conditional, geared toward influencing behavior and more normatively-oriented. The result is that there is less freedom of choice in these programs. The family-related benefits, on the other hand, have become less conditional; implicit behavioral requirements have been relaxed and the decisional latitude is widened. Thus, the "philosophy" underpinning these programs stands in clear contrast to the thinking underlying reforms in the Social Insurance programs. One might even say that there is a polarization in the philosophy of the Social Insurance programs, on the one hand, and the philosophy of family programs on the other. The Social Insurance reforms are intended to increase labor market participation for both genders while the official intentions behind family policy reforms are indifferent with regard to this issue.

Reforms in welfare and family policies may be rather similar in their differential effects on men's and women's living conditions.

This, we argue, is because of the different social, economic circumstances among, and cultural expectations directed toward, men and women. Unless these structures change fundamentally and rapidly, a scenario highly unlikely in the foreseeable future is welfare institutions, and the (prospected) reforms in them, will tend to reproduce or exacerbate the present gender inequalities in the future. Obviously, the gender implications of welfare reform are difficult to tease out, but the main argument based on our analyses is that gender-neutral reforms implemented in a gender-differentiated society will maintain, or perhaps even increase, gender inequalities in work as well as welfare.

## Notes

1.  The demographic support ratio, i.e. the number of people in the economically active age-groups, twenty to sixty-five, divided by the number of people over sixty-five, has declined from 3.9 to 2.6 between 1967 and 2003 (NOU 2004:1).
2.  The Special Supplement explains why the replacement rate for a one-earner couple has remained very high while replacement rates for other family types have deteriorated significantly since 1967—see table 4.4.
3.  Figures on average pension benefits broken down by gender are not available before 1985. One might say that changes in the compilation of statistics reflects societal change in distributive concerns from the family as the natural unit of analysis to the individual – a change that is of course intimately tied to the rise of public and political concerns for issues related to gender equity.
4.  Such a scheme was introduced under the current system in 1992, but the Pension Commission suggests to make the provisions more generous as part of their overall reform proposal.

## References

Andersen, E Grimsmo A, Westin S (1995) Hvordan går det med dem som får avslag på uførepensjon? *Tidsskrift for den norske lægeforening* 115: 1754-8.

Atkinson, A.B., Rainwater, L., Smeeding, T.M. (1995) *Income Distribution in OECD Countries.* OECD Social Policy Studies No. 18. Paris: OECD.

Barr, Nicholas. (2002) Reforming Pensions: Myths, Truths and Policy Choices. *International Social Security Review*.55 (2):3-36.

Barth, E. Moene, K. Wallerstein. M. (2003). *Likhet under press. Utfordringer for den skandinaviske fordelingsmodellen.* Oslo: Gyldendal.

Birkelund GE and Petersen, T (2003) Det norske likestillingsparadokset. Kjønn og arbeid i velferdssamfunnet. In Frønes and Kjølsrød (eds) *Det norske samfunn.* Fjerde utgave. Oslo: Gyldendal norsk forlag.

Cichon, Michael (1999) "Notional defined-contribution schemes: Old wine in new bottles?" *International Social Security Review.* 52 (4):87-105.

Dahl, Espen (1997) Den som har, ham skal gis. Inntektsulikheter blant eldre i Norge. Fafo-report no. 231, Oslo: Fafo.

Dahl, E, JA. Drøpping. (2001) The Norwegian Work Approach in the 1990s: Rhetoric and Reform. In Neil Gilbert and Rebecca A. Van Voorhis (eds) Activating the Unemployed. A Comparative Appraisal of Work-Oriented Policies. New Brunswick, NJ: Transaction Publishers.

Dahler, B (2003) Inkluderende arbeidslivsvirksomheter—plass til alle? ECON Analyze Rapport 47, Oslo: ECON.

Disney, Richard (1999) "Notional accounts as a pension reform strategy: An evaluation." Pension reform primer. Nr.1. Washington, DC: World Bank.

Ellingsæter, AL & Gulbrandsen L (2003). Barnehagen—fra selektivt til universelt gode. Report 24/03. Oslo: NOVA.

Esping-Andersen, G. (1990) TheThree Worlds of Welfare Capitalism. Oxford: Polity Press

Esping-Andersen, G. (1999) Social Foundations of Postindustrial Economies. Oxford: Oxford University Press.

Erikson, R. & Goldthorpe, J.H. (2002) "Intergenerational inequality. A sociological perspective," Journal of Economic Perspectives, 16: 31-44.

Erikson R, Hansen E J, Ringen S, Uusitalo H, (eds) (1987) The Scandinavian Model. Welfare States and Welfare Research. Armonk, NY: M E Sharpe.

Fevang E. Røed, K. Westlie, L. Zhang, T (2004) Veier inn i, rundt i, og ut av det norske trygde- og sosialhjelpssystemet Report 6/2004, Oslo: Ragnar Frisch Center for Economic Research.

Fox, Louise and Palmer, Edward (2001) "New approaches to multi-pillar pension systems: What in the World is going on?" I Holzman, Robert and Stiglitz, Joseph E. (red): New ideas about social security. Washington, DC: World Bank.

Frederiksen, Dennis (1998) Minstepensjon, særtillegg og regulering av grunnbeløpet. Økonomiske analyzer 3/98. Oslo: Statistics Norway.

Frederiksen, Dennis og Koren, Charlotte (1993) Kvinners forsørgelsesmønster og folketrygden. Økonomiske analyzer. 8/93. Oslo: Statistics Norway.

Fritzell, J. (2001) "Still different? Income distribution in the Nordic Countries in a European Comparison," in Kautto, M., J. Fritzell, B. Hvinden, J. Kvist & H. Uusitalo (eds.) Nordic Welfare States in the European Context. London: Routledge.

Gilbert, N. (2002) Transformation of the Welfare State. The Silent Surrender of Public responsibility. Oxford/New York: Oxford University Press.

Huber E and Stephens JD (2001) Development and Crisis of the Welfare State. Parties and Policies in Global Markets. Chicago: The University of Chicago Press.

Kautto M, Heikkilä M, Hvinden B, Marklund S, Ploug N (eds) (1999) Nordic Social Policy, London: Routledge.

Kautto M, Fritzell J, Hvinden B, Kvist J, Uusitalo H (eds) (2001) Nordic Welfare States in the European Context. London: Routledge.

Kavli, H. (2001) En dråpe, men i hvilket hav? Konstanstøttens konsekvenser for barnehagebruk blant etniske minoriteter. Fafo report 349, Oslo: Fafo.

Kjølsrød, L (2003) En tjenesteintens velferdsstat. In Frønes og Kjølsrød (ed) (2003) Det norske samfunn. Fjerde utgave. Oslo: Gyldendal norsk forlag.

Koren, Charlotte (2001) Minstepensjon og minstepensjonister. Report 19/01. Oslo: NOVA.

Korpi, W. & J. Palme (1998) "The Paradox of Redistribution and the Strategy of Equality: Welfare State Institutions, Inequality and Poverty in the Western Countries." American Sociological Review, 63:661-687.

Leira, A (2003) Familier og velferdsstat. Familieendring og politisk reform i 1990-åra.. i Frønes og Kjølsrød (ed) Det norske samfunn. Fjerde utgave. Oslo: Gyldendal norsk forlag.

Lødemel I and Trickey H (2001) An offer you can't refuse? Bristol: Polity Press.

Marshall, TH. (1964) Class, Citizenship and Social Development. New York: Anchor Books.

Midtsundstad T (2002) Tidlig pensjonering i stat og skoleverk. Fafo notat 2002:12. Oslo: Fafo.

National Insurance (2002)"Gjennomsnittlig pensjoneringsalder i Norge 1970-2001," (Expected retirement age) Rapport 06/2002 Oslo: National Insurance.

National Insurance (2003) Basisrapport 2002 Mellomlangsiktig budsjettering og rapportering, Report 01/2003. Oslo: National Insurance.

NOU 2004:1. Modernisert folketrygd. Bærekraftig pensjon for framtida.

Orloff, A.S. (1993) "Gender and the social rights of citizenship: the comparative analysis of Gender relations and welfare states", *American Sociological Review*, 58: 303-328.

Ot. prp. nr 17, 1965-66.

Palme J., Bergmark, Å., Bäckman, O., Estrada, F., Fritzell, J., Lundberg, O., Sjöberg, O. and Szebehely, M. (2002) "Welfare trends in Sweden: balancing the books for the 1990s," *Journal of European Social Policy*, 12: 329-346.

Pedersen, Axel West (1990) Fagbevegelsen og folketrygden. LOs målsetninger, strategi for innflytelse i pensjonspolitikken 1945-1966. Fafo-report no. 110. Oslo: Fafo.

Pedersen, Axel West (1997) "Do public pensions hamper the growth of private pensions? A comparative study of time series data for Denmark and Norway." CWR Working Paper No.7/1997. Copenhagen: Center for Welfare State Research, The Danish National Institute for Social Research.

Pedersen, Axel West (1999).

Petersen, T (2003) Likestilling i arbeidsmarkedet. *Tidsskrift for samfunnsforskning* vol 43, nr 4: 443–478.

Smeeding ,T. M. (2002) "Globalization, Inequality and the Rich Countries of the G-20: Evidence from the Luxembourg Income Study (LIS)," LIS Working Paper Series No. 320. Luxembourg.

Skrede, K (2004) Familiepolitikkens grense—ved "likestilling" light? In Ellingsæther AL and Leira, A (eds) *Velferdsstaten og familien. Utfordringer og dilemmaer*. Oslo: Gyldendal Akademisk.

St. meld. nr. 75, 1963-64.

Statistics Norway (2000) Kvinner og menn i Norge 2000. *Statistical Analyzes* 43, Oslo: Statistics Norway.

Williamson, John B (2004) Assessing the pension reform potential of notional defined contribution pillar. *International Social Security Association*. 57(1):47-64.

# 5

# Active Aging and Pension Reform: The Gender Implications in France

*Christel Gilles*
*Antoine Parent*

## Introduction

A major trend has gained strength over the past decades in France: the decline of the participation rate[1] of workers fifty-five-years-old. Despite a recent tick upward the employment rate among the fifty-five to sixty-four-year-old age group remains very low in France in contrast with OECD countries (39.3 percent versus 49.4 percent in 2002, OECD, 2004). The French Pension debates have focused on the question of the demographic ratio between the working and non-working populations, as well as on the necessity to extend the working lifecycle. Various resolutions of the European Council have already gone in that direction defining a target of 50 percent in the employment rate among the population aged between fifty-five and sixty-four-years-old by 2010 (resolution of the Stockholm European Council of March 2001) with a five-year progressive increase in the average effective retirement age also starting that year (resolution of the Barcelona European Council of March 2002).

France might find reaching these objectives very difficult considering the trend, fueling early retirement via the existence of early retirement schemes, might have contributed to what Anne Marie Guillemard (2003) defines as a "culture of early age of exit." It follows this issue emerges now in France as a crucial challenge for preserving the equilibrium of its pay-as-you-go (PAYG) system.

In an effort to do just this, the Pension Reform Act of August 21, 2003 reaffirms the choice of a pay-as-you-go system, which is based upon the principle of pensions attached to work. The goal of the Pension Reform is to adapt the pension insurance system to demographic and economic trends by 2020 in order to secure the equilibrium of pension regimes. Specifically, its aim is to stabilize at two-thirds and one-third. respectively, the distribution between two periods, working life and retirement. The objective for the replacement rate is set at two-thirds of the salary (and 85 percent of the net minimum wage for low income) by 2020. Another major orientation outlined by the 2003 Law is to "give more flexibility and choices to pensioners" regarding their decisions to retire. To that end, various mechanisms have been introduced, such as bonuses and penalties, easing of the rules regarding the combination of pension and wage and the progressive retirement scheme.

According to the text of the 2003 Pension Law, the extension of the contribution period "only makes sense if the working life cycle expands"; this suggests "a national mobilization in favor of the employment of people over sixty-years-old." The objective of the law is meant to encourage the work participation of the older-age people (over sixty) and to prompt firms and public administrations which employ them to help increase their working lifecycle. This orientation is a major break from the former ones.

In more detail, the Fillon Law adopted on August 21, 2003 supercedes the Balladur Reform of 1993[2] (the latter bringing the number of compulsory contribution years for wage earners in the private sector to forty years). Specifically, the Fillon Law of August 21, 2003:

- first increased the compulsory contribution period in the public sector from 37.5 years to forty years by 2008 and then, for all workers, from forty years to 41.9 years over the 2009- 2020 period;
- introduced, in the public sector, penalties on the benefit level of pensioners whose number of contribution years are below the required contributing lifetime as well as bonuses when above this; (these rules were already applied to civilian labor force covered by the *Régime General*, see appendix 1);
- modified the indexation rules for all regimes from an indexing by wage to an indexing by inflation

The implementation of penalties for workers exiting the workforce before reaching a total tenure can be seen as a signal of a new aging policy in France. More generally, this pension reform option aims at easing transitions from work to retirement which, up until now, has been considered a rupture in working life. In order to defer the effective retirement age other provisions have been adopted by the Fillon Law, including raising taxes on early pensions. The Fillon Law also revisited and relaxed the rules forbidding the simultaneous holding of wage and pension benefits, a decision which can be perceived as an element of this new aging policy. This clears the way today, in France, for a new debate on so-call pension gap-filling "bridge jobs" as transitional job markets, at the end of people's career pathways, could now appear as one of the solutions to the problem of financing pensions.

In the first section, we show the issue of *bridge jobs* is recent in France and explain why.

Does the increase of working lifetime of women stand as a solution to gender inequalities within the pension system? The rise in the female labor participation rate plays a similar role as demographic growth. An increase in the contribution period leads to higher pensions. Hence, it can be argued, in theory, the rise in the female labor participation rate reduces pension inequalities between men and women. In the second section, we discuss this point.

In the third section, we examine, from a gender perspective, other pension reform options that may, in theory, provide greater gender equality, but that are, in practice, far from the implementation phase.

## Bridge Jobs: A New Issue in France

*Incentives to Extend the Employment Lifecycle After the Legal Age for Retirement*

*The effect of the institutional context.* Many research studies have shown that the old aged workers' labor supply behavior is affected by financial incentives induced by public and private schemes, that is, by the institutional context. For example, Gruber and Wise (1999) found that in OECD countries, strong financial incentives to retire early are associated with low participation rates and conclude a major incentive effect is produced by pension and social protection schemes.

However, the dynamics of pathways to retirement are complex since transitions can infer movements from in and out of the labor market as well as "intermediary states" (part-time jobs, unemployment). Hence, the analysis, based on the observation of stocks (participation rates), can be improved by the analysis of flows (changes in situations on the labor market). Research based on flows has shown most of the exiting flows of the labor market take place at specific ages conditioned by the legislation on pensions (Bommier, Magnac, Roger, 2001). The probability to exit the labor force changes dramatically with age. In France, over the 1995 to 1996 period, the exit rate reached 50 percent for individuals aged sixty (and 40 percent for women) and 40 percent for individuals aged sixty-five (55 percent for women), (Blöndal et Scarpetta, 1998). The irregular pattern of exit rates is observed in most western countries. In Italy, like in France, two peaks of exit rates can be identified: one at sixty-years-old and the other at sixty-five (Miniaci, 1998); in the U.S. as well, two peaks are observed at respectively sixty-two and sixty-five-years-old (Quinn, Burkhauser, Cahill and Weathers, 1998). These changes of exit rate according to age suggest pathways from the labor force to retirement are highly dependent on the regulation of the social protection systems. Taking the example of the U.S., Stock and Wise (1990) show the peak of exit rate at sixty-two-years-old can be attributed to the particularities of U.S. pension schemes; Rust and Phelan (1997) give evidence the second peak of exit rate at sixty-five-years-old could be created by the health care schemes targeted to the elderly. In France, research on the link between the effective exit age and pension schemes remains scarce; Blanchet and Mahieu (1999) show the age profile of workers exiting the labor force is framed by the features of the French Pension System. However, institutional factors cannot be the only explanation of the timing of retirement. Retirement behavior depends, as well, on the situation on the labor market of the husband (or wife): Sedillot and Walraet (2002) show within the household the decisions of each individual to retire are inter-dependent[3]; women seem, however, more sensitive to the situation of their husbands than men to the situation of their wives. Retirement behavior seems also to depend on the socio-demographic characteristics of the household: for given income, highly educated workers have longer careers (Marchand, Minni and Thélot, 1998) and retire later than low educated workers (Blöndal, Scarpetta, 1998). Having dependent children as well as a health condition (workers with bad health retire earlier) act as discriminant factors in the decision to retire.

*The Work and Retirement Behavior of Elderly Individuals*

According to standard economic theory, the old aged worker defines his/her age of retirement at the end of an arbitrage between the level of the pension benefit, obtained when retiring at time (t), and the level of his/her pension entitlements when postponing his/her age at exit by one more period.[4] In a Life Cycle Model, under the assumption of a non-risky environment (uncertainties about wages and unemployment risks are ignored) the potential gain in income derived from a one year's delay in retirement depends not only on the difference between the levels of wage and pension entitlements, but also on changes in the deferred wage provided by the pension benefits derived from the supplementary year of activity. Research studies having applied this type of model to the case of France (Pelé and Ralle—1998, 1999; Blanchet and Mahieu—1999) find changes in pension schemes can strongly influence the decisions to retire.

The effect of the pension schemes on the age of exit is of great magnitude: Anderson, Gustman and Steinmeier (1997) find that in OECD countries, the features of the basic public pension system are an explanatory factor of the decline in the age of retirement. Hence, the dynamic modelling of labor supply's behavior of old aged workers allows for making the first analysis of the systemic incentives to retire and provides predictions on the future flows of individuals exiting the workforce in keeping with the facts presented above.

However, these models are based on the assumption that the environment is non-risky and ignores the fact that old aged workers could suffer from labor market risks, such as unemployment, which may erode their future income. Stock and Wise (1990) propose an "option value model" which takes into account uncertainty of future income. The decision to retire is considered irreversible. At this time (t), the individual calculates the actual value of his/her expected income gained from work and accumulated over his/her working life if s/he retires at time (t). At each period (t), the individual can choose to extend his/her working life if the expected return of work is superior to the expected return of retiring at time (t). Stated differently, considering the available information at the time (t), the individual makes the decision to carry on working if the value of the option "stay at work" is greater than the value of the option "exit the workforce." Econometric estimates of this model, on U.S., German and French Data (Stock and Wise—1990, Börsch-Supan—1998,

Blanchet and Mahieu—1999) show the estimated exit rates are very close to those observed in reality; workers substantially respond to public and private incentives to retire. Mahieu and Walraet (2002) using a Stock and Wise (1990) option value model, in order to simulate the impact of changes in retirement rules on a cohort of people aged fifty-five years, find "a large impact of behavioral responses to modifications in the Social Security provisions." In the case of a "reform introducing a unique normal replacement rate of 60 percent at age sixty-five and a strictly actuarial adjustment," their results show a "sharp increase in the average retirement age" (p. 21).

The Option Value models are, therefore, compatible with the stylized facts, as are the Life Cycle Models.

A third generation of models, called "dynamic programming" (Rust and Phelan, 1997), is not contingent upon the irreversibility of retirement. The individual is said to be free to choose between staying retired or accepting a new full-time or part-time job. This assumption matches the existing possibilities of pathways between work and retirement, such as the progressive retirement schemes and bridge jobs. The individual decides at each period to change or maintain his/her situation on the basis of financial observable variables (wages, level of pension benefits), non-financial ones (leisure), and according to the different states on the labor market (unemployment, part-time or full-time job). The probability of moving from one state to another depends on the features of the pension system and on the parameters known by the individual. Each individual moves from one state to another according to his/her own sets of rules used in maximizing his/her inter-temporal function.

The results of the econometric estimates on U.S. data suggest current public pension schemes act as an important disincentive for old-aged individuals to participate in the labor market. Rust and Phelan (1997) show the patterns of the pension schemes contribute to explain the high exit rates observed at the ages of sixty-two and sixty-five-years-old. The incentives to participate to the labor market are particularly strong amongst low-income employees who do not have access to other forms of social coverage than those provided by employment (health insurance scheme).

The development of "transitional markets" between full activity and full retirement (the question of the so-called bridge jobs[5]) needs to be considered from the side of the rationality of old-aged workers and the institutional context. In a given national institutional context, a rational reason for pursuing work after the legal age for retirement could be a low level of income. The latter can result from a deficient social protection system; then the job search of old-aged individuals should then be facilitated by a flexible regulation of the labor market. Rix (2001) underscores the bridge Jobs, held by American workers above sixty-five-years-old, present all the characteristics of a flexible labor market (part-time jobs with flexible working hours for two-thirds of old-aged workers). Herz (1995) stresses on his side the low replacement rates provided by companies' pension funds as an influential factor in the decision to continue working. Equally, the costs of health care services and the absence of a universal public health system can explain this decision (Bruce, Holtz-Eakin and Quinn, 2000). A funded pension system could facilitate the extension of working life in the following way: under the assumption of a fall in stock prices and, therefore, a decline in savings, the individual is rationally encouraged to carry on working, employment becoming a risk coverage against a fall in income (Eschtruth and Gemus, 2002). Finally, favorable macro-economic conditions, coupled with the capacity of the labor market to create jobs, are a prerequisite for extending working life after the legal age of retirement.

If it is possible to explain the rise in participation rate among old-aged workers in the U.S. with the above sets of factors, in France, they do not act this way: the pay-as-you-go system, and the universal minimum income support scheme targeted at the poor elderly, cover most of the population and prevents an age-dependent poverty risk; furthermore, each pensioner has access to a health care coverage; also, job creation in France is, in the long-run, less abundant than in the U.S.; the old age French person having reached the legal age for retirement is, therefore, less encouraged to extend his/ her working life in France. Quite the reverse, until the 2003 Fillon Law was passed; most of the previously existing schemes supported decisions in favor of early retirement.

*The Legal Devices*

Before the 2003 Pension Reform, the law made the transitions from work to retirement difficult

Before the 2003 Pension Reform, there was a complex set of legal devices aiming at creating bridges between employment and retirement: the progressive retirement scheme (*Retraite progressive*)

and the scheme allowing the holding of wage and pension benefits simultaneously (*Cumul Emploi-Retraite*).

*Progressive Retirement Scheme* The law on progressive retirement of January 1988, applied initially to wage earners covered by the basic general scheme *(Régime General)*, had been extended in 1992 to craftsmen and trades-people. The entitlement to a progressive pension scheme was opened to all individuals meeting the requirements for a full-rate Social Security pension. The law authorized working people sixty-years of age scoring at least 150 quarters of contribution to pension schemes, or being at least sixty-five-years-old, to work on a part-time basis beyond the legal age of retirement. The beneficiary had, then, the possibility to move progressively from full-time to part-time employment: that is,, the level of the pension entitlement varied accordingly from zero, when the individual held a full-time job, to a full-rate pension once exiting the workforce; with the pension becoming progressive in between these two employment situations.

In 2002, only 723 persons benefited from a progressive pension scheme, up slightly from 183 in 2001. These unreasonably small figures clearly illustrate that the solution of a progressive transition from full-time employment to full-time pension did not match the aspiration of those French people sixty and over. It is not off-base to say these schemes had no social relevance in France.

**Table 5.1**
**Employment Rates in 2001 Among the Population**
**ages Fifty to Sixty-Five-Years-old in France**

| Age | Employment rate (%) | | Age | Employment rate (%) |
|-----|--------------------|---|-----|--------------------|
| 50 | 79,9 | | 58 | 45,9 |
| 51 | 78,9 | | 59 | 38,3 |
| 52 | 78,4 | | 60 | 31,2 |
| 53 | 74,7 | | 61 | 14,6 |
| 54 | 73,7 | | 62 | 9 |
| 55 | 70,9 | | 63 | 8,2 |
| 56 | 61,2 | | 64 | 6,5 |
| 57 | 55 | | 65 | 5,4 |

*Source: INSEE*

On the other hand, the private sector's early progressive retirement scheme (*Préretraite Progressive*), created in 1982 and modified in 1993, targeted to wage earners below sixty-years-old, matched the public's expectations. Its number of beneficiaries rose from 13,100 in 1993 to 48,700 in 2003. In the public sector, the progressive pension scheme (*Cessation Progressive d'Activité*) gradually expanded and included 28,000 persons in 2001. These developments aptly reflect the preferences of the French society for early retirement as opposed to deferred retirement[6]. Table 5.1 provides a further illustration of this trend.

As the Report *Boulanger* (2003) highlighted prior to the 2003 Pension Reform, "a step-by-step transition from full activity to full pension was an exception whereas early retirement tended to become the norm or, at least, the best possible outlook once the opportunity came up" (Report on "Cumul Emploi Retraite " Conseil d'Orientation des Retraites, March 2003, p29).

*Holding wage and pension benefits simultaneously* The prevailing principle for twenty years, from the 1982 Law until the 2003 Pension Act, was to limit the possibility of holding pension benefits and wages concurrently after sixty-years of age (before sixty-years-old, there were no limitations unless employment took place in the public sector). The core principle of the Law was as follows: obligation to stop working at the legal age of exit while also having the possibility of being re-employed under certain conditions, namely holding a job different from the previous one. This ban on taking up the same job was applied to both wage earners from the private sector and self-employed.[7]

Nevertheless, if the entitlement of the basic pension scheme relied only on the obligation to stop working for the previous employer, compulsory complementary pension schemes (*Régimes ARRCO and AGIRC*, see appendix 1) complied with different rules that, in the end, contributed to limit financial incentives to work. The complementary pension schemes were entirely suspended when taking on a job[8] leading to a total level of income (wage plus Social Security and Complementary Pensions) greater than the last career's wage.

In order to empirically appreciate the importance of the pension system's phenomenon prior to the 2003 Reform, the only available study, done by DREES (Coëffic, 1999), has been utilized(see Appendix 2). This analysis, based upon the former scheme, may, nonetheless, deliver precious comparison information regarding the possible outlook of the 2003 reform when focusing on the gender issue.

*The 2003 Reform facilitates transitions from work to retirement*
With the 2003 Pension Reform, the access to early retirement schemes (progressive and non-progressive) has been made more difficult: early retirement schemes concluded after May 27, 2003, and signed between the State and firms from the private sector, are tied to a specific financial contribution from the employers; the progressive early retirement scheme in the private sector (*Préretraite Progressive, PRP*) was removed on January 1, 2005. In the public sector, the regulation of the progressive early retirement scheme (Cessation Progressive d'Activité) has been strengthened by limiting eligibility to workers aged fifty-seven-years or more and having thirty-three contribution years among which twenty-five years in the public sector.

On the other hand, the 2003 Pension Act improved the incentives to extend the working lifecycle above sixty years. By and large, it aims at creating financial incentives to work after the legal age of exit and to lift the related various barriers produced by the Laws on Employment:

- Creation of a 3 percent bonus (in the private and public sectors) on the level of the pension for each year of work achieved by January 1, 2004, benefiting the insured individual over sixty-years-old and entitled to full-rate pension. This mechanism has been set up in order to defer professional activity earning salary-scale work pay;
- The legal age at which an employer can decide to make a worker retire has been changed from sixty to sixty-five-years-old;
- The progressive retirement scheme opened to public sector wage earners has been eased: the liquidation of the pension changed from definitive to provisional allowing the insured individuals holding a part-time job to improve their pension rights;
- The rules on the combination of wages and pensions have been simplified in the private sector and alleviated in the public sector. In the private sector, the related rules applied in the *Régime Général* have been brought into line with those applied to complementary schemes—the pensioner can simultaneously hold a pension and earn wages up to a level set at his last career's salary and also accumulate further rights for pension.
- The combination of pension benefits and wages, both dependent on the same *Regime*, is now made possible, although capped and restricted: for a wage earner, the combination is possible only within the limit of his/her last career's wage or the total amount of pension benefits (basic pension benefit plus complementary pension benefit) which can not

exceed the level of his/her last career's wages. If the job occurs with the former employer, the same limit applies after a six-month work interruption.

- In the public sector, there is no income limit when the pensioner takes a job in the private sector (it is capped when employment occurs in the public sector, the pension being reduced by the amount above the ceiling).

Hence the Pension Reform of March 1, 2003 took pressure off the rules limiting the possibility of simultaneously working and benefiting from a pension. Whatever his/her former occupation and regime, the individual now has the opportunity to accumulate wages and a pension up to his/her last career's salary. It is worth mentioning these new guidelines have been in force since January 1, 2004. Not enough time has elapsed to assess the efficiency of these measures. However, one can highlight any old-aged individual now has the opportunity to maintain his/her standard of living to the level prevailing when employed since the effect of the inactivity trap is effective only above the level of the last career's wage. In sum, the reform facilitates the transition between work and retirement.

## Pension and Gender Inequalities

### Large Disparities

Disparities amongst men and women are large.

**Table 5.2**
**Level of Pension Benefits by Sex and Age in 2001 (Monthly Average in Euros)**

| | 65- 69 | 70- 74 | 75- 79 | 80- 84 | 85 years or | Total |
|---|---|---|---|---|---|---|
| | Direct pension entitlements drawn | | | | | |
| Men | 139 | 137 | 137 | 139 | 118 | 137 |
| Women | 666 | 619 | 587 | 566 | 506 | 606 |
| Ratio | 0.48 | 0.45 | 0.43 | 0.41 | 0.43 | 0.44 |
| | Total pension benefit (direct pension entitlement plus secondary benefits | | | | | |
| Men | 146 | 145 | 146 | 148 | 128 | 145 |
| Women | 805 | 808 | 833 | 864 | 837 | 822 |
| Ratio | 0.55 | 0.55 | 0.57 | 0.58 | 0.65 | 0.56 |

Field: retired people aged sixty-five-years-old or more benefitting from a direct pension entitlement.
Note: the total pension benefit includes the minimum income support for the elderly.
Sources: échantillon interrégimes de retraités (EIR) 2001 in Bonnet and alii (2004).

The gender gap of 50 percent in the level of the direct pension benefits (*Droits directs*) is reduced to 44 percent when the indirect entitlements are included (table 5.2). In 2001, among retired people aged sixty-five-years-old or more, the average number of contribution years reached 42.25 for men versus 29.75 for women (including the bonuses for women having raised children) (table 5.3).

**Table 3**
**Number of Contribution Years [1] of Pensioners**
**Benefiting from Direct Pension Entitlement, by Age and Sex, in 2001**

|  | 65- 69 years | 70- 74 years | 75- 84 years | 80- 84 years | 85 years and more | Total |
|---|---|---|---|---|---|---|
| Men | 41,5 | 42 | 43 | 44 | 41 | 42,25 |
| Women | 30,5 | 29,75 | 29,75 | 28,75 | 28,25 | 29,75 |

[1] Number of contribution years drawn from work as well as unemployment, early retirement, sickness etc...plus bonuses given for children.
Field: retired people aged sixty-five-years-old or more benefitting from a direct pension entitlement.
Sources: échantillon interrégimes de retraités (EIR) 2001 in Bonnet and alii (2004).

In 2001, only 40 percent of women (versus 80 percent of men) have retired at full-pension rate. Amongst the male and female population of those having retired with the required number of contribution years to obtain a full-rate pension, the gap between men and women's pension reached 35 percent (in favor of men, 2001 data).

Pension benefits among women are more scattered than those of men: the ratio of the last tier to the first tier of the pension benefits' distribution (of the basic general scheme) came to 7 for women versus 4.3 for men in 2001; 50 percent of retired women from the basic general scheme were beneficiary of the minimum income support allowance targeted on the elderly (*Minimum Vieillesse*) versus 20 percent of the men (Bonnet et al. 2004).

*The explanatory factors.* Several factors are widely cited to explain these disparities:

- Women have shorter careers than men. For example, in 2003, 22.8 percent of employed women worked part-time versus 4.7 percent of men (OCDE 2004); women are also more likely than men to have a short-term contract and more likely to hold a subsidized job than men;
- Their wages are, on average, lower;
- They have a higher probability to end their career with a period of inactivity;

- They are more frequently beneficiaries of the survivor benefit which limits their pension benefit to the indirect type of entitlement (see section 3);
- The increasing participation of women to the labor market causes a substitution effect between direct and indirect entitlements; the first ones are logically higher whereas the second ones diminish. This leaves uncertain the global effect of employment on the disparities of the levels of pension benefits.
- Women also face more *accidents* on their career paths than men.

These uneven careers[9] have a mechanical effect on the level of pensions. It can be easily understood a higher exposure to unemployment risk, discontinuous career paths and low wages all contribute to a low level of pension benefits. A part-time job leads to a lower year based average wage than a full-time job; in addition, the level of the basic pension benefit is calculated on the average salary gained over the best twenty-five years. Furthermore, working part-time has a direct effect on the number of points the worker accumulates during his/her career, an item used for the calculation of the complementary pension benefit (see appendix 1).

It is nevertheless true French Law offers some protections against the risk of uneven career pathways through:

- the guarantee of a minimum income support for people whose income is below a threshold set at 40 percent of the minimum wage (on an annual basis);

**Table 5.4**
**Labor market indicators in 2002 by sex**

| 2002 | Total | Men (1) | Women (2) | Difference (2) - (1) |
|---|---|---|---|---|
| Employment rate (15-64 years), in % | 62,2 | 68,6 | 55,8 | -12,8 |
| Employment rate (55-64 years), in % | na | 44,2 | 34,6 | -9,6 |
| | | | | |
| Labor Force participation rate (15-64 years), in % | 68,3 | 74,5 | 62,1 | -12,4 |
| Labor Force participation rate (55-64 years), in % | | 47 | 36,6 | -10,4 |
| | | | | |
| Unemployment rate (15-64 years), in % | 8,9 | 7,9 | 10,1 | 2,2 |
| Unemployment rate (55-64 years), in % | | 6 | 5,5 | -0,5 |
| | | | | |
| Long-term unemployment rate (15-64) years [(1)], in % | 33,8 | 32,2 | 35,2 | |
| | | | | |
| Part-time employment as % of employment (15-64 years) | 13,7 | 5,2 | 24,1 | 18,9 |

Source: OECD, Employment Outlook, 2004
(1) twelve months and older

- the existence of rules, applied to the basic general scheme, related to the accumulation of contributory quarters, which allow people earning more than 40 percent of the minimum wage to legitimate four contributory quarters per year;
- the validation of "free" quarters during periods of *subsidized* unemployment

Recalling women are more exposed to career up and downs, they should benefit the most from the above sets of laws.

In total, considering the factors described in this section, it is apparent gender inequalities in the labor market largely contribute to gender inequalities in pensions.

### Will the Rise in the Participation Rate of Women[10] Help to Reduce Gender Inequality in Pensions?

Women's participation rates have been rising with generations and reached 62.5 percent in 2003 for women aged twenty-five to sixty-four years. The difference in participation rates between men and women has steadily declined from thirty-five points in 1970 to eleven points in 2003 (figure 5.1).

**Figure 5.1**
**Labor Force Participation Rates, Men and Women Aged 15-64 (%)**

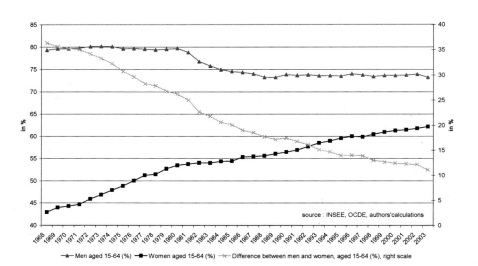

source : INSEE, OCDE, authors'calculations

—▲— Men aged 15-64 (%)   —■— Women aged 15-64 (%)   ⋯✕⋯ Difference between men and women, aged 15-64 (%), right scale

Wage discrepancies have slowly closed over time as well: "the average salary of women for a full-time job as a percentage of the average male salary, rose from 64 percent in 1960 to 81 percent in 2001" (Bonnet et al. 2001). Thus, under the driving forces of the rising participation rate of women, the gap in the level of pensions between men and women is apparently decreasing. This reduction in wage disparities could also be related to the increase of women's educational attainments. This trend contributes logically to diminishing the gap in direct pension entitlements and, therefore, to reducing gender inequalities. With the arrival of female cohorts more active than their parents, the gender gap in pensions could close even more rapidly.

*Will the rise in the participation rate of women eliminate gender inequalities in pension? If so, will the process be fast or not?* In order to answer to these questions, two projections done with the micro-simulation model Destinie[11] of INSEE by Bardaji, Sedillot and Walraet (2002) and Bonnet, Buffeteau and Godefroy (2004) are presented here. This latter simulation shows the advantage to taking into account the major pieces of the 2003 Pension Reform.

According the first simulation, under the assumption the participation rate of women will continuously rise and converge with the male participation rate by 2010, the level of the pension benefit (basic general scheme, direct entitlement) of women from the generations of 1965 to 1974 will be lower by 32 percent than that of men compared to a difference of 50 percent for the 1935 to1944 generation. Given the situation of retired people reflects past inequalities and/or disparities on the labor market, gender gaps in pensions are currently more important than gender wage gaps. However, the results obtained by the first simulation exhibit a substantial remaining gender gap in pensions despite the favorable assumption made on participation rate of women. This reveals the effect of career ups and downs described above which is highly discriminant for women.

Under the assumption the female participation rate will  continue to rise by 2010 to a level of 10 points below the male participation rate, Bonnet, Buffeteau and Godefroy (2004) find an average contributing years of 32.5 for women belonging to the 1965 to 1974 cohort versus 29.3 years for the 1940 to 1944 generation. This rise in the contributory period for women, coupled with the assumption of a gender wage gap stabilized at 25 percent by 2040, would lead to a gender pension gap (for a population aged between sixty-five and sixty-nine-years-old) of 29 percent in 2040 versus 50 percent in 2001.

These results show if the gender gap in the level of pensions is narrowing, the move is slow. Hence, the rise in women's participation rate is not the miraculous solution to the problem of gender inequalities.

In addition, the results of these simulations strongly rely on the assumptions made on changes on the labor market: if we suppose that flexible types of jobs (short-term contracts and part-time jobs) expand without women being less exposed to career misfortunes, then the scenario could be that of deepening the pension disparity amongst women and men.

It is easy to comprehend the difficulty of dealing with the question of pension gender inequalities: in short, the comfortable assumption of a rising participation rate among women as the solution to the problem does not hold, at least in the short-run. Besides, a rise in the rate of women participation in the labor market makes the system more contributory-based. This could worsen the pension gender gap. As underlined by Bonnet and Colin (2003), in a system in which pension benefits are highly dependent on career pathways, "reforms consisting in reinforcing this link with the labor market generally bring about disadvantages for women."

If strengthening the principle of contribution can lead to a result opposite to the objective, that is, in penalizing women, do other scenarios of pension reform produce more fairness and equality regarding to the gender issue?

### Pension Reforms: The Paradox of Equality

*Indirect Entitlements Versus More Egalitarian Systems of Pension: The pros and cons*

Female economic self-sufficiency stands at the center of most programs of European Welfare States. For example, in Scandinavian countries, eligibility to social rights has been inspired by the single-earner model encouraging women to participate in the labor force. In France, the tradition relies on the "breadwinner" model characterized by the "familialization" of social rights.

Rights to benefit from a pension in France rely on the traditional family-based model of the breadwinner in which the husband supports his family through work. The husband is the owner of the pension rights and the spouse and the children benefit from indirect pension entitlements. The spouse, as "the second half," is entitled to the survivor benefit allowing women, at the death of their husband, to benefit from his pension (capped though by a ceiling). This system secures the full protection of women against health risks. It ensures the family-based model of social rights stands at the heart of the French Social Protection System. Indirect entitlements help to secure women outside the labor force by giving them access to the social protection of their husbands without supplementary contributions on their own.

Various problems are commonly identified with such a system. First, from a fairness perspective, how is it justified that a woman who worked full-time her whole life at the minimum wage receives a lower pension than the widow of a company chairman, who did not work or contribute to the system, but qualifies for a survivor's benefit ? Should it be considered a gift, financed by individuals who do work, to women who never did?

Three main criticisms emerge: indirect entitlements are unfair since married women standing outside of the labor force cash in survivor's benefits without any contribution; they create a dependency vis à vis the person entitled to the social rights; they deter women from entering the labor market since they benefit from the social protection of their husband.

Different arguments against the "familialization" of social rights are put forward by those in favor of their individualization:

- The survivor benefits would be very expensive: 15 percent of pension expenditures in France in 2002 (Lanquetin and al, 2004);
- The reason for indirect entitlements to subsist depends on a strong condition, which is not true anymore: the employment stability of the husband.
- The individualization of social rights would hamper women from falling into a "dependency trap." This is the main economic criticism made about "familialization" which is it hinders women from participating in the labor market. The joint taxation equalizes the income tax rate between each member of the couple. A move to a separate taxation would lower the marginal tax rate on women and help to increase their labor force participation rate. It would, therefore, correct for the effects mentioned above.
- The individualization of social rights would put into effect the principle of gender equality (the choice to work would be individual-based)

*Would the individualization of social rights stand as the miraculous solution to gender inequalities in France?* It is worth mentioning a higher female participation in the labor market is an essential prerequisite for a change of the formal gender equality into an effective equality in terms of income and pensions. Sterdyniak (2004) questions the argument of the cost of the survivor benefits: he estimates the survivor benefit prevents the society from paying for the old-aged means-tested benefits. According to the author's calculations, "if the man is two years older than his wife, the society saves on average the equivalent of twenty-eight years of means-tested benefit while financing the equivalent of eight years of survivor benefit" (p. 443). Besides, the author estimates "the abolition of the survivor benefit would reduce by 17.5 percent the level of pension benefiting to women" which would, in the end, produce a result opposite to the pursued objective of more equality in pensions between women and men.

Does the logic of an advanced disincentive effect of indirect entitlements on female employment hold true? This argument is based upon the assumption marginal tax rates play a crucial role on the labor supply's behavior. But it is not clear-cut the French tax system discourages female employment in particular. The female labor market participation rate of persons between twenty-five and fifty-five years old in France is one of the highest in Europe: 79 percent versus 78 percent in Germany, 75 percent in the Netherlands, 76.7 percent in England (2002 data, cited by Sterdyniak, 2004). As underscored by the author, "the employment disincentive effects are not gender-related: they do play a role for single persons or couples with two individuals not of the labor force benefiting from a minimum income support (*Revenu Minimum d'Insertion, Allocation de Solidarité Spécifique*)" (p458).

Finally, the individualization of social rights in its universal dimension entails a paradox. The question of universal social benefits reveals most explicitly the ambiguity of the choice for individualization. As Sterdyniak (2004) asks, "how would the individualization of social rights materialize? Each individual's social rights will depend on his/her own financial situation and no more on the household's one. Hence, the idle spouse of a wealthy city businessman would be entitled to the minimum income support whereas a two-person couple earning the minimum wage would not, given that their individual income stands above the income threshold" (p. 456).

One might wonder, as Sterdyniak (2004), does, if the individualization of social rights represents the wrong answer to the question of reducing gender inequalities.

We show in the following section the French survivor benefit system presents a number of advantages compared to more egalitarian models of pension.

### Survivor Benefits: A Correction for Gender Inequalities

A willingness to replace the occupational-based system by a universal system assuring formal benefits is evidence of misunderstanding the main characteristics of the French pension system. Although organized on an occupational base, this system guarantees a quite large redistribution between men and women through three legal devices:

- *The non-adjustment of contribution rates to the differences in life expectancy between men and women;* the French system is going away from a pure insurance system based on the principle of actuarial neutrality. Given the differences in life expectancy between men and women, this non adjustment corresponds to a redistributive mechanism in favor of women; various projections suggest that women do have an advantage because of the current methods of calculation of the pension and that they benefit from a higher internal rate of return than men;
- *The introduction of a minimum income support scheme for the poor elderly* has a mechanical effect of reducing the pension gender gap; in the same manner, the introduction of various corrective items for uneven career pathways in the formula of pensions has a relative favorable incidence for women in the sense that women do generally have lower wages, shorter working lives and longer unemployment spells;
- *The introduction of family advantages to women* aims at correcting for the career disadvantages women face because of their difficulties in reconciling work and family life: a bonus taking the form of some additional contribution years (two years per child in the basic general scheme, a rule maintained in the 2003 Pension Act) for women having had their children; possibilities in the civil servants' regime, counties' regime, National Railways and Subways Companies' regimes, to advance the age at exit for women having three children or more and totaling fifteen years of contribution years.

Therefore, the French occupational-based system is not, at present, more penalizing for women than the so-called universal systems, in particular when it is strictly contributory-based and when it relies on the principle of actuarial neutrality. In this context, as Zaidman (1998, p. 592) points out, "it is not quite certain offering entitlements to women not in the labor force instead of assuring them an indirect entitlement, will not be even more problematic." The author discusses the pros and cons of a reform guaranteeing women entitlements to pensions, independent from the social status of their husband, when not participating in the labor force or when having a reduced type of job. Various simulations show both single and married women will loose with such a system. This suggests keeping the existing occupational and contributory-based system could be more efficient, from a gender point of view, than a universal system.

## Conclusion

In the first section we showed the drop in participation rates at old ages in France comes from the financial incentives created by the system and more generally, from public policy favoring early retirement. The implementation of "bridge jobs" to facilitate the transition from full employment to full retirement, enhanced in the 2003 Reform, could, in theory, lessen the long-term decline in employment rates of men and women. But it is hazardous to draw any conclusion on the effects of these measures based on the expected narrowing of pension gender inequalities. It is also too early at this stage to assess the effects of this reform and, in particular, to evaluate the degree of satisfaction working women will express regarding its main elements.

In the second section, we question the idea rising participation rates among women are adequate to narrow pension inequalities between men and women. In regard to this point, we also note since women's careers are generally shorter than men's and their labor income remaining, on average, lower, an increase in their labor force participation would lead, in an occupational-based system, to a substitution effect between direct and indirect entitlements. The impact of this effect on pension gender inequalities remains uncertain.

How does the French pension system affect women in particular? In the third section, we presented the net outcome of various options of pension reforms, founded on the strict principle of equality between men and women. We highlighted the individualization of pension entitlements could lead to a counter-productive effect in worsening the situations of single and married women. Our arguments provided evidence the French pension system, based on occupations and entailing a few corrective mechanisms, guarantees, in fact, a noticeable redistribution between men and women.

Finally, in response to the challenges of an aging society, innovative policies have been implemented in France in order to recalibrate the relationship between active aging and retirement. We stressed that the 2003 Reform introduced a large set of measures aimed at promoting active aging. The developments we have analyzed in this case study tend to reveal, in a way, a perceivable change in the philosophy of aging policy France.

### Appendix 1: The French Pension System

This appendix is a contracting form of the presentation done by Mahieu and Walraet (2002), pp 3-6.

**1. For wage earners in the private sector pensions rely on two pillars**

1.1. The basic general scheme

The basic general scheme (Social Security) offers contributory benefits corresponding to the share of wages below a Social Security ceiling (2352 euros per month in 2002). The pension is proportional to the number of quarters of contribution to the system. The number of quarters is truncated to a maximum, $N_{max}$ and to a reference wage that is the average wage of the twenty-five best years of the pensioners' career (and no more the best 10 years like previously). The level of pension is given by:

Pension = $\alpha$.([number of quarters truncated to $N_{max}$ ]/$N_{max}$).(average wage of the best 25 years).

The proportionality coefficient $\alpha$ is maximal when the pensioner leaves at age sixty with a full number of quarters of contribution. It is then equal to 50 percent. The same value of 50 percent is also automatically applied to the leaver at age 65, whatever the number of contributed years.

In all other cases, the coefficient is reduced by 1.25 percentage point for each quarter missing to reach either the age of 65 or the value of $N_{max}$.

People who were successively affiliated to different schemes (for instance people moving from the situation of self-employment to wage-earner) will cumulate two pensions, one from their original scheme, the other from the general scheme in proportion of the number of years spent in each one.

For women, $N_{max}$ is increased by two years for each child they had.

## 1.2. Complementary schemes

The numerous complementary schemes (more than 180) are organized according to the occupation of the individuals. Nevertheless, they are federated in two core organisms: AGIRC for executive workers and for the fraction of their wages over the Social Security ceiling; and ARRCO, for other workers and executives' wages below this ceiling.

These schemes are contributory: workers accumulate "points" during their careers in proportion to their contributions. These points are the pension's basic unit of calculation.

Let $PP_t$ be the purchase price (*salaire de référence*) of one "point", the pension is then equal to the total number of points accumulated over the pensioner's career, multiplied by a coefficient V (*valeur du point*) which is the value of the point defined every year.

Thus, the pension level at time t for a pensioner who worked between time $t_0$ and time $t_1$ is given by:

$$\text{Complementary pension} = V(t).\sum_{t'=t_0}^{t_1} \tau(t')w(t')/PP(t')$$

where $\tau(t')$ and $w(t')$ are respectively the contribution rate and the worker's wage at time t'.

For executives, contributions are collected by ARRCO for the share of the wage below the ceiling, and by AGIRC for the segment of the wage between one and four ceilings. For non-executives, the wage is truncated to three times the Social Security ceiling and contributions are collected by ARRCO.

## 2. A unique pension for civil servants

Civil servants have a unique pension scheme funded by the State budget calculated as:

Pension = 0.75.([number of quarters truncated to $N_{max}$ ]/$N_{max}$ ).(last gross wage, excluding bonuses)

## 3. Survivor benefits

Civil servants' and private sector wage earners' widowers and widows can claim for survivor benefits. Benefits are capped.

The 2003 Pension Act reshuffled the survivor benefit program in the basic general scheme (*Régime Général*): the eligibility conditions for the survivor benefit in respectively the self- employed and the farmers' regimes have been mapped on those applied in the basic general scheme. From July 1, 2004, the survivor benefit is granted under a unique condition: the conditions on, age (fifty-five years), the possibility to cumulate a pension with the survivor benefit, and finally the condition on marriage, all have been eliminated. From now on, income should not exceed a threshold (different for a single person from that of a couple). When total income stands above these thresholds, the benefit is reduced in due proportion. The survivor benefit takes the form of a differential benefit.

## 4. Non-compulsory saving pension plans

The 2003 Pension Act recognises the right for each person to acquire, either on a private or professional setting, one or more saving pension plans, on top of the pensions guaranteed by the compulsory PAYG pension regimes. To that end, two new products have been created:

- an individual saving pension plan: the "Plan d'Epargne Retraite Populaire" (PERP)
- a collective saving pension plan: the "Plan d'Epargne pour la Retraite Collectif" (PERCO)

## Appendix 2: The available statistics show the restricted nature of combining pension and work prior to the 2003 Reform

The data[12] used in the DREES study (Coeffic, 1999) have to be considered cautiously since they are based on pensioners' statements.

According to this study, in 1996, the number of individuals drawing a pension benefit and wage concurrently was very small, 300 000 persons that is, 3 percent of the whole retired population. After sixty-years-old, pensioners having a job accounted only for 2 percent of the whole population of pensioners. The percentage of people holding wage and pension simultaneously was declining with age: from 19 percent for those below sixty-years-old to 2 percent for those above sixty-years-old.

Besides, it concerned essentially men: women, drawing pension benefits and wage concurrently accounted only for 15 percent of the total. Whatever the age, the proportion of men drawing concurrently both items was constantly well above that of women.

Among the retired population aged between fifty-four and fifty-nine years old, the military sub- group showed the highest proportion holding wage (40 percent), followed by the miners (23 percent, but this occupation is disappearing). In comparison, for all other occupations, this proportion reached less than 10 percent. It is worth emphasizing 40 percent of those who drew concurrently these two sources of income, exited the labor force before fifty-years-old, which put them in a second career pathway.

Did wage stand as an important complementary source of income for retired people aged between fifty-four and seventy-years-old? The following four points partially answer this question:

- a U-shape curve existed between wage and pension benefits: wages as a percentage of pension benefits were greater at the two extremes of the scale (for low and high pension benefits) than in the middle of the distribution;
- wage earned above sixty-years-old, accounted on average for less than 50 percent of wage gained below sixty years of age; on the other hand, the pension benefit level was on average 25 percent higher above sixty-years-old than below;
- after sixty-years-old, educated people were the most concerned; the probability to obtain a job was increasing with the level of education; prior to 2003, the law encouraged this practice in allowing lawyers, scientists, experts, consultants and self employed to pursue an activity after sixty years;
- wages of women below sixty, combining pension and income from work, were very low compared to those of men in the same situation; the median wage for women accounted for less than a fourth of the median wage of men;

In total, this practice concerned a minority of retired people in France; it was more frequent amongst the retired population aged less than sixty-years-old; it was a male phenomenon, and after sixty-years-old, this practice was limited to highly educated people.

# Notes

1.  The participation rate is defined as the percentage of people participating to the labor force (employed or unemployed) to the whole population, for given ages.
2.  Law no 93-936 of July 26, 1993 and Law no 2003-775 of August 21, 2003
3.  Considering a couple is not an addition of independent individuals, it is logical to find out inter- dependent decisions within the couple in terms work behavior and retirement. This leads to favor a modelling of collective retirement choices (Bommier, 2002).
4.  For a full survey of literature, see Bommier, Magnac, Roger (2001). Our synthetic presentation of the models of work behavior of elderly individuals and couples, is based on the logic of presentation of their authors.
5.  Surveys undertaken in specific states.
6.  It is worth not neglecting in the study of the phenomenon the component (demand for old-aged workers) emanating from employers: the increase in wages with age, in part due to the role played by the seniority bonus remains a very widespread phenomenon in France. The European Commission Study (2003, chapter 3, table 32), which consists in regressing for each member country, the wage by sector on work productivity, finds France is the only country where there is a positive correlation between the level of wages and the proportion of old-aged workers in the workforce. Crépon and alii (2003), measuring the difference between productivity and wage in France, find all levels of education aggregated, old-aged workers are more paid than their work productivity. This result could explain why French firms use massively the early retirement schemes as a means to cut payrolls. Surprisingly, it is in firms that use the most early retirement schemes the demand from workers for these programs is the highest... (Alexandre- Bailly and alii, 2004).
7.  This obligation enclosed however a few exceptions: artists, persons having activities related to literature and science when held occasionally, members of academic jury, legal consultants when, again, done sporadically. An agreement of 1984 introduced few changes: it exempted "activities of little importance" from the general obligation of interrupting work: the exiting for retirement did not apply to wage earners receiving the equivalent of less than a third of the annual minimum wage. Finally, it is excepted personal services which could not be interrupted without engendering negative externalities: nannies and children related occupations, housekeepers, home helps for the elderly, the invalid and for the handicapped people.
8.  The complementary regime (régime complémentaire) of trades persons and industrial workers did not allow to combine the complementary pension benefit with wage even though the occupation differed from the former one; self-employed workers (doctors, lawyers, nurses) had to fully retire with a few exceptions possible though in the medical environment for (marginal activities), drawing the complementary pension with wage at the same time being however capped.
9.  The break in career for children and the question of family advantages included in the pension benefit is developed in section 3.
10.  The female aggregated participation rate is the percentage of women in the Labor Force among all women of working age (between fifteen to sixty-five-years-old). Unlike what is commonly thought, this indicator did not show any spectacular trend: it remained stable around a declining trend between 1950 (50 percent) and 1970 (45 percent), rose slightly there after and reached 60 percent at the end of the century. In fact, this relative stability seen over the cycle is understood when looking at the female participation rate by age. Female participation rate of young women dropped considerably over the last century and the same is observed for young men.

The increase of female participation rate concerns only intermediary ages: the participation rate doubled among thirty-year-old women between 1950 and 2000, the decrease of participation rates at extreme ages offsetting this phenomenon.

11. The model Destinie of INSEE allows to make simulation until 2040 of economic and demographic development (labor market, wages, pension) of a population of 50,000 individuals ending their career in the private and public sector, self-employed included. The studies mentioned make the same following assumptions: stability to its 1990 level of the percentage part-time jobs in the total until 2040; an unchanged distribution of part-time jobs among men and women. All else being equal, a relaxation of these strong assumptions leads to accentuate the gap in pension benefits among men and women.

It is worth mentioning two other models not referred to in this article: the model ARIANE of the Division of the Budget (from the Ministry of Economy and Finance), related to the pension system in the public sector; the model MARS of the Division of Social Security which makes forecast of the accounts of the basic general scheme (Régime Général).

12. These data come from the exploitation of the survey Enquête Budget de Familles (1995), from the sample of retired people of all regimes (Echantillon interrégimes de retraités), from the annual statements of social data (Déclarations annuelles des Données Sociales), from the file on the payrolls of the civil servants ( Fichier de Paie de la Fonction Publique).

# References

Alexandre-Bailly F., Gautié J., Guillemard A.M., Jolivet A. (dir.), (2004), Gestion des âges et rapports intergénérationnels dans les grandes entreprises: études de cas, Rapport Commissariat Général du Plan – DARES – Ministère de la Recherche, juin.

Anderson P., Gustman M., Steinmeier A.L. and T.L. (1997), *Trends in Male Labor Force Participation and Retirement: Some Evidence on the Role of Pensions and Social Security in the 1970s and the 1980s.* NBER WP6208.

Bardaji J., Sédillot B., Walraet E., (2001), Evaluation de trois réformes du régime général d'assurance vieillesse à l'aide du modèle de microsimulation Destinie, *Document de travail Insee*, G2002/07, 38p.

Blanchet D., Mahieu R., (1999), *Une analyse microéconométrique des comportements de retrait d'activité*, miméo.

Blanchet D., Pelé L.P. (1999), Social Security and Retirement in France in *Social Security and Retirement all Around the World*, NBER/The University of Chicago Press.

Blöndal S., Scarpetta S., (1998), *The Retirement Behavior in OECD Countries*, OECD Economics Department Working Papers no. 202.

Bommier A., (2002), Les choix de départ en retraite: une affaire de famille, *Economie et Statistique*, no. 357-358, pp99-102.

Bommier A., Magnac T., Roger M., (2001) Quels sont les effets des modifications des systèmes de retraite sur les taux d'activité des travailleurs âgés?, *Revue Française d'Economie*, vol 16, pp79-124.

Bonnet C., Buffeteau S., Godefroy P., (2004), Retraite: vers moins d'inégalités entre hommes et femmes?, *Population et Sociétés*, no. 401, mai.

Bonnet C., Colin C., (2003), Les retraites des femmes: situation actuelle et perspective, *Travail, Genre et sociétés*, no. 9, pp. 226-233.

Börsch-Supan A., (1998), *Incentive Effects of the Social Security on Labor Force Participation: Evidence in Germany and Across Europe.* NBER WP7339.

Boulanger J.M. (2003), Cumul emploi retraite, rapport remis au Conseil d'Orientation des retraites, mars.

Bruce D., Holtz-Eakin D., Quinn J.F., (2000), *Self-Employment and Labor Market Transitions At Older Ages.* Chestnut Hill, MA: Center for Retirement Research at Boston College.

Burricand C., Roth N., (2000), Les parcours de fin de carrière des générations 1912-1941: l'impact du cadre institutionnel, *Economie et Statistique*, n°335, pp63-79.

Charpin J.M. and alii (1999), *L'avenir de nos retraites*, La documentation française.

Coëffic N. (2003), L'âge de liquidation de la génération 1934, *Etudes et Résultats*, n°237, Insee.

Coëffic N. (2002), Les montants des retraites perçues en 2001, *Etudes et Résultats*, n°183, Insee.

Coëffic N. (1999), Le cumul emploi – retraite, *Etudes et Résultats*, n°14, avril, DREES.

Colin C., Mette C., (2002), Impact des différents aléas de carrière sur les pensions de retraite: inactivité, chômage, travail à temps partiel, Retraite et Société, n°40, pp22-51.

Conseil d'Orientation des Retraites (COR), (2004) Retraites: les réformes en France et à l'étranger, le droit à l'information, deuxième rapport.

Crépon B., Deniau N., Perez-Duarte S., (2003), Productivité et salaire des travailleurs âgés, *Revue Française d'Economie*, vol. 18, n°1, pp 157-185.

Dupeyroux J.J., (2000), *Droit de la sécurité sociale*, Dalloz, 9ème ed.

Eeschtruth A.D., Gemus J., (2002), Are Older Workers Responding To The Bear Market? *Just The Facts On Retirement Issues* CRR, September (5).

Gazier B., Schmidt G., (2002), The dynamics of full- employment. Social Integration by Transitional Labor Markets, Cheltenham, Edward Elgar.

Gautié J., (2004), Les marchés internes du travail, de l'emploi et les salaires, *Revue Française d'Economie,* vol. 18, n°4, pp33-63.

Gautié J., (2003), Les travailleurs âgés face à l'emploi, *Economie et statistique*, n°368, pp33-42.

Gruber J., Wise D.A., (1999), *Social Security and Retirement Around The World*, NBER: New York.

Guillemard E.M., (2003), *L'âge de l'emploi*, Armand Colin.

Herz D.E., (1995), Work after Retirement: An Increasing Trend Among Men, *Monthly Labor Review*, 118(4), pp 13-20.

Lanquetin M.T., (2003), Femmes et retraites, *Travail, Genre et sociétés*, n°9, pp234-239.

Lanquetin M-T., Letablier M-T., Périvier H., (2004) « Acquisition des droits sociaux et égalité entre les femmes et les hommes », Revue de l'OFCE, juillet n°90, pp 461-488.

Leseman F., Beausoleil J., (2004), Les emplois «post- carrière » aux Etats-Unis: un bilan des connaissances, Retraite et Sociétés, No 42, La documentation Française.

Mahieu R., Walraet E., (2002), Simulating Retirement Behavior: The Case of France, NBER, november.

Majnoni d'Intignano B.(dir.), (1999), Egalité entre hommes et femmes: aspects économiques, Rapport du Conseil d'Analyse Economique.

Marchand O., Mini C., Thélot C., (1998): La durée d'une vie de travail, une question de génération?, *Premières synthèses*, DARES, 12-N50.2.

Meurs D., Ponthieux S., (1999), Emploi et salaires: les inégalités entre hommes et femmes en mars 1998, *Premières synthèses*, 99.08 – n° 335.

Miniaci R., (1998), Microeconometric Analysis of the Retirement Decision: Italy. OECD Economics Department Working Papers n°205.

OCDE (2003), Perspectives de l'emploi

OCDE (2004), Perspectives de l'emploi

Pelé L.P., Ralle P., (1998), Vers un âge de la retraite plus élevé?, *Insee Première*, 578.

Pelé L.P., Ralle P., (1999), Les choix de l'âge de la retraite: aspects incitatifs des règles du régime général et effets de la réforme de 1993, *Economie et prévision*, N° 138-139.

Quinn J., Burkhauser R., Cahill K., Weathers R., (1998), Microeconometric Analysis of the Retirement Decision: United States. OECD Economics Department Working Papers n°203.

Rix S.E. (2001), Restructuring Work in an Aging America: What Role For Public Policy, in Marshall, Heinz, Kruger, and Verma (eds), *Restructuring Work and The Life Course* (pp 375-396). Toronto: University of Toronto Press.

Rust J., Phelan C., (1997), How Social Security and Medicare Affect Retirement Behavior in a World of Incomplete Markets, *Econometrica,* 65, pp 781-831.

Sédillot B., Walraet E., (2002), La cessation d'activité au sein des couples: y a-t-il interdépendance des choix?, *Economie et Statistique*, N° 357-358, pp79-98.

Sterdyniak H., (2004) Contre l'individualisation des droits sociaux, Revue de l'OFCE, juillet n°90, pp 419-460.

Stock J., Wise D., (1990), Pensions, the Option Value of Work and Retirement, *Econometrica*, 58, pp 1151-1180.

Zaidman C., (1998), L'individualisation des droits réduirait-elle les inégalités hommes/femmes, *Droit social*, N°6, juin, pp 590-595.

# 6

# Pension Reforms and Gender:
# The Case of Sweden

*Ann-Charlotte Ståhlberg, Marcela Cohen Birman,*
*Agneta Kruse and Annika Sundén*

## Introduction

Sweden, like most other industrialized countries, has an aging population. This is caused by decreases in fertility as well as increases in life expectancy. Table 6.1 shows the percentage of the population over sixty-five and eighty-years-old.

**Table 6.1**
**The Share of the Population Sixty-Five Plus and Eighty Plus, Percent**

| Year | 65+ | 80+ |
|------|-----|-----|
| 1975 | 15.1 | 2.7 |
| 2000 | 17.3 | 5.0 |
| 2015 | 21.4 | 5.7 |
| 2030 | 25.1 | 8.6 |

*Source*: An Aging World 2001

In 2000, the share of sixty-five plus is 17.3 percent and will increase to 25.1 percent in the year 2030. The share of people eighty plus increases from 5.0 to 8.6 percent between 2000 and 2030.

The labor force participation rate in the age groups from sixteen to sixty-four has decreased from 87.0 to 79.8 for men and from 82.6 to 76.1 for women between 1990 and 2002. This is shown in table 6.2. The decrease is especially pronounced among those approaching retirement, in the age group fifty-five to sixty-four. The decrease is less pronounced among women than among men. As a result, retirement age has been decreasing.

Table 6.2
Labor Force Participation Rate in 1990 and 2002

| Age | 1990 Men | Women | 2002 Men | Women |
|---|---|---|---|---|
| 55-59 | 87.4 | 78.8 | 83.9 | 79.1 |
| 60 | 74.2 | 69.0 | 73.7 | 70.3 |
| 61 | 70.9 | 62.2 | 67.3 | 63.1 |
| 62 | 65.9 | 54.5 | 60.7 | 55.4 |
| 63 | 58.0 | 46.7 | 51.2 | 42.5 |
| 64 | 48.8 | 37.3 | 43.7 | 31.7 |
| 16-64 | 87.0 | 82.6 | 79.8 | 76.1 |

*Source:* SCB, AKU

Aging, together with declines in the labor force participation rates, will cause financial pressures in the future. Although the recent pension reform has created a pension system that should be financially sustainable, the described demographic development will provide challenges. For example, expenditures for health care and old age care will increase. Also, annual pension benefits may become lower as a result of increases in longevity. One solution is to increase labor supply. Increased labor force participation and hours of work would lead to a lesser burden for those of active age. Measures for increasing female labor force participation and working hours might be an option.

In 1998, the pension system in Sweden was changed from a defined benefit system to mainly a notional defined contribution system. The purpose of this study is to analyze the effects of the pension reform for men and women by comparing the outcomes in the system after reform to the outcomes in the old system. We also study the incentive effects on labor supply. However, labor supply is also influenced by the rules for early retirement, other social insurance programs (e.g. sickness insurance and unemployment insurance), negotiated collective agreements and seniority rules in the labor market. Therefore, we briefly examine these areas in order to spot "system errors" vis-à-vis labor supply effects.

The chapter is organized as follows: In the next section we give a description of the old and the new old age pension systems and analyze the incentive effects. The analysis is conducted with a gender perspective. We then briefly describe James et al.'s (2003) estimates of the gender effects of the pension reforms in Chile, Argentina and Mexico. Following this, we add to James et al.'s assessments of the gender effects by providing estimates of the Swedish reform. We use a simulation model to compare women's pension benefits and contributions to men's in the new Swedish system and in the old. The analysis includes simulating the wage and employment histories of representative men and women and the pension benefits these are likely to generate under the old and new rules. After showing the results of this model, we describe and discuss the supplementary pension systems, that is, the negotiated collective agreement schemes and different pathways to retirement. Based on empirical evidence from Swedish and Latin America simulated data, the final section discusses gender impact of pension rules and how to design pension systems to ensure adequate pension benefits for both women and men.

### The Swedish Pension System: A Gender Perspective

Retirement income in Sweden comes mainly from two sources: public national pensions covering all individuals, and occupational pensions building on collective bargaining agreements and cover practically all employees. There are four main schemes: one for private sector white-collar workers, one for private sector blue-collar workers, one for state employees and one for local authority and county council employees. The occupational pensions are, in particular, important to high earners because most of the plans replace earnings above the ceiling in the national scheme.

In 1998, Sweden passed pension legislation replacing the public defined benefit scheme with a notional defined contribution plan. In addition, a second tier of funded benefits was established. The reformed pension system went into effect in 1999 with the first benefit payments in 2003. During a transition period, benefits will be paid both from the old and the new systems. Also most of the occupational pension systems have been fundamentally changed in recent years. Three of Sweden's four collective-agreement pension schemes have followed the path taken by the public pension and have been changed from defined benefit to defined contribution. It is only the private sector white-collar workers who have kept the main part of their pensions defined benefit.

The old public old age pension system consisted of a portion independent of income (national basic pension), a special pension-tested supplement to those with a low or no ATP and a portion tied to earnings (ATP). Normally the basic pension and ATP combined made up about 60 percent of a person's fifteen years of highest earnings up to a ceiling. Thiry years of labor force participation was required for full pension. The normal retirement age was sixty-five but benefits could be withdrawn from age sixty or postponed until age seventy, with actuarial adjustments. The system was financed by a payroll tax in principle on a pay-as-you-go basis, although the financing of the basic flat pension was supplemented by general tax revenues. Negotiated collective agreement pensions provided a further 10 to 15 percent of final salary.

The reformed pension system is a defined contribution system financed primarily on a pay-as-you-go basis (notional defined contribution) but with a small funded component. The contribution rate is 18.5 percent: 16 percent of earnings will be credited to the notional account and 2.5 percent will be contributed to a self-directed individual account (the premium pension). Pension rights are credited from age sixteen and for every year individuals have income earning pension rights. Hence, lifetime contributions will determine benefits. Individuals earn pension rights from labor income as well as from income from transfers, such as parental leave benefits, unemployment insurance and sickness benefit insurance. Individuals also earn complementary pension rights for having young children. Parents with young children are apportioned a fictive pension-based income according to one of three options, from which the custodian, who can be either the mother or the father, may choose the one most advantageous to him or her. There is no requirement to give up paid work in order to receive the subsidy. Credits for having children are paid until the youngest child is four-years-old, with a maximum of four years per child.

The rate of return on the notional accounts is determined by average wage growth. Using average wage growth introduces a possible instability in the system. For example, if the work force decreases, benefit and pension rights will grow faster than the contributions base from which benefits are paid. In order to deal with this possible instability, an automatic balancing mechanism is built into the system reducing the indexation of earned pension rights and the outgoing pensions if the system faces a deficit.

In the self-directed accounts, the rate of return is determined by the investment allocation. Participants have more than 600 funds to choose from, most of them equity funds. For individuals who do not want to pick their own investments, the government provides a default option. The premium pension allows married individuals to transfer pension rights between spouses. This means, for example, if one spouse has low earnings while the other has high earnings, the spouses could equalize expected pension benefits by transferring credits from the high-income spouse to the low-income spouse.

Retirement age is flexible and benefits can be withdrawn from age sixty-one. At retirement, annual benefits are calculated by dividing the balance in the notional account by an annuity divisor. The divisor is determined by average life expectancy at retirement for a given cohort and an imputed real rate of return of 1.6 percent. Since the annual pension benefit is equal to the net present value of benefits using a real interest rate of 1.6, the initial benefit at retirement is higher than if benefits were adjusted for economic growth each year. The divisor is the same for men and women. Benefits are price indexed plus/minus the deviation from this 1.6 percent growth norm. The account balance in the premium pension will be converted to either a fixed or a variable annuity using standard insurance practices. This annuity is nominal and not indexed for inflation.

In addition to the earnings-related benefits, the pension system also includes a guaranteed minimum pension, currently equal to approximately 40 percent of an average industrial workers wage before tax. This benefit is pension-tested and is payable from age sixty-five. The guarantee pension is only offset by the earnings-related benefit in the national scheme; at low levels of earnings-related benefits, the offset is one-for-one and then declines. Individuals without any earnings-related benefit are eligible for the full guaranteed benefit.

The public pension reform was motivated by a severe long-term financing deficit, however several other problems were present in the old system. The system was sensitive to changes in economic growth because benefits, as well as earned pension rights, were indexed to follow prices rather than wages. There was no link between the pensioners' pensions and the wages of the current working population. All adaptations to changes in demographic and economic contexts were effected by means of changes in the rate of pension contributions; that is, the adaptation was laid in its entirety on the section of the gainfully employed population. The scope pensioners had for consumption was fixed, no matter what happened to the economy. In "lean" years pensioners' living standard rose relative to that of the working population, whereas in "fat" years the reverse was the case. The new system is intended to change this. The working population is to be relieved of some of the pressure through the introduction of wage-indexing.

In the old pension system, the working population took on all of the increased costs resulting from increased life expectancy. Because of its defined-benefit pay-as-you-go design, a rise in expenditure on pensions had to be matched by increased contribution rates. Under the new scheme, it is the pensioners themselves who bear the cost resulting from increasing life expectancy, since the individual's accumulated capital, up to retirement, is divided by the number of years a particular age group is expected to have left to live.

With wage growth a large proportion of the pensioners in the old ATP would have pensions limited by the ceiling. The ATP would cease to function according to the principle of compensation for loss of income and would, instead, function as an augmented national basic pension. This was not originally intended. In the new pension the ceiling automatically increases with the growth in real wages.

In the old ATP pension, there was no systematic redistribution between higher and lower wage earners but there was redistribution between people with a long working life but weak real wage growth over time, and people with a relatively short working life with unevenly distributed lifetime incomes. This was one consequence of ATP's fifteen- and thirty-year rules. Those who had their (covered) income distributed unevenly over their life (often intermediate level white-collar workers and also senior white-collar workers whose income did not exceed the ceiling) received a much higher ATP pension if it was calculated on the basis of their fifteen "best years" than they would have if it were calculated on the basis of their entire life cycle income. By contrast, pensions for those with a flat (covered) life cycle income (often lower level white-collar workers and blue-collar workers) did not increase more with the fifteen-year rule than they would without it. Thus, since the pension contribution was proportional to the life cycle wage, blue-collar workers and lower level white-collar workers paid more for their pensions than intermediate-level and senior white-collar workers did (Ståhlberg 1989, 1990).

The new system was designed to address this. In principle, it will not redistribute income other than over individual life cycles. However, there are exceptions. For example, parents of small children are awarded "free" pension rights during their children's infancy.

It is often thought the design of the Swedish national earnings-related system (the ATP system) prior to the 1999 reform was more favorable to women than to men. The fact this pension was determined by the fifteen best-paid years and thirty years were enough to qualify for a full pension, while pension contributions were proportional to earnings in all years, may, to a certain degree. have compensated women for the years they spent at home. But these rules are also to the advantage of those who gained promotions and had successful careers, that is, often men. The ATP-ceiling on pensionable earnings, on the other hand, is favorable to low-income earners and the special pension supplement is advantageous to those who have low or no ATP. The situation is such the rules can work in a contradictory fashion from the point of view of redistribution. Consequently, only empirical studies can reveal the true pattern of redistribution.

How ATP pensions systematically redistributed income between women and men born between 1944 and 1950 has been studied in Ståhlberg (1990, 1995).[1] In these studies, pension benefits and contributions were calculated for each individual in the population sample on the basis of his or her actual and estimated life cycle income. It was found the average ratio between expected lifetime benefits and lifetime contributions was higher for men as a group than for women as a group. However, female senior white-collar workers have the highest ratio because they often couple a relatively short professionally active life with relatively good income. The reverse is true for female unskilled blue-collar workers who derive the  least benefit from their contributions to the earnings-related scheme because they work for many years and have a weak wage progression. This is shown in table 6.3.

When we combine ATP and the national basic pension, no group among women is at a disadvantage (see table 6.3). This is due to the progressiveness of the national basic pension system.

Table 6.3

**The ratio of present value of expected lifetime benefits/lifetime contributions of women and the present value of expected lifetime benefits/lifetime contributions of men for five socio-economic groups in the Swedish national pension prior to the 1999 reform**

| Socio-economic group | (B/C for women)/ (B/C for men) | (B/C for women)/ (B/C for men) |
|---|---|---|
| | The earnings-related pension (ATP) | The earnings-related pension (ATP) and the basic pension |
| Senior white-collar workers | 1.26 | 1.45 |
| Intermediate level white-collar workers | 1.00 | 1.30 |
| Lower level white-collar workers | 0.87 | 1.29 |
| Skilled blue-collar workers | 0.96 | 1.34 |
| Unskilled blue-collar workers | 0.83 | 1.28 |
| All | 0.94 | 1.35 |

*Source*: Ståhlberg (1995)

The tight connection between contributions and benefits in the new system increases work incentives compared to the old one. As every Swedish crown paid in contributions gives rise to a corresponding increase in expected benefits, market work is encouraged from early age and beyond.

One exception to the tight connection between contributions and benefits is the child credits. However, these are not restricted in the sense the parent has to abstain from market work. The credit is paid also when the parent continues to work in the labor market. This, again, is an increase in work incentives compared to the old system which subsidized all kinds of non-market activities whether the time was spent caring for infants, healthy husbands or doing some other activity. Two other exceptions are the guarantee pension and the contributions paid on income above the ceiling without giving any benefits. The first one may reduce labor supply incentives in the lower part of the income scale, while the second one may do so among high-income earners.

## Pension Reforms and Gender Issues in James et al. 2003

The pension systems of a number of countries have been reformed during the past twenty years, including in Latin America, in what was previously the Eastern Bloc and in a number of OECD countries. These countries have chosen different designs of their respective systems. James et al. (2003) estimated the gender effects of the pension reforms in Chile, Argentina and Mexico and also discussed conceivable effects of the pension reforms in Australia as well as in the transitional economies of Poland, Kazakhstan and Latvia. What is the relationship between women's and men's pensions in the new as compared to the old systems—e.g., in regards to monthly benefits and total pension benefits over one's lifetime? What is the relation between the ratio of expected lifetime pension benefits and lifetime pension contributions for women as compared to men? What are the effects of women's incentives compared to men's? Which rules play a key role from the point of view of gender? This section summarizes some of the results in James et al. (2003).

The old pension systems in Chile, Argentina and Mexico were benefit defined pay-as-you-go. Pension benefits were determined by the wages or salaries received during final working years together with the number of years worked. The new pension systems are defined contribution funded systems with individual accounts. In addition, Chile has a guaranteed minimum pension (MPG), Mexico a "social quota" (plus a minimum-guarantee) and Argentina a flat benefit pension. In the old systems married women received a tax-financed widow's pension. In Chile, it was 50 percent of the husband's pension, in Argentina 75 percent and in Mexico 90 percent. In Chile and Argentina women had to relinquish their own pensions when they received a widow's pension. In the new systems, married men pay for a joint annuity (or joint withdrawal), and the widow can retain her own pension while receiving widow's pension.

*Chile*

The old system was a defined benefit one. The pension was determined by wages or salary over the last five working years. Less than ten working years provided no pension. Twenty years' work guaranteed a minimum pension. Widows received 50 percent of their husband's pensions, but at the same time had to relinquish their own pensions. Men could retire at sixty-five, women at sixty with no actuarial penalty.

The new system is a defined contribution with individual accounts plus a guaranteed minimum pension (MPG). The obligatory pension premium is 10 percent of earnings (plus about 3 percent for administrative fees and premiums for disability and survivors insurance).[2] Those who have worked at least twenty years are guaranteed a tax-financed minimum pension (MPG) which is tested against their earnings-related pensions. In 1994 the MPG corresponded to 27 percent of the average wage/salary for men, 37 percent for women and 125 percent of the poverty line. Poor elderly persons who are not qualified for pension receive in the new system social allowances (PASIS), which correspond to about half of the MPG. Married men have to purchase a joint annuity (or joint withdrawal) providing the widow with a pension that is at least 60 percent of her husband's. A woman cannot do the same with respect to her husband unless he is disabled. The widow can receive her widow's pension as well as her own pension.

As may be expected when it comes to earnings-related pensions, women's pensions are lower than men's. But the pension gap is reduced with the MPG and joint annuities (or joint withdrawals). The MPG allows redistribution from higher income earners to lower, while joint annuities/withdrawals allow redistribution within the family. The new defined contribution system contains incentives encouraging women to work outside the home. For low-paid women, the MPG carries a negative incentive to work after twenty years and an incentive to take an early pension.

Women and men with little education gain the most from the reform. They have a flat wage profile and begin to work early in life, while the highly educated have a steep wage profile with high final salaries which was an advantage in the old system. Single men benefit relative to married men in the new system as compared to the old. In the old system unmarried men (and women) had to contribute to widow pensions while in the new system married men themselves pay for their wives' widow pensions. The position of married, as compared to unmarried women, is improved in the new system. In the old system married women could not retain their own pensions while receiving widow's pensions while now they can.

*Argentina*

The old system was defined benefit and pay-as-you-go. It was highly fragmented, distinguishing between the public and private sectors and between different occupations within each sector. James et al. (2003a, 2003b) describe the largest pension plan in the private sector. Before the reform it was very similar to the old Chilean system. Employees with twenty or more years of contribution received 70 percent of their "basic wage" plus an extra 1 percent for each year over thirty. The basic wage was defined as that of the three best of the last ten years. Men retired at sixty, women at fifty-five. Those who had only worked for ten years received 50 percent of their basic wage plus an extra 1 percent for every year over ten, and were retired at agesixty-five. There was no automatic price- or wage-indexing, which in practice made the pensions less generous.

The new system has as its first pillar a flat benefit that is paid to men when they turn sixty-five and to women when they reach sixty. In order to qualify, thirty years of contribution are required—which excludes most women. But anyone who has turned seventy and has contributed for ten years receives 70 percent of the full amount. Widows receive 70 percent of men's flat benefit. The amount received is neither price- nor wage-indexed. The flat benefit in 1994 corresponded to 30 percent of the average wage for men, 45 percent for women and 130 percent of the poverty line. The incentives for women to work in the formal sector are strong the first ten years, but weak after that.

The second pillar is either similar to Chile's or is defined benefit and earnings related. Employers can choose either of the two. In 2001, 80 percent of employees, including most women, belonged to the defined contribution system with individual accounts. 7.75 percent of the wage is invested (administrative fees and survivors and disability insurance fees are 3.25 percent of the wage[3]). The retirement age is sixty-five for men and sixty for women. Married men and women must have a joint annuity. The widows/widowers pension is 70 percent of the pension of the deceased. In the new system the widow retains her own pension while receiving her widow's pension.

The Argentinean system provides a strong subsidy to women who only work for ten years. They receive a return on their pension contributions higher than that of any other group. The estimates in James et al. (2003a, 2003b) show women gained from the pension reform in comparison to men, despite the fact many rules in the old system already benefited women—a high level of compensation for only ten years' work, a minimum pension and an early retirement age. The result depends on the levelling-out effect of a flat benefit on the transference within the family as a result of joint annuity, and by the fact that women do not have to relinquish their own pensions when they receive widow's pension. That early pension contributions have greater weight in the new system is also of significance.

## Mexico

The James et al. (2003a, 2003b) estimates concern the pension reform in Mexico's private sector. The old system was defined benefit. Just as in Chile and Argentina, ten years' pension contributions sufficed to qualify a person for pension. The rules were such the incentives were strong for low-wage earners to work in the formal sector for ten years and then move over to the informal sector. Those who had career salaries benefited from their pension's being determined on the basis of their last five years' salary. There was a minimum pension that was as large as the minimum wage. The widow received 90 percent of her husband's pension while also receiving her own pension. The retirement age was sixty-five for both men and women, and there was no indexing.

The new system has two pillars. The first is, as in Chile and Argentina, directed towards low-wage earners. However, it is distinct from these two countries in it encourages work in the formal sector. Those who work more receive more. What is termed the "social quota" (SQ) is a flat benefit per day worked. It was initially set at 5.5 percent of the minimum wage, which corresponded to 2.2 percent of the average wage, and is price-indexed. The state guarantees a minimum pension (MPG) which was originally on a level with the minimum wage (which was 33 percent of men's average wage and 46 percent of women's). It is price-indexed; twenty-five years' of work is required to qualify for MPG, which excludes many women.

The second pillar is defined contribution. 4.6 percent of the wage/salary (administrative costs are 1.9 percent[4]) is invested in individual accounts. Both men and women are pensioned at sixty-five. Married men and women must purchase a joint annuity providing the widow/widower with 60 percent of their own old-age pension in the event of death.

What mainly distinguishes the Mexican pension system from that of Chile and Argentina is Mexico's SQ. It is a flat benefit directed to those who have low incomes due to low hourly wages, as opposed to a low level of participation in the workforce.

When the link between payroll contributions and benefits was tightened, women in Chile, Argentina and Mexico began to receive a lower defined contribution pension than men. Women have lower wages, spend less time in the labor force and often retire earlier than men. However, female/male ratios of lifetime benefits in the new systems exceed those in the old systems in all three countries. Intra-household transfers from husband to wife in the form of joint annuities play the largest role. Women who work no longer have to give up their own annuity to get the widows' pension as they did in some old systems. In the new system women have a higher return on their pension contributions than do men. This is due partly to the minimum pension directed to low-wage earners and partly to the joint annuity.

In the following section we add our own estimates of the Swedish pension reform to the assessments of the gender effects in James et al.

## A Simulation of Women's Pension Benefits and Contributions in Sweden

In order to examine the effects of the Swedish reform we simulate the wage and employment histories of representative men and women, and the pension benefits and contributions these are likely to generate under the new and old rules. The following hypotheses follow from the previous pension descriptions:

In the old pension system:

- The fifteen- and thirty-year rules redistribute income from those who have long professionally active lives and weak real wage growth over time to those who have their covered income spread unevenly over their lives and do not work for so many years.
- The ceiling (indexed by prices) on benefits but not on contributions redistribute income from those who have income above the ceiling to those who have income below the ceiling (that is, from men as a group to women as a group).
- The life expectancy of women is higher than that of men. The pension system relies on "unisex" life tables and redistributes income in favor of women.
- The (uniform) basic pension including the special (pension-tested) supplement redistributes income from those who have high incomes during their years of paid work to those who have low incomes (that is, from men as a group to women as a group).

In the new pension system:

- No income is redistributed in a pure defined contribution system.
- Fictive pension rights for those who have young children are, in practice, in favor of women.
- The ceiling (indexed by wages) on benefits but not on contributions redistribute income from those who have income above the ceiling to those who have income below the ceiling (that is, from men as a group

to women as a group). However above the ceiling only half of the contributions are paid.

- The life expectancy of women is higher than that of men. The pension system relies on "unisex" life tables and redistributes income in favor of women.
- The (pension-tested) guarantee pension redistributes income from those who have high incomes during their years of paid work to those who have low incomes (that is, from men as a group to women as a group).

In order to illustrate how the Swedish pension system affects women's pension benefits, we calculate benefits for groups of "typical" women. In constructing the groups, we build on James et al. (2003a, 2003b). The purpose of these groups is to illustrate how different women fare under the system. The groups are chosen so that they represent a majority of women. The groups include:

- Full career woman: same labor force participation and retirement age as men—works full-time for most or all of her career.
- Full time/Part-time woman: working full-time until having children, alternates between parental leave and part-time as long as the children are young and then goes back to full time work.
- ten-year woman: participate in the labor force during ten years early in life, before marriage and birth of children.[5]
- Part-time woman: women who work part-time for most of their careers.

For each case, a wage profile is constructed using earnings data for five levels of education: no upper secondary school, upper secondary school, undergraduate education two years or less, undergraduate education more than two years and postgraduate education. For women with children we calculate benefits in one scenario when she has children early and one scenario when she has children late (not shown as the results turned out to be very similar to "children early"). In each case, she has two children and stays home for a full year collecting parental benefits. Details on the construction of the earnings profile are discussed in the Appendix (and earnings-profiles are illustrated).

Pension benefits are calculated for the new system as well as the old system. Comparisons of the new and old pension systems are problematic as the old system was unable to disburse future benefits and, therefore, could not be sustained. We do not know what adjustments would have been made to make the old system solvent (for example higher contributions or lower benefits). Therefore it is impossible to determine absolute gains or losses from the change into the new system. To avoid this problem we calculate relative changes in the position of men and women in different groups. We study different female earnings profiles compared to the earnings of full career men. Did the reform result in a larger or smaller gender ratio?[6]

Another important fact is in the old system the ceiling was indexed by prices. We have used a scenario with an annual growth rate of 1.8 percent. The consequence of this is, particularly among full career men and highly-educated women, the ceiling quickly becomes effective, putting a cap on the benefits, that is, the system turns into an augmented basic one and the benefits no longer compensate in relation to loss of income. With the ceiling effective, the system is more progressive than without an effective ceiling, that is, the old system seems to favor women as a group more than if the ceiling was not effective. Thus, we can not expect the kind of outcome shown in table 6.3.

Our measures are:

1)  Replacement rates calculated as the annual benefit as a percent of final salary
2)   annual own annuities
3)  lifetime annuities (women live longer than men)
4)  ratio of present value of expected lifetime benefits/lifetime contributions

In all these measures we calculate the ratio between women old (new) system / full career men old (new) system. A gender ratio of 1 means that men and women have the same replacement rate, annual annuities etc. A gender ratio greater (smaller) than 1 means that women have a higher (lower) replacement ratio, higher annual annuities etc. than men.

*Results*

Replacement rates and rates of return

Table 6.4 presents replacement rates calculated as *the annual benefit as a percent of final salary* for the four typical earnings profiles. For each typical case, the replacement rate is presented for the five education levels in the new system.

The results show for women with upper secondary school and less education, replacement rates vary between 45 and 51 percent for all earnings profiles except for the ten-year woman. The woman who alternates between full-time and part-time work have slightly lower replacement rates. The ten-year woman receives guarantee pension benefit in all cases and because of her lower earnings she receives a

Table 6.4

**Replacement Rates in the Reformed Swedish Pension System for Four Typical Earnings Profiles. Replacement Rate is Calculated as Annual Benefit as a Percent of Final Salary.**

A. Full Career

|  | Men | Women |
|---|---|---|
| No upper secondary school | 49 | 50 |
| Upper secondary school | 42 | 47 |
| Undergraduate education  2 years | 45 | 45 |
| Undergraduate education > 2 years | 36 | 44 |
| Postgraduate education | 28 | 34 |

B. Full-time/Part-time Woman

|  |  |
|---|---|
| No upper secondary school | 48 |
| Upper secondary school | 45 |
| Undergraduate education  2 years | 43 |
| Undergraduate education > 2 years | 42 |
| Postgraduate education | - |

C. 10-year Woman

|  |  |
|---|---|
| No upper secondary school | 71* |
| Upper secondary school | 55* |
| Undergraduate education  2 years | 55* |
| Undergraduate education > 2 years | 51* |
| Postgraduate education | 40* |

* guarantee pension

D. Part-time Woman

|  |  |
|---|---|
| No upper secondary school | 51 |
| Upper secondary school | 49 |
| Undergraduate education  2 years | 47 |
| Undergraduate education > 2 years | 45 |
| Postgraduate education | - |

higher replacement rate. For full career women with undergraduate education, replacement rates are around 45 percent. The replacement rate for full career women with postgraduate degrees is 34 percent with the lower replacement rate being explained by their higher earnings; their benefits are, therefore, restricted by the ceiling.

Women's replacement rates are fairly similar to those of men. In general, men have higher earnings and, therefore, reach the ceiling in more cases than women, which explains their somewhat lower replacement rates.

In table 6.5 the ratio of the replacement rates, calculated as in table 6.1, are shown for four typical earnings profiles. The gender ratio decreases in the new system compared to the old one. In almost all cases the ratio is still above 1, that is, women still have a higher replacement ratio than men. Again, this is due to the ceiling being effective in more cases for men than for women. When it comes to women working only ten years however, the ratio increases in all cases but for those with highest education. These women have only the guarantee pension. Concerning full career persons with the highest education, the gender ratio in the new system is the same as in the old one, 1.21.

In table 6.6 the gender ratio of *annual own annuities* in the reformed and the old system is shown for the four typical earnings profiles. In the old system this ratio is close to 1 in full career and full-time/part-time career. In the new system the ratio is less than 1 except for those with the highest education. The ratio varies between 0.8 and 0.9. For women working ten years the gender ratio is rather low, between 0.3 and 0.4. It increases in the new system compared to the old one for low educated women. For women working part-time all their lives the gender ratio decreases with the new system.

When it comes to *lifetime annuities* the gender ratios are higher than for annual own annuities depending on women's higher life span. The ratio of lifetime annuities is shown in table 6.7.

In table 6.8 we compare the *rate of return* ratios in the new and the old system. The rate of return is calculated as the ratio of the present value of expected lifetime benefits and lifetime contributions.[7] The gender ratio is well above 1 in all cases. This goes for both the old and the new system. However it has decreased in the new system. The gender ratio is exceptionally high for ten-year women. In the new system it lies between 3.1 and 3.9. In the old system this ratio varied between 10.8 and 14.8!

Table 6.5

The Ratio of the Replacement Rate in the Reformed and the Old Swedish Pension system for Four Typical Earnings Profiles. Replacement Rate is Calculated as Annual Benefit as a Percent of Final Salary

A. Full Career

|  | Women old system/Men old system | Women new system/Men new system |
|---|---|---|
| No upper secondary school | 1.12 | 1.02 |
| Upper secondary school | 1.33 | 1.12 |
| Undergraduate education  2 years | 1.13 | 1.00 |
| Undergraduate education > 2 years | 1.32 | 1.22 |
| Postgraduate education | 1.21 | 1.21 |

B. Full-time/Part-time Woman

|  | Women old system/Full career men old system | Women new system/Full career men new system |
|---|---|---|
| No upper secondary school | 1.14 | 0.98 |
| Upper secondary school | 1.33 | 1.07 |
| Undergraduate education  2 years | 1.16 | 0.96 |
| Undergraduate education > 2 years | 1.39 | 1.17 |
| Postgraduate education | - | - |

C. 10-year Woman

|  | Women old system/Full career men old system | Women new system/Full career men new system |
|---|---|---|
| No upper secondary school | 1.24 | 1.45 |
| Upper secondary school | 1.20 | 1.31 |
| Undergraduate education  2 years | 1.24 | 1.22 |
| Undergraduate education > 2 years | 1.35 | 1.42 |
| Postgraduate education | 1.54 | 1.43 |

D. Part-time woman

|  | Women old system/Full career men old system | Women new system/Full career men new system |
|---|---|---|
| No upper secondary ŝchool | 1.16 | 1.04 |
| Upper secondary school | 1.33 | 1.17 |
| Undergraduate education  2 years | 1.16 | 1.04 |
| Undergraduate education > 2 years | 1.39 | 1.25 |
| Postgraduate education | - | - |

Table 6.6
The Ratio of Annual Own Annuities in the Reformed and
the Old Swedish Pension System for Four Typical Earnings Profiles

A. Full Career

|  | Women old system/Men old system | Women new system/Men new system |
|---|---|---|
| No upper secondary school | 0.96 | 0.88 |
| Upper secondary school | 0.98 | 0.83 |
| Undergraduate education   2 | 1.00 | 0.88 |
| years | 1.00 | 0.91 |
| Undergraduate education > 2 | 1.00 | 0.99 |
| years Postgraduate education |  |  |

B. Full-time/Part-time Woman

|  | Women old system/Full career men old system | Women new system/Full career men new system |
|---|---|---|
| No upper secondary school | 0.94 | 0.82 |
| Upper secondary school | 0.98 | 0.79 |
| Undergraduate education   2 | 1.00 | 0.84 |
| years | 1.00 | 0.84 |
| Undergraduate education > 2 years Postgraduate education | - | - |

C. 10-year Woman

|  | Women old system/Full career men old system | Women new system/Full career men new system |
|---|---|---|
| No upper secondary school | 0.35 | 0.41 |
| Upper secondary school | 0.37 | 0.40 |
| Undergraduate education   2 | 0.35 | 0.35 |
| years | 0.34 | 0.35 |
| Undergraduate education > 2 years Postgraduate education | 0.42 | 0.40 |

D. Part-time woman

|  | Women old system/Full career men old system | Women new system/Full career men new system |
|---|---|---|
| No upper secondary school | 0.72 | 0.66 |
| Upper secondary school | 0.75 | 0.62 |
| Undergraduate education   2 | 0.93 | 0.66 |
| years | 0.94 | 0.67 |
| Undergraduate education > 2 years Postgraduate education | - | - |

Table 6.7

The Ratio of the Lifetime Annuities in the Reformed and the Old Swedish Pension System for Typical Earnings Profiles

A. Full Career

|  | Women old system/Men old system | Women new system/Men new system |
|---|---|---|
| No upper secondary school | 1.10 | 1.00 |
| Upper secondary school | 1.11 | 0.94 |
| Undergraduate education 2 years | 1.14 | 1.00 |
| Undergraduate education > 2 years | 1.14 | 1.03 |
| Postgraduate education | 1.14 | 1.03 |

B. Full-time/Part-time Woman

|  | Women old system/Full career men old system | Women new system/Full career men new system |
|---|---|---|
| No upper secondary school | 1.07 | 0.93 |
| Upper secondary school | 1.11 | 0.90 |
| Undergraduate education 2 years | 1.14 | 0.95 |
| Undergraduate education > 2 years | 1.14 | 0.95 |
| Postgraduate education | - | - |

C. 10-year Woman, Children

|  | Women old system/Full career men old system | Women new system/Full career men new system |
|---|---|---|
| No upper secondary school | 0.40 | 0.47 |
| Upper secondary school | 0.42 | 0.45 |
| Undergraduate education 2 years | 0.40 | 0.40 |
| Undergraduate education > 2 years | 0.39 | 0.40 |
| Postgraduate education | 0.48 | 0.45 |

D. Part-time woman

|  | Women old system/Full career men old system | Women new system/Full career men new system |
|---|---|---|
| No upper secondary school | 0.82 | 0.75 |
| Upper secondary school | 0.85 | 0.70 |
| Undergraduate education 2 years | 1.05 | 0.75 |
| Undergraduate education > 2 years | 1.07 | 0.76 |
| Postgraduate education | - | - |

Table 6.8

**The Ratio of Present Value of Expected Lifetime Benefits/Lifetime Contributions of Women and the Present Value of Expected Lifetime Benefits/Lifetime Contributions of Full Career Men, in the Reformed and the Old Swedish Pension System for Four Typical Earnings Profiles**

A. Full Career

|  | Women old system/Men old system | Women new system/Men new system |
|---|---|---|
| **No upper secondary school** | 1.27 | 1.16 |
| **Upper secondary school** | 1.41 | 1.15 |
| **Undergraduate education   2 years** | 1.43 | 1.21 |
| **Undergraduate education > 2 years** | 1.54 | 1.28 |
| **Postgraduate education** | 1.54 | 1.28 |

B. Full-time/Part-time Woman

|  | Women old system/Full career men old system | Women new system/Full career men new system |
|---|---|---|
| **No upper secondary school** | 1.31 | 1.18 |
| **Upper secondary school** | 1.44 | 1.17 |
| **Undergraduate education   2 years** | 1.47 | 1.23 |
| **Undergraduate education > 2 years** | 1.47 | 1.23 |
| **Postgraduate education** | - | - |

C. 10-year woman

|  | Women old system/Full career men old system | Women new system/Full career men new system |
|---|---|---|
| **No upper secondary school** | 11.51 | 3.69 |
| **Upper secondary school** | 10.79 | 3.22 |
| **Undergraduate education   2 years** | 13.72 | 3.65 |
| **Undergraduate education > 2 years** | 14.81 | 3.92 |
| **Postgraduate education** | 13.35 | 3.07 |

D. Part-time woman

|  | Women old system/Full career men old system | Women new system/Full career men new system |
|---|---|---|
| **No upper secondary school** | 1.31 | 1.19 |
| **Upper secondary school** | 1.49 | 1.19 |
| **Undergraduate education   2 years** | 1.83 | 1.25 |
| **Undergraduate education > 2 years** | 2.04 | 1.32 |
| **Postgraduate education** | - | - |

As long as the ceiling on covered earnings is ineffective, the best-year rule in the old ATP redistributes from women as a group to men as a group. When effective, the covered lifecycle income pattern becomes more or less flat and consequently more similar between women and men. The regressive effect of the fifteen-year rule will be low or none at all. That explains our different result from the earlier studies in Ståhlberg (1990, 1995).

### Unisex Tables and Child Credits

This section describes the effects of unisex tables and child credits. The distributional effects of unisex tables are high while the child credits have less influence on women's pension amounts. This is shown in table 6.9 and table 6.10.

*Early Exit*

Swedish social insurance schemes are set up as pay-as-you-go systems and are, therefore, sensitive to changes in the factors determining expenditures and the total wage sum. Early exit from the labor force, high absenteeism because of sickness, unemployment (in particular long-term absenteeism) reduce the number of contributors to the system and increase the number of those receiving benefits, resulting in a greater financial burden on those in employment.

In the new old age pension system, incentives to work are strengthened compared to the old one because of the tight connection between contributions and benefits. However, the occupational pension systems, disability insurance, sickness insurance and unemployment insurance can be (and are) used for early exit from the labor market and these schemes include incentives far less in favor of work.

Sweden experiences a trend toward increased absenteeism due to illness and increasing numbers of people taking early retirement. While obvious impairments in physical or mental functions can make it difficult to carry on working in an increasingly demanding labor market, it has become more common to release employees whose competitiveness in the labor market has declined to a greater or lesser extent and to compensate them for the loss of earnings with an early retirement pension. The incentive to leave working life before the formal retirement age can be influenced by rules governing compensation. Negotiated collective agreement supplements and similar arrangements specific to individual companies reduce the excess

Table 6.9
The Ratio of the Replacement Rate in the Reformed Swedish Pension System
When Unisex Tables are Used and When the Probability of Surviving is
Diversified According to Sex
(Replacement Rate is Calculated as Annual Benefit as a Percent of Final Salary)

A. Full Career

|  | Women/Full career men unisex tables | Women/Full career men Survival probabilities calculated by sex |
|---|---|---|
| **No upper secondary school** | 1.02 | 0.89 |
| **Upper secondary school** | 1.12 | 0.97 |
| **Undergraduate education 2 years** | 1.00 | 0.90 |
| **Undergraduate education > 2 years** | 1.22 | 1.03 |
| **Postgraduate education** | 1.21 | 1.04 |

B. Full-time/Part-time Woman

|  | Women/Full career men unisex tables | Women/Full career men Survival probabilities calculated by sex |
|---|---|---|
| **No upper secondary school** | 0.98 | 0.86 |
| **Upper secondary school** | 1.07 | 0.95 |
| **Undergraduate education 2 years** | 0.96 | 0.85 |
| **Undergraduate education > 2 years** | 1.17 | 1.00 |
| **Postgraduate education** | - | - |

D. Part-time woman

|  | Women/Full career men unisex tables | Women/Full career men Survival probabilities calculated by sex |
|---|---|---|
| **No upper secondary school** | 1.04 | 0.98 |
| **Upper secondary school** | 1.17 | 0.97 |
| **Undergraduate education 2 years** | 1.04 | 0.90 |
| **Undergraduate education > 2 years** | 1.25 | 1.03 |
| **Postgraduate education** | - | - |

in the public social insurance schemes and, therefore, provide an incentive for some people to leave the labor force early, thus leading to a decrease in labor supply. In Palme and Svensson (2003) pathways out of the labor force are studied. In table 6.11 some of their results are presented.

Table 6.10

**The Ratio of the Replacement Rate in the Reformed Swedish Pension System With and Without Child Credits. (Replacement Rate is Calculated as Annual Benefit as a Percent of Final Salary**

A. Full Career

|  | Women/Full career men with child credits | Women/Full career men without child credits |
|---|---|---|
| No upper secondary school | 1.02 | 1.02 |
| Upper secondary school | 1.12 | 1.12 |
| Undergraduate education  2 years | 1.00 | 1.00 |
| Undergraduate education > 2 years | 1.22 | 1.22 |
| Postgraduate education | 1.21 | 1.21 |

B. Full-time/Part-time Woman

|  | Women/Full career men with child credits | Women/Full career men without child credits |
|---|---|---|
| No upper secondary school | 0.98 | 0.94 |
| Upper secondary school | 1.07 | 1.05 |
| Undergraduate education  2 years | 0.96 | 0.93 |
| Undergraduate education > 2 years | 1.17 | 1.14 |
| Postgraduate education | - | - |

D. Part-time woman

|  | Women/Full career men with child credits | Women/Full career men without child credits |
|---|---|---|
| No upper secondary school | 1.04 | 1.00 |
| Upper secondary school | 1.17 | 1.12 |
| Undergraduate education  2 years | 1.04 | 1.00 |
| Undergraduate education > 2 years | 1.25 | 1.22 |
| Postgraduate education | - | - |

Table 6.11

**Percentage share of pathways to permanent exit from the labor market showing main source of income (more than 50 percent from the indicated source); cohorts born 1927-32**

| Source | Men | Women |
|---|---|---|
| State old age pension (the old system) | 33.70 | 26.94 |
| Occupational pension | 13.68 | 14.21 |
| Disability pension | 6.55 | 6.59 |
| Private pension | 0.86 | 0.76 |
| Sickness insurance | 20.53 | 26.88 |
| Unemployment insurance | 8.35 | 6.42 |
| Partial retirement benefit | 10.04 | 6.83 |
| No income source more than 50% | 5.67 | 4.64 |

*Source*: Palme and Svensson (2003), p. 218.

The most common pathway out of the labor market is to use one of the labor market insurances, that is, disability pension, sickness insurance, or unemployment insurance. These ways are used by more than 35 percent of men and almost 40 percent of women. Note also the very small proportion who use private pensions for early exit. Also, there are pronounced gender differences in the modes of early exit, women using sickness insurance far more than men, while the opposite is true for old age pension. Palme and Svensson also calculate the expected change in benefits of working an additional year. They conclude that incentives to stay in the labor force decrease rapidly at the age of sixty (p. 231).

Increased labor force participation and employment will lead to a lesser burden for those of active age. Measures for increasing female labor force participation and working hours may be an option. Other measures are those intended to increase the labor supply and employment among older workers. One measure is to raise the formal retirement age. In Sweden, the law on job security has been changed (2003) so that mandatory retirement agreements at an age lower than sixty-seven years are prohibited. Other measures aim at raising the actual retirement age by counteracting early exit, for example by changes in the compensation rates and the possibilities of access to different social security schemes. Special labor market programs for older workers may also be a possibility.

*Concluding Remarks*

Recent pension reform in Sweden tightens the link between payroll contributions and benefits. The old system resulted in a higher return on men's pension contributions than on women's. However, with increases in real wages, an increasing number of persons will have incomes above the stipulated ceiling of covered earnings which reduces the old earnings-related pension to no more than a basic pension for employees, albeit at a higher level. This erases the regressive effect of the best-year rule. Given the ceiling in the old system has not become effective, the pension reform would result in a higher ratio between women's and men's rate of return on pension contributions. Women would be better off, compared to full career men, in the new system than in the old system. Given the ceiling has become nearly effective among full career men, the pension reform results in a lower ratio between women's and men's return on pension contributions. Women will be worse off relative to full career men in the new system than in the old system. However the gender ratio is well above one in all cases. This is true for both the old and the new system.

The outcome for women in the *new system* is summarised in table 6.12.

**Table 6.12**
**Women's Outcome in Percent of Full Career Men's**

| | Full career woman | Women / Full career men Full time/part time woman | 10-year woman | Part-time woman |
|---|---|---|---|---|
| Annual own annuities | 80-100 | 80 | 35-40 | 60-70 |
| Replacement rate | 100-120 | 100-120 | 120-145 | 100-125 |
| Rate of return | 115-130 | 120 | 310-400 | 120-130 |

*Note*: The interval goes from no upper secondary school to postgraduate education.

The results show women, on average, get lower pension benefits than men. Despite this, women have a higher replacement rate and a higher rate of return on lifetime contributions than men. Part-time women's annual pension is 60 to 70 percent of full career men's. However, they have a replacement rate up to 25 percent higher than men's and a rate of return which is 20 to 30 percent higher than men's. If for example men's rate of return would be 3 percent part-time women would have a rate of return of 3.6 to 4.0 percent. Full-time/part-time women have a rate of return which is 20 percent higher than men's. The ten-year woman get the minimum pension guarantee. Her rate of return on lifetime contributions is 300 to 400 percent higher than men's.

Any pension system having a tight link between benefits and contributions is likely to produce lower benefits for women. Despite this, women have a higher replacement rate and a higher rate of return on their pension contributions than men. This is due to the uni-sex life tables, the guaranteed minimum pension and pension credits for child rearing. The distributional effects of unisex tables are high whereas the child credits have less influence on women's pension amounts.

The response to the challenges of an aging society

The reformed system in Sweden shows dramatic change in the philosophy of how to organize support in old age. The system consists of a guarantee pension financed over the state budget, a notional defined contribution part and a funded component with individual accounts.

Firstly, the defined contribution feature means that each individual bears her or his own costs which also means that one generation can not impose a burden on future generations. The defined contribution design also includes strong incentives to work in the labor market which is one way of lessening the burden of aging.

Secondly, in the reformed system the benefits are determined by accumulated contributions (plus interest) divided by a factor determined by the cohort's expected life time at the time of retirement. In this way the system takes care of increased longevity.

## Appendix

Figure 1 presents the career profile for a full career man and four *types* of women:

1. Full career woman: same labor force participation and retirement age as men—works full time for most or all of her career.

2. Full-time/Part-time woman: working full time until having children, alternates between parental leave and part-time as long as the children are small and then goes back to full-time work. The woman is assumed to have two children and the earnings profile is constructed for two cases: one where the first child is born when she is age twenty-four and one when the first child is born when she is age twenty-eight.

3. Ten-year woman: participate in the labor force during ten years early in life, before marriage and birth of children.[8] The woman is assumed to have two children and the first is born when she is age twenty-eight.

4. Part-time woman: women who works part-time for most of her career. The woman is assumed to have two children and the earnings profile is constructed for two cases: one where the first child is born when she is age twenty-four and one when the first child is born when she is age twenty-eight.

The career profile is based on published income data from Statistics Sweden in 2001. We use the *average* wage for a given age/education group and, therefore, does not include any cohort effects. In addition to earnings from work, income also can come from education transfers and parental benefits. The career profile is constructed by dividing the income at each age with the starting income, that is, the income for the first age a person earns pension rights. As a result, the career profile is shown as an index where the index takes the value 1 at the first age a person has income, and then shows how income grows over the lifecycle. For example, an index of 3 at a given age indicates that the earnings are three times the starting income for the group.

The career profile reflects women who stay home to take care of children are eligible for parental benefits. For the full/part-time woman and the part-time woman, the wage she receives when returning to work is her wage prior to parental leave multiplied by the average wage growth (assumed to be 1.8 percent). This means her wage will be lower compared to the woman who does not have any children (full-time woman).

**Figure 6.1**
**Career profiles for a Full Career Man and for Four Groups of Women.**

Panel 0: Full Career Man

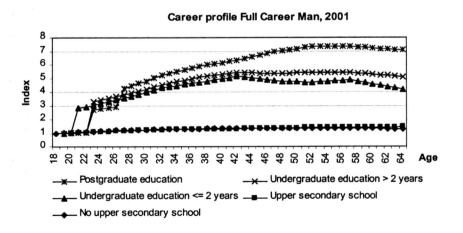

Panel A. Full Career Woman

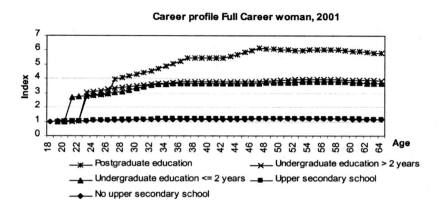

**Career profile Full Career woman, 2001**

Panel B: Full-Time/ Part-Time Woman

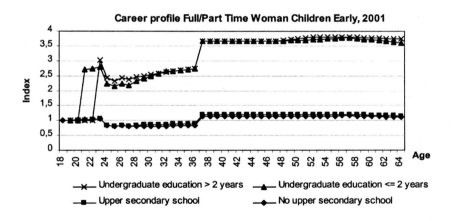

**Career profile Full/Part Time Woman Children Early, 2001**

## Panel C: 10-year Woman

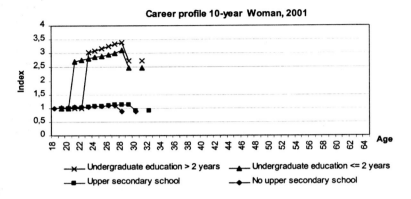

**Career profile 10-year Woman, 2001**

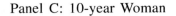

## Panel D: Part-Time Woman

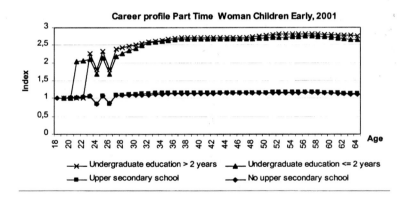

**Career profile Part Time Woman Children Early, 2001**

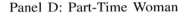

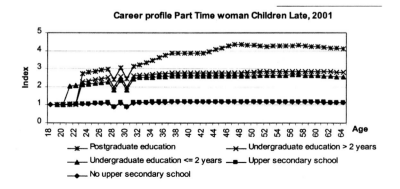

**Career profile Part Time woman Children Late, 2001**

# Notes

1.  The 1944 cohorts are the first not favored by the transition period, since they have to pay during their whole active life cycle.
2.  Data on administrative fees and premiums for disability and survivors insurance are from James et al. 2003b.
3.  See footnote 3.
4.  See footnote 3.
5.  The ten-year woman is an exception in Sweden. Most Swedish women work far more than that. The case is chosen for comparability with James et al.: also it illustrates how persons with no own pension fare in the new system.
6.  We assume the lifecycle incomes are unaffected by the pension system. That means we do not consider that a higher contribution rate in the old system, in order to cope with pension commitments, would result in lower wages, or that the increased work incentives in the new system could affect the lifecycle incomes.
7.  The calculation of lifetime contributions includes an estimate of the tax paid for the guarantee benefit.
8.  The ten-year woman is an exception in Sweden. Most Swedish women work far more than that. The case is chosen for comparability with James et al. (2003): also it illustrates how persons with no own pension fare in the new system.

# References

James, Estelle, Alejandra Cox Edwards and Rebeca Wong (2003a), "The Gender Impact of Pension Reform: A Cross-Country Analysis," *Journal of Pension Economics and Finance* 2(2).

James, Estelle, Alejandra Cox Edwards and Rebeca Wong, (2003b), *The Gender Impact of Pension Reform: And Which Policies Shape This Impact*, The World Bank.

Palme, Mårten and Ingemar Svensson (2003), "Pathways to retirement and retirement incentives in Sweden," chapter 9 in Andersen T. M. and P. Molander (eds.), *Alternatives for Welfare Policy. Coping with Internationalisation and Demographic Change*, Cambridge University Press.

Ståhlberg, Ann-Charlotte (1989), "Redistribution Effects of Social Policy in a Lifetime Analytical Framework," in Gustafsson Björn and Klevmarken Anders (eds.), *The Political Economy of Social Security*, 51-65, North-Holland.

Ståhlberg, Ann-Charlotte (1990), "Lifecycle Income Redistribution of the Public Sector: Inter- and Intragenerational Effects," in Persson, Inga (ed), *Generating Equality in the Welfare State. The Swedish Experience*, 97-121, Norwegian University Press, Oslo.

Ståhlberg, Ann-Charlotte (1995), "Women's Pensions in Sweden," *Scandinavian Journal of Social Welfare*, Vol. 4, 19-27.

# 7

# Reforming Social Security for a Long-Life Society: What Impact on Women?

*Roland Sigg and Rebecca Taylor*

## Introduction

Countries around the world are reforming their welfare systems to tackle the challenge of demographic aging, declining labor participation and low fertility rates. These trends, combined, are eroding dependency ratios and calling into question the sustainability of existing social security measures for the older population. Longer life spans are creating new opportunities but also new risks necessitating a fundamental rethink of social security policy in long-life societies. The preceding chapters explore the gender impact of recent reforms in a range of different welfare states.

The issues surrounding sustainability of income in old age are typically magnified for women. Women generally live longer but earn less over their lifetime than men because, on average, they tend to command lower wages, are more likely to work part-time or on a temporary basis and to interrupt employment for domestic work. Women account for three-quarters of all part-time work in OECD countries (Sarfati 2003). In the EU, only 37 percent of working age women are employed full-time (Ginn 2002). Sixty-nine percent of women working part-time in Germany, and 48 percent in the U.K., attribute the need to work part-time to doing housework and other family commitments (Daly and Rake 2003:78).

This suggests women perform a significant amount of unpaid domestic labor, but generally have less opportunity to accumulate adequate resources in their own right for what is usually a longer retirement than for men. The risk of poverty in old age is, thus, generally higher for women than for men. The 2002 data on the EU-15 shows, on average, 10 percent of EU women aged sixty-five-plus were at risk of poverty (measured as below 50 percent of median income) compared with 7 percent of men.

In the U.K., 75 percent of pensioners claiming means-tested financial support from the state are women; and the declining value of state pensions is eroding their effectiveness in addressing poverty (Ginn 2003). The data also show one in four single women pensioners in the U.K. lives in poverty (Reday-Mulvey 2004). In France, there was a gap of 50 percent in the level of direct pension benefits between men and women in 2001 (see chapter 5).

This book has focused on the gender aspects of retirement and active aging but, as can be seen from the preceding chapters, it is impossible to divorce the question of income in old age from income during years of employment, which is closely linked to an individual's ability to accumulate resources for retirement.

Traditional family and gender roles are changing rapidly, however. Women's labor force participation is rising; participation in EU countries rose from 40 percent of twenty-five to fifty-four-year-old women in 1970 to 60 percent in 1999 (Sarfati 2002:22). The growth in unmarried and single-parent households is breaking the link between marriage and parenthood.[1] These trends together are eroding the significance of the traditional "male breadwinner model" of family life in many countries. Although this is less true in Latin America, for example, where there is still significant gender segmentation in the labor market, there are indications the participation gap is closing Expectations of retirement are similarly changing. A clear trend towards early retirement in recent decades is now being met by policies emphasizing later retirement, flexibility and individual choice.

These changes pose many challenges for social security and for ensuring equality between the genders in a long-life society, but they also offer opportunities for society and for both men and women. Growing work participation and the extension of working lives has the potential to improve the productiveness and well being of society as a whole, as well as contribute to the long-term funding of retirement benefits. For many individuals, it may provide greater scope for accumulating resources for retirement and a chance to take a fresh approach to gender roles throughout the life course. At the same time, it needs to be recognized that choice is often the luxury of wealth, and, for some, a longer working life will, in fact, be the only option in future.

How can social security adapt to changing family structures and the expected increase in retirees in a way not discriminating between men and women? To what extent will policy interventions impact differently on men and women? What is "fair" in terms of future pension contributions and benefits?

This concluding chapter attempts to address these questions. It reviews the main policy reforms countries have undertaken to address the long-life society challenge, considers the gender impact of such reforms and identifies the key questions policy-makers need to grapple with in ensuring fairness of outcome for men and women.

## The Gender Impact of Long-life Policies

We have seen in the preceding chapters the wide range of policy interventions being made in post-industrial and emerging economies to address the challenge a long-life society poses for social security systems. Initiatives typically include reform of pension systems to create a tighter link between life-long contributions and benefits; measures to improve dependency ratios by increasing labor market participation rates, particularly of women and older workers; and measures targeted at the family. This section considers what differential impact such measures may have on the genders and on equality of income in old age.

### Pensions

Faced with population aging, all countries studied have recently reformed, or are about to reform, their pension systems with a clear trend toward tightening the link between contributions and benefits, usually with the stated intention of improving long-term financial sustainability.

The radical pensions reform in Chile in 1981 introduced a system based on individualized savings accounts with benefits calculated using mortality tables by sex. Given the same amount of funds in their savings account, annuities for women are automatically lower due to their longer life expectancy. The reform incorporated no specific measures to compensate for differences in gender roles, implicitly assuming women would be provided for within the family. Bertranou finds in chapter 3 that, as a result, labor market differences between men and women lead not only to differences in income during their working lives, but also exacerbates the problem in retirement.

As returns of defined contribution accounts are proportionate to effort in the paid labor market, such a system might be seen as "fair" in a world where gender offered no advantage for employment opportunities or wage differentials. In practice, however, labor market inequalities persist. Without the use of specific redistributive measures, benefits based on defined contributions are likely to result in increasingly unequal outcomes as long as real differences remain in the paid and unpaid employment of men and women.

The most notable recent example is the Swedish pension reform in 1998 which introduced a system of "notional defined contribution" (NDC) accounts with benefits linked to lifetime contributions and life expectancy. Under this system, each individual bears the risk of increased life expectancy, relying on their own lifetime contributions (real or credited) for their pension, instead of on the contributions of the current generation as was previously the case. This has significantly strengthened the notion of individual responsibility. In contrast to the Chilean system, however, Sweden has retained a substantial degree of social solidarity through the provision of a generous minimum guarantee, credits for certain unpaid periods (such as caregiver work or study) and the use of unisex life tables to calculate annuities.

Proposals to adopt a similar system in Norway are, nevertheless, proving controversial from a gender perspective. Projections by Dahl and Pederson in chapter 4 find although the difference between men and women's pension income is projected to be relatively modest under the proposals, it will, nevertheless, contribute to some widening of the gender gap. Similarly, Gilles and Parent argue in chapter 5 women's interests would be best served by maintaining the existing occupation-based pay-as-you-go system in France which, due to the inclusion of corrective mechanisms, guarantees a significant redistribution from men to women.

A general shift to pension systems with a tighter link to contributions seems inevitable however. Policy-makers face the compelling challenge of how to design these pension reforms in a way achieving "fair" outcomes for both men and women. Chapter 1 studied the gender aspects of pension design in some depth.

Many of the countries studied in this book have introduced or retained special redistributional features intended to provide a degree of solidarity between men and women, largely—but not only—through the pension system. These include measures compensating directly for unpaid domestic work in a gender-neutral way; those compensating indirectly by redistributing income to women (e.g. unisex life tables or minimum guarantees); and non-pension measures enabling all to compete in the paid labor market and, thus, build resources for retirement on equal terms.

*Direct Compensation.* Direct measures to redistribute income from the main breadwinner to a dependent partner provide a means of recognizing unpaid domestic work along traditional gender lines.

In familialist welfare states, the emphasis is on derived rights through the family. *Joint annuities* are an important feature of new pension systems in Latin America, for example, with annuities calculated on the basis of both the beneficiary's age and sex and that of dependents. This can ensure a degree of redistribution within the family and may reduce the differences in pensions between men and women (see chapter 3). Benefits are dependent on marriage (or in some cases long-term partnership) to the main breadwinner.

*Joint-survivor pensions* similarly ensure family income is redistributed to support a partner who has carried the burden of unpaid domestic work when the main breadwinner passes away. In many countries the measure is gender neutral. In Chile, however, men have no right to survivor's pensions unless they are invalids; as a result, just 0.3 percent of Chilean men were covered by survivor's benefits in 2000 compared with 22.5 percent of women (see chapter 3)—arguably a discriminatory measure against men.

Such measures may lead to a levelling down of entitlements rather than a levelling up however. Derived rights may also act as work disincentives by encouraging reliance on family income and do little to boost overall funds for retirement. Indeed, where schemes are voluntary, families may well choose to minimize contributions and maximize annuities by paying into an individual pension based on the main breadwinner, leaving widows in poverty when the beneficiary dies. *Mandatory joint-survivor pensions* have been introduced in some Latin American countries to address this problem (although there is some evidence of evasion). As in the case of joint annuities, the pensions are dependent on marriage (or in some cases long-term partnership) and, in and of themselves, offer no support for the rising number of divorcees and single parents.

Provision for *pension-splitting* is an important tool ensuring women (or indeed men) who have spent many years outside paid employment during their marriage due to caregiver responsibilities or other domestic work, do not lose their rights to the accumulated family pension upon divorce. This allows for the individual pension rights each spouse has accumulated during the marriage (whether through employment or through credits for child-rearing) to be spread evenly between the partners upon divorce.

The rapidly changing nature of family formation and gender roles suggests family-derived benefits—which assume a strong link between marriage and socially valuable unpaid labor (such as childcare)—need to be fundamentally reviewed. Where survivor pensions are funded by the state, the result is redistribution from the unmarried to the married, irrespective of whether those who benefit have performed unpaid labor or socially valuable roles such as child-rearing. Single parents, on the other hand, would receive no such benefits.

Conversely, if it is considered child-rearing (and other caregiver work) is of value to society as a whole, should not state pensions be structured so as to ensure women (or indeed men) who perform such activity are not penalized but, rather, valued accordingly, on an individual basis and proportionate to their actual contribution?

While all of the pension systems studied maintain some elements of derived benefits, there has been a clear move toward individualization of pension rights. Provision for pension-splitting upon divorce is one example of this. A further prominent example of this is the provision in many of the countries studied for direct compensation for parenting work, in an individual and gender-neutral way, through a system of *pension credits*. A key difficulty many primary caregivers face in accumulating pension resources is a requirement to meet qualifying period conditions (often a minimum of forty years to receive a full pension). Pension credits ensure periods of unpaid labor are recognized for the purposes of the state pension.

In Sweden, such credits for childcare are provided for up to four years for each child, irrespective of previous income and with no requirement to give up work; the credits can be apportioned to either the mother or the father. In Finland, unpaid leave up to one year (within employment) is credited, while in the U.K. credits are available toward the (rather lower) basic state pension for those caring for children up to the age of sixteen, or eighteen while enrolled in full-time education. (see chapter 2).

This is arguably a fair mechanism for compensating non-working parents—at least in terms of basic state pension income—for their unpaid but socially valuable work in raising the next generation. It does not provide direct compensation for occupational pension income foregone if parents do not return to work after any paid parental leave; however, it does secure a basic pension income to ensure caregivers have more flexibility to choose whether or not to balance their domestic responsibilities with work.

*(Indirect) Redistribution to Women.* In many countries where mandatory private savings schemes have been introduced, such as in Latin America, there is no pension solidarity between men and women. Lifetime contributions are converted to an annuity rate based on life expectancy and differentiated by sex resulting in either higher annual contributions, or significantly lower annuities, for women. While this is actuarially fair in terms of returns for contributions from paid employment, it fails to recognize gender inequalities in both the paid and unpaid labor market.

Conversely, the use of *unisex life tables* to calculate annuities under public schemes redistributes pension income in favor of those with longer life expectancy. Such schemes need to be public and mandatory, as in the case of the Swedish NDC system, to enable pooling of risk and solidarity between those with different life expectancies. (The private sector would automatically favor those with shorter life expectancies). The use of such tables arguably favors women and discriminates against men due to gender differences in life expectancy. In Sweden and Finland it is seen as an important means of compensating women indirectly for unpaid caregiver work.

However, life expectancy is determined not only by gender but by a complex matrix of factors such as education, employment, income and life-style. Use of standardized, unisex life tables is, therefore, likely to disadvantage those with low life expectancy due to socio-economic status or health, for example, as well as the average man. So it is unclear, for example, whether the use of such tables would advantage a woman with lower socio-economic status relative to a wealthy and successful man (who might have a higher life expectancy). Nevertheless, as the average woman lives longer than the average man, a move away from unisex life tables could be expected to widen overall gender inequalities and such a proposal is, therefore, likely to be politically unacceptable in many countries.

A basic state pension or *minimum income guarantee* for older people ensures a degree of redistribution to those in lower income brackets and, therefore, plays a significant role in underpinning pension provision for women under contribution-based systems. In 2000, 55.1 percent of women pensioners in Norway received minimum benefits (the "Pension Supplement"), while just 12.7 percent of male pensions claimed (see table 4.5 in chapter 4). The difference reflects the difficulty many women have in meeting minimum qualifying period conditions under occupational pension schemes. In the U.K., this seems poised to play an increasingly important role for women as the value of the state pension (indexed to prices) drops ever further below the minimum income guarantee (indexed to earnings) projected to drop to just 7 percent of average male earnings by 2050 (DSS 1998, quoted in Ginn 2003, p.15).

Although the general rise in female labor market participation has the potential to reduce the proportion of women relying on minimum benefits in future, Tuominen and Laitinen-Kuikka suggest in chapter 2 they are likely to continue to play a bigger role in pension provision for women than for men for some time to come due to women's shorter working careers. And in some emerging economies the participation rate of women seems likely to lag behind that of men for many years. In Chile, for example, the 2002 female participation rate in the (formal) labor market was just 34 percent compared to 72 percent for men, meaning a much higher share of women are excluded from contributory pensions and rely solely on means-tested minimum assistance (see chapter 3).

A minimum pension guarantee could potentially have the effect of excluding some women from the labor market however. The Pension Supplement in Norway has been strengthened in recent years and is awarded to married women with no, or low, individual pension rights without infringing on their husbands' entitlement. It could be argued this provides a work disincentive to those women who would otherwise enter employment partially (e.g. part-time or temporary) and at low pay rates as the marginal financial incentive to work is reduced. A minimum pension guarantee, nevertheless, helps to provide some compensation for gender inequalities in the labor market.

Other countries rely on *means-testing* to ensure that public resources reach those who need them most. The U.K. directs support toward the most needy via a basic, means-tested, minimum pension; this underlines the fact that the state pension is not about earnings replacement but about guaranteeing a minimum level of income. Although relatively low, it has been successful in raising minimum income of the poorest pensioners, of which a relatively high proportion are women. However, means-testing arguably penalizes work and savings and is likely to create a particular disincentive for those on low incomes for whom the marginal incentive to work or save will be lower. Beside the disincentive effect, it is questionable whether means-testing is "fair" toward those who put in greater effort or forego consumption today in order to save for retirement.

*Indexing* pensions to consumer prices or wages is a key tool for ensuring that the value of pension income is maintained in real or relative terms. This is of particular significance for women, who are more likely than men, to be dependent on the minimum guarantee or low pensions and to live longer. Since 1980, the U.K. state pension has been indexed to prices only and has fallen to just 15 percent of average earnings (Ginn, in Sarvati 2002); as 75 percent of pensioners claiming the means-tested state pension in the U.K. are women, this has had a disproportionate impact on the income of female pensioners. In Sweden, the earlier pension system was linked to prices rather than to the wages of the working population; the new system is intended to change this through wage-indexing.

The indirect redistribution mechanisms discussed in this section were not designed with the express purpose of redistributing income from men to women. Rather, they are primarily intended as poverty alleviation tools. The indirect result—due to inequalities in the labor market—is they tend to benefit women more than men. Removing them, though, would almost certainly result in furthering wider gender inequalities.

Such measures do not necessarily create a direct link between effort and reward, however; indeed, in some cases, they may create work disincentives. Conversely individualized measures, such as pension credits for child-rearing, specifically target those who take time out of the paid labor market to perform socially valuable activity and, therefore, create a more direct link between reward and effort.

*Fair compensation* From the above analysis it would seem that generic redistribution tools that favor all women over all men do not necessarily result in "fair" outcomes in terms of rewarding people for unpaid labor. Gender is by no means the only characteristic impacting on income or poverty; indeed, the income gap between women can be as large as the gap between men and women. It is, therefore, important not to assume that all women (or indeed all men) have similar employment patterns, make the same life choices or will be affected equally by reforms or interventions.

In chapter 1, Kruse, Ståhlberg and Sundén show that the pre-1999 defined benefit system, under which annuities were calculated on the basis of a limited number of "best years," favored female senior white collar workers compared to female unskilled blue-collar workers as the former tend to work for fewer years but command higher salaries. Conversely, the new system favors those who work continuously from an early age.

Dahl and Pederson similarly find in chapter 4 that, in terms of pension income, the move to contribution-based systems is likely to benefit those who work full-time continuously; and that supporting safety nets, such as the minimum guarantee, will benefit women who stay at home in terms of the rate of substitution for their (relatively low) lifetime income. However, they argue such a system it is not well suited to the majority of women who fall somewhere in between. The contributions-based system is likely to weaken work incentives for those on lower incomes (including many women) and, as these same people are generally more sensitive to effective marginal tax rates, cause a polarization of work incentives.

Safeguards are, thus, needed within such schemes to provide compensation for socially valued but unpaid activity on the basis of individualized rights. Such measures require the redistribution of resources from other sectors of society however. Policy-makers need to consider what activities warrant such solidarity. Should those without primary care responsibilities for children or elderly dependents subsidize those who do on the basis of the public good they provide? Or should such solidarity be provided primarily from within the individual family? As we have seen, the erosion of the traditional family unit can make the latter course a risky one for the individuals concerned.

*Coverage* In developing and emerging economies, the question of securing income for old age is typically a more fundamental one of coverage. In Latin America, a high proportion of people (including many women) work in the informal labor market and are, thus, excluded from contributory pension systems and other occupation-linked social security coverage. It is estimated that in 1998, 45 percent of working age women in Chile, and 46 percent of working age women in Uruguay, were employed in the informal sector.

These workers depend on minimum pension guarantees providing a basic safety net, but for many it is not sufficient to guard against poverty. Relative poverty amongst older women continues to rise. There is a need for either much greater generosity in non-contributory pensions or an extension of contributory pensions to the informal sector, if social security systems are to be effective in addressing poverty and ensuring some equality of outcome for men and women.

## Employment Measures

All of the countries studied are in parallel taking steps to improve the overall employment rate by increasing labor market participation of women and older workers, often regarded as two major potential—and relatively untapped—sources of labor.

*Increasing Women's Employment* Greater female employment has the potential to move many women, and their families, out of poverty during both employment and retirement. At the same time, it encourages self-sufficiency and can raise the overall level of contributions to, and sustainability of, pension systems. The EU has set a target of a 60 percent overall female employment rate by 2010 compared to an average of 55 percent in 2001 (including both full-time and part-time workers).

Those countries in which female participation is highest, such as in Scandinavia, support working parents with a wide range of measures including parental leave and ample good quality, affordable childcare . The U.K., by contrast, has a relatively weak infrastructure for supporting working caregivers making it difficult for many women to reconcile the dual roles of worker and parent. The impact motherhood has on employment accordingly varies across Europe: Harkness and Waldfogel (1999) found that 76 percent of British women without children were employed full-time compared with just 26 percent of those with children; the equivalent rates were 72 percent and 40 percent in Germany, 75 percent and 61 percent in Sweden and 79 and 66 percent in Finland (Ginn 2003).

Measures to increase women's employment need to address both supply (making it easier to combine paid employment with caregiver work) and demand (ensuring a level playing field and good availability of more flexible jobs in the labor market). Interventions typically focus on good quality, affordable childcare and, in some cases, also on training, skills and life-long learning. Other examples include working tax credits and cash allowances for childcare in the U.K. Wider issues, such as school hours and availability of related services, are also likely to have a major impact. The key lies in linked policies with policy-makers and their delivery agents, individuals, particularly women, considering such practical issues overall.

However, do measures to improve access to work necessarily improve equality of outcome? Dahl and Pederson find in chapter 4 although the Norwegian system is considered to be family- and woman-friendly, with a range of generous provisions enabling women to combine work and family life, it has not necessarily contributed to more equality between the genders. Work participation of women is particularly high (67 percent of population aged sixteen to sixty-four in 2000, compared with 75 percent of men) and they describe a relocation of caregiver work from the informal, family sphere to the formal, public sphere during recent decades. But they also find a significant gender gap in wages (20 to 30 percent), due to the nature of employment and that Norwegian women continue to carry out a disproportionate share of unpaid household work. Gilles and Parent find in chapter 5 that although the gender gap in pensions in France is narrowing through increased female participation in the labor market, the move is, in fact, rather slow, as in practice gender disparities in the paid labor market are hard to change.

Nevertheless, it seems likely that, with time, such measures will gradually increase women's ability to accumulate their own resources for retirement and reduce their dependence on minimum guarantees.

*Productive Aging: Increasing employment of older workers* Many of the countries studied have begun to encourage the extension of working lives as a central means of improving dependency ratios between workers and retirees and, therefore, the funding base of pensions—whilst utilizing the skills and experience of the older population. In 2001 the average employment rate of those aged fifty-five to sixty-four in the EU was just 38.8 percent (European Commission

2003) suggesting there is a lot of scope for better utilizing the experienced resource available in this age group.

The need to extend working lives is central to current debate in France where there is a strong culture of early retirement and a particularly low employment rate amongst those over fifty-five (31 percent of sixty-year-olds and just 5 percent of sixty-five-year-olds).[2] Gilles and Parent highlight in chapter 5 how the structure of pension schemes provide strong incentives to those over sixty to exit the labor market permanently (as it is based on a pay-as-you-go system with good minimum income support and ready access to health care) while early retirement schemes over the past two decades have offered positive incentives not to do so.

The extension of working lives provides an opportunity not only to improve the funding base of pensions, but also to harness the skills and experience of those who are able and willing to work in an aging society. The ability to work longer could also give parents, who have taken time out to raise a family ,(mainly women) the flexibility to build more resources for retirement.

As in the case of female participation, policies in the countries studies tend to address both supply and demand, on the one hand making it easier and more attractive for older people to remain in or return to work and, on the other, removing real or perceived barriers to their employment (such as age discrimination). On the supply side, many countries are in the process of equalizing the public retirement age (the age at which one becomes eligible for state pension) between men and women. All EU member states are obliged to do so by 2010. On the demand side, a number of countries have introduced labor market measures to ensure older workers are able to continue working if they choose to.

Measures often combine both incentives and penalties. Typical incentives include measures to facilitate a more flexible transition from work to retirement, such as the ability to combine pension and income and financial rewards for extending working life in the form of pension bonuses for extra years worked. Penalties include tougher access to, or financial penalties for, early retirement, delaying retirement by increasing the statutory retirement age or lengthening the contributory period for first pillar state pensions. Employment measures include investment in end-of-career training, anti-ageism measures and more flexible working conditions.

France has employed a combination of measures: they have recently tightened rules on early retirement whilst improving incentives to extend work beyond age sixty. Measures include a pension bonus for each additional year worked and the concept of "bridge jobs"—the right to combine state pension with continued earnings (and continued accumulation of pension) after the official retirement age up to the limit of their last career earnings level.

A flexible retirement age has similarly been introduced as part of the contribution-based system in Sweden. Benefits can be withdrawn from age sixty-one and are calculated by dividing the balance in the notional account by an annuity divisor (determined by average life expectancy for a given cohort, equal for men and women). At the same time, the law on job security has been changed (2003) to prohibit mandatory retirement agreements below age sixty-seven.

Finland is also introducing a flexible retirement age from 2005 which will offer higher accrual rates of pension rights for those who work between ages sixty-two and sixty-eight. Reform proposals would move Norway in a similar direction, introducing a flexible retirement age from age sixty-two, with actuarial deductions for those retiring before the standard retirement age of sixty-seven and premiums for those retiring after.

Indeed, it is questionable whether a mandatory retirement age is necessary, or appropriate, any longer in long-life societies in which contribution-based systems can give individuals the flexibility to work longer and save more if they choose to. This is the case in the (private) scheme in Chile, for example, for which there is no longer an official retirement age. The risk of such schemes is they may simply lead to greater relative poverty amongst those who are unable to work beyond the traditional retirement age, or more ill health amongst those who can, and potentially a greater burden on the state. Ideally, safeguards would be incorporated to such a scheme to ensure the focus is on providing greater opportunity to those who want to continue working and in no way penalizes those who do not.

Other measures aim to increase the *effective* average retirement age for everyone—recognizing that many people choose to retire before the official retirement age either formally (based on early retirement incentives or simply accepting a lower pension) or informally through substituting disability benefits as a transition to retirement. The EU has a target of increasing the effective labor market exit age by five years by 2010 for the EU as a whole and achieving an employment rate of 50 percent of those aged fifty-five to sixty-four.

Some countries have focused on labor market measures to extend the age of retirement. The U.K. New Deal for those over fifty, although voluntary, provides targeted support for those who wish to stay active in the labor market offering personal advice, assistance with job-seeking, a small training grant and an employment credit. The U.K. has also used anti-ageism legislation and has introduced an Age Positive Campaign to promote a mixed-age workforce with a code of practice for employers. Elsewhere, affirmative action for older workers has been introduced, such as in Korea, where companies are offered wage subsidies if those over-fifty-five represent at least 6 percent of their workforce.

Thus a fundamental change of philosophy can be seen in many countries. The "all or nothing" mutually exclusive approach to work and retirement seems to be a thing of the past. Governments are taking a more pragmatic approach to utilizing the skills and experience of the older generation, with an emphasis on individual choice and flexibility. People approaching retirement will have different views as to whether it is preferable to work a little longer to earn a little more pension income or to sacrifice pension income of tomorrow in return for a lighter workload today. In contrast to the fixed retirement age that has so far existed in most welfare states, measures are now being introduced that give individuals the ability to make a gradual transition from work to retirement and to decide for themselves when and how to do so.

Winning popular support for the extension of working lives is more difficult however. A recent Eurobarometer survey showed raising the age of retirement was less popular in EU member states than the alternatives of increasing pension contributions or reducing benefits, winning the approval of just 23 percent of respondents compared to 68 percent and 40 percent respectively for the two alternatives (Kohl 2003). Interestingly, the order of preference was, on average, the same across all age groups (from fifteen to twenty-five to over sixty-five) and different employment categories (self-employed, employed and unemployed). In contrast, the same survey showed strong support for the proposal "older workers should be allowed to retire gradually from work (e.g. to combine partial pension with reduced work").

What impact will these measures have on men and women in later life? It seems likely those who lack alternative sources of income will have little choice but to continue to work until the higher retirement age. This is arguably more often the case for middle age women who are more reliant on state pensions than men (Ginn 2003:11). As in the case of encouraging women to work, it is also important to bear in mind the potential cost in terms of the loss of socially valuable roles that would otherwise be fulfilled by these people, for example, in the family (perhaps in terms of grandparents as primary caregivers) or in unpaid community work.

The key however, is flexibility and individual choice. The measures outlined above will help to give both men and women much greater ability to manage and change the balance of work and family over their full lifetimes.

It should be noted extension of work is a major, but not the sole, aspect of active aging. The World Health Organization describes active aging as:

> The process of optimizing opportunities for physical, social and mental well-being throughout the life course, in order to extend healthy life expectancy, productivity and quality of life in older age.

In terms of a "fair" retirement, active aging might be seen rather in the context of a contract with society: solidarity between the generations based on reciprocal gains. For example, older women are often more vulnerable to poverty and, on average, have less work skills or experience than older men; but older women are often more active in relation to family caregiving responsibilities. Support can, thus, be repaid through socially valuable activity. In the future, it can be expected people will switch between paid and unpaid employment throughout their lives and will probably be more active in old age than previous generations (Sigg 2004). Long-life societies offer a wealth of opportunities in this respect.

*Family Policies*

The review of employment measures highlights the range of ways in which different countries are seeking to increase women's employment. In view of the stark decline in fertility rates in recent years, the potential impact, or contribution to, fertility rates is a key concern. Are working women discouraged from starting a family or helped by measures to aid those seeking to balance work and family life? In chapter 2, Laitinen-Kuikka and Tuominen note that contrary to what might be expected, higher fertility rates, in fact, go together with high female employment.

Esping-Anderson (2004) shows provision of good quality affordable childcare and other family services in (mainly) Nordic states not only results in higher employment rates overall for women, but also high fertility rates—perhaps because women have less reason to fear the career consequences of starting a family. As well as the availability of childcare services, he attributes the combination of high female participation and rising birth rates since the 1970s to a considerable expansion of public sector services and employment which provide a "soft economy" and more flexible employment options for working mothers (while noting however, these countries also rank amongst the most segregated labor markets in the world).

However, encouraging primary caregivers to work is arguably not without social cost. While it brings clear economic benefits, it does not necessarily recognize, or value, the socially important activity these people would have carried out at home, such as caregiving and educational activity. From a global perspective, it unquestionably makes economic sense for such activities to be pooled within communities, through professional carers for example. Still there may be hidden social costs—and, ultimately, perhaps, also economic costs—of requiring the primary caregivers of young children to work, which have yet to become evident; the increasing rate of family breakdown is to be considered in this respect.

Esping-Anderson (2004) makes the case for both a new social contract to enable both parents to combine work with family and for more gender equality in the division of unpaid roles. He suggests that the only route to equality will be through the 'masculinization' of women's roles finding its natural counterpart in a 'feminization' of men's life course options. If both sexes were to engage in similar careers and to perform more evenly balanced domestic roles, it does seem likely there would be a more equal outcome for men and women both during and after working age. The extent to which the state can or should play a role in this respect is debatable however.

### Policy Issues

The precise impact of similar policy reforms will always vary according to the status of women and gender roles in different countries. Nevertheless, it seems clear the general trend toward contributions-based pensions to meet the challenge of long-life societies could result in greater inequalities in retirement—both between men and women and between women—unless underpinned by compensatory measures based on solidarity between different sectors of society.

Much effort was made during the 1970s and 1980s to address gender inequalities in the labor market and with some success. The gender gap has been narrowing to various degrees around the world—though has not yet been closed. Yet now pension reforms are being introduced in many countries with seemingly little consideration of the possible gender impact, almost taking us a step back. This fact that labor market inequalities persist in practice implies that some form of compensatory mechanism will continue to be required, at least for the foreseeable future, if there is to be some equality or fairness of outcome for men and women.

A further paradox of these developments is while countries around the world are considering how to boost fertility rates in order to improve dependency ratios, many are reforming pension systems in such a way discouraging potential parents from taking time out of the work place to have children. Again, this suggests a need for compensatory or other family-friendly interventions to ensure that those who want to have children can, without severe penalties in terms of pension income. Experience in Scandinavia has shown that higher fertility rates are compatible with higher female work participation in these circumstances.

Can the state afford *not* to intervene when fertility rates become dangerously low? The extent to which state intervention could, or should, be used in this respect is debatable. Many states are now considering how best to boost reproduction rates but past policies of direct intervention in the family sphere, particularly in relation to reproduction, have a dubious history.

Rather, perhaps the state's role should be focused on creating a genuinely level playing field: removing obstacles and structuring social security and services so as to enable women to have the children they wish to have without being penalized financially and also to enable men to take on the role of primary caregiver on equal terms should they wish to. Pension systems could then become genuinely gender neutral. Until then, compensatory measures will be necessary.

Such redistributive mechanisms need to be designed carefully however, in order to minimize possible work or savings disincentives and to avoid preserving the very stereotypes that lead to gender inequalities. A complementary, and arguably fairer, approach is to address the root cause of inequalities by promoting greater equality in both the paid and unpaid labor market. Perceptions of gender roles are shifting with the rise in female employment and breakdown of the traditional family unit, raising new questions about who should perform traditional family caregiving work. Social policy needs to adapt and take a broader approach to policy and delivery across the full range of social services, linking the many different measures necessary to enable parents to combine work and family in practice.

Decision-makers also need to consider what public goods the state wishes to pay for. For example, should the individual or family internalize the costs of childrearing or should this cost be at least shared by the state on the basis parents are providing a service of value to society as a whole? For example, the employment gap between men and women aged twenty-four to forty-four in Great Britain in the mid-1990s was 7 percent, but the employment gap between women with and without children was much larger at 29 percent (Ginn 2003, with reference to Harkness and Waldfogel 1999). This suggests that there is perhaps not so much a gender gap as a "family" gap in employment and, thus, potentially in retirement.

The cumulative effect of many of the policy reforms discussed in this volume is a general transferral of risk from the state to the individual. However, the days of a "job for life" are gone and declining fertility rates and family instability show that domestic lives are also increasingly hard to predict. The range of options and incentives an individual faces for providing for their future is widening all the time. Young workers face the seemingly impossible task of choosing the pension option that is likely to provide the best outcome based the pattern of their future life; with the task of prediction often being more difficult for women than for men (Ginn 2003).

In summary, policy-makers need to consider the following issues in pursuing equality of outcome in retirement for men and women:

- As long as labor market inequalities exist, compensatory mechanisms will be required within pension systems. These should be designed so as not to discourage or create barriers to work and to recognize unpaid contributions that society values (such as caregiving work).

- Inequalities should continue to be tackled at the root cause—through family-friendly labor market policies. The momentum created in the 1970s and 1980s should be built upon.
- Policies need to focus on creating a genuinely level playing field: not assuming any particular life pattern or creating incentives to certain types of family arrangements but rather removing obstacles and structuring social security and services to ensure men and women have maximum flexibility to make their own individual choices throughout the life cycle, in particular to allow them to have the children they wish to have.
- Social policies and services and labor market policies need to be designed in an integrated way, considered from the perspective of the individual.
- Clear and effective information about options and incentives is paramount to ensure individuals are able to make informed choices.

## Conclusion

Welfare states of all types are moving toward greater individualization of pension rights and a tighter link between work and reward—between contributions (paid or unpaid) and benefits. There is a strong new emphasis on work at all ages with associated benefits and support services. The underlying philosophy is of an individual responsibility to support oneself in retirement—that each individual should bear his or her own costs and the 'risk' of a longer life without imposing an unfair burden on the next generation.

In parallel, derived, family-based rights are becoming ever less relevant as the predominance of the traditional family unit diminishes. This has not necessarily led to an erosion of certain familial aspects of social security as yet, such as using family resources to compensate women for unpaid domestic work through joint annuities. But there has been a trend toward gender neutrality and individualization.

Moreover, there has been a fundamental strengthening of the principle of *choice*. This is reflected both in the growth of multi-pillar pension systems, which give individuals flexibility to opt for additional pensions depending on what will best suit their lifestyle; and also in measures that facilitate a more flexible transition between work and retirement.

The questions addressed in this volume are not simply a matter of gender equality. Policies need to take account of gender roles but recognize that no two individuals will interpret them the same way. Gender roles are evolving, creating the scope for a new type of family or gender contract in terms of division of both paid and unpaid labor. At the same time, the prospect of a long-life society offers new opportunities in terms of extended capacity for both work and reproduction.

It seems essential that social security must ensure equal access to employment and services while facilitating individual choices by both men and women on how to balance both work and family during the different life stages. This has the potential not only to lift women and families out of poverty, but to create greater equality throughout the life course and to give fertility rates a much-needed boost in redressing dependency ratios. Maybe in this way policymakers can regard long-life society less as a risk and more as a positive opportunity.

## Notes

1.  For example, single parents represent a quarter of all families in the U.K.; over 90 percent of single parents are mothers (Ginn 2002:55 based on Office of National Statistics data).
2.  See Chapter 5.1. Source: INSEE

## References

Daly and Rake. 2003. Mary Daly and Katherine Rake. *Gender and the Welfare State.* Polity Press in association with Blackwell Publishing Ltd. Cambridge.

Esping-Anderson. 2002. Gøsta Esping-Anderson, with Duncan Gallie, Anton Hemerijck and John Myles. *Why We Need a New Welfare State.* Oxford University Press, 2002.

Esping-Anderson. 2004.

European Commission. 2003. *Adequate and Sustainable Pensions. Joint Report by the Commission and the Council.* Directorate-General for Employment and Social Affairs, European Communities, September 2003.

Ginn. 2002. Jay Ginn. "Gender and Social Protection Reforms" in Sarfati 2002 (see below).

Ginn. 2003. Jay Ginn. *Gender, Pensions and the Lifecourse: How pensions need to adapt to changing family forms.* Polity Press, June 2003. Cambridge.

Kohl. 2003. Jürgen Kohl. "Citizens' Opinions on the Transition from Work to Retirement: Evidence from a Recent Eurobarometer Survey". Paper submitted for International Research Conference on Social Security in Antwerp, May 2003.

Reday-Mulvey. 2004. Geneviève Reday-Mulvey. "Women and the Fourth Pillar", in *The Four Pillars*, No.35/August 2004. Four Pillars is Geneva Association Research Program.

Sarfati. 2002. Hedva Sarfati and Guiliano Bonoli (Eds). *Labor Market and Social Protection Reforms in International Perspective: Parallel or Converging Tracks?* Ashgate Publishing Ltd, 2002. Hampshire, U.K.

Sarfati. 2003. "Gender, discontinued careers and low activity rates—the challenges and responses in a long-life society." Paper submitted for International Research Conference on Social Security in Antwerp, May 2003.

Sigg. 2004. "Social security and change: The case for confidence". In *Developments and Trends 2002-2004*, International Social Security Association.

# Contributors

*Fabio M. Bertranou* is a Senior Social Security Specialist at the International Labour Office in Santiago, Chile

*Agneta Kruse* is a senior lecturer at Department of Economics, Lund University, Sweden

*Eila Tuominen* (DSocSc) is a Head Researcher at the research department of Finnish Centre for Pensions.

*Sini Laitinen-Kuikka* is a Development Manager and researcher at the Research Department of the Finnish Centre for Pensions, Helsinki.

*Axel West Pedersen* is a senior researcher at NOVA - Norwegian Social Research, Oslo

*Antoine Parent* is an associate Professor of Economics at the University of Paris 8, Researcher at MATISSE, University of Paris 1 – Sorbonne.

*Christel Gilles* is an economist, Matisse, University of Paris 1-Sorbonne

*Ann-Charlotte Stååhlberg* is an Associate Professor of Economics at the Swedish Institute for Social Research, Stockholm University, Sweden

*Annika Sundéén* is a Senior Economist at the Social Insurance Agency in Stockholm, Sweden.

*Marcela Cohen Birman* is a Senior Economist at the Premium Pension Authority in Sweden

*Espen Dahl* is a professor of health and social welfare at Oslo University College.

*Neil Gilbert* is the Chernin Professor of Social Welfare at the University of California, Berkeley

*Roland Sigg* is the Head of Research at the International Social Security Association

*Becky Taylor* is a Consultant at the International Social Security Association

# Index

## DATE DUE

| | | | |
|---|---|---|---|
| | | | |
| | | | |
| | | | |
| | | | |
| | | | |
| | | | |
| | | | |
| | | | |
| | | | |
| | | | |
| | | | |
| | | | |
| | | | |
| | | | |
| | | | |
| | | | |
| | | | |
| | | | |
| | | | |

GAYLORD

PRINTED IN U.S.A.